OPERATION CHIFFON

Beating the Terrorists? Interrogation at Omagh, Gough and Castlereagh
Smoke Ring: The Politics of Tobacco
Stalker: The Search for the Truth
Families at War
States of Terror: Democracy and Political Violence
Provos: The IRA and Sinn Féin
Loyalists
Brits: The War Against the IRA
Talking to Terrorists: A Personal Journey from the IRA to Al Qaeda

OPERATION CHIFFON

The Secret Story of MI5 and MI6 and the Road to Peace in Ireland

PETER TAYLOR

BLOOMSBURY PUBLISHING

LONDON · OXFORD · NEW YORK · NEW DELHI · SYDNEY

BLOOMSBURY PUBLISHING
Bloomsbury Publishing Plc
50 Bedford Square, London, WC1B 3DP, UK
29 Earlsfort Terrace, Dublin 2, Ireland

BLOOMSBURY, BLOOMSBURY PUBLISHING and the Diana logo are trademarks
of Bloomsbury Publishing Plc

First published in Great Britain, 2023

A catalogue record for this book is available from the British Library

ISBN: HB: 978-1-5266-5963-7; TPB: 978-1-5266-5962-0; EBOOK: 978-1-5266-5961-3;
EPDF: 978-1-5266-5960-6

2 4 6 8 10 9 7 5 3 1

Typeset by Newgen KnowledgeWorks Pvt. Ltd., Chennai, India
Printed and bound in Great Britain by CPI Group (UK) Ltd, Croydon CR0 4YY

To find out more about our authors and books visit www.bloomsbury.com
and sign up for our newsletters

To Michael Gilbey – the bravest and the best

Forsan et haec olim meminisse iuvabit

(Perhaps one day it will be good to remember even these things)

Virgil, *Aeneid,* Book I, line 203

Contents

Author's Note

The photograph on the cover needs an explanation. It was taken in 'Free Derry' on 13 June 1972, and captures the moment that marks the first step in the British Government's engagement with the IRA. The secret talks that followed continued on and off over the next twenty years, culminating in 'Operation Chiffon', which helped make the historic Good Friday Agreement and peace possible. It shows the leadership of the Provisional IRA, Seán MacStíofáin (Chief of Staff), Seamus Twomey (Commander Belfast Brigade), David O'Connell (Political Strategist) and Martin McGuinness (Commander Derry Brigade) outside the hall where they are about to hold a press conference inviting the British for talks. The unidentified person in the foreground is believed to be Sean Keenan Jr, son of the veteran Derry republican.

'Operation Chiffon' and the secret talks between the British Government and the IRA is the centrepiece of the story, told against the background of the bloody history of the conflict to explain why covert dialogue was necessary to help persuade the IRA to end its 'armed struggle' and embrace the political process.

The anonymous MI5 officer I simply call 'Robert' was at the centre of 'Operation Chiffon'. His extraordinary story, told here for the first time, brings home what was at stake and the heavy price he paid in helping make peace possible. Although I've longed to tell Robert's story for more than twenty years, in the end the opportunity to do so came about by pure chance...

Acknowledgements

I am indebted to more people than I can mention, including all those colleagues and friends at the BBC and ITV with whom I've worked for over half a century. I could not have reported on Ireland and other conflicts without their help, support and advice.

I am greatly indebted to Robert, the former MI5 and MI6 officer officer without whom this book would never have been written and the full inside secret story of the peace process told. I am also indebted to his MI6 predecessor, Michael Oatley, who introduced me to the labyrinthine workings of the 'back channel' and trusted me with his remarkable first-hand account. Sadly, I cannot thank two others who shared their precious, first-hand insights: Michael Oatley's MI6 predecessor, Frank Steele, and Brendan Duddy, the crucial and enduring link in the back channel, as both are now deceased.

Nor could I have written this book without the love and support of my family and my partner, Irene Barrett, and her family too. Irene kickstarted the process by selflessly refurbishing my study and then by telling me I would have to sit down and do something in it. That turned out to be *Operation Chiffon*. Irene showed infinite patience, encouragement and advice throughout its gestation.

Some years ago my agent, Annabel Merullo of Peters Fraser and Dunlop, said it was time I wrote another book. I said I needed to find a suitable subject first. Astonishingly Robert came along completely out of the blue and Annabel reunited me with Bloomsbury, publisher of my previous trilogy on the conflict, *Provos*, *Loyalists* and *Brits*. *Operation Chiffon* now completes the story and makes the trilogy a quartet. Senior Commissioning Editor Jasmine Horsey enthusiastically embraced the book, and my managing editor, Elisabeth Denison, skilfully orchestrated the publication process. Bloomsbury thoughtfully commissioned Bill Swainson, who edited *Brits*, to edit this manuscript, which he did with inexhaustible patience, expertise and calmness. He was my indispensable guide, my *vade mecum* throughout the process. Peter James was a dedicated and meticulous copy editor, and Catherine Best a sharp proofreader. Lesley Hodgson trawled the archive for photos, and Phil Beresford contributed design support on the plate section. Together, my publicist, Anna Massardi, and Rights Manager Callum Mollison helped to bring the book to a wider readership. I also wish to thank the BBC's Malcolm Balen, who so assiduously read the manuscript, and Auriol Griffith-Jones, who expertly compiled the index. Finally, there are those I would like to thank but cannot name. They know who they are. *Operation Chiffon* is a tribute to the efforts and support of many.

Image Credits

Frank Steele in Derry: copyright untraceable

William Whitelaw: © Don Smith/Radio Times/Getty Images

Seamus Twomey on Lenadoon Avenue: © Victor Patterson

Brendan Hughes: © David Barker

Peter Taylor and the Thames TV Crew on Lenadoon Avenue: © Victor Patterson

Brendan Duddy: courtesy of Peter Norrey

Michael Oatley: © David Barker

Billy McKee and Proinsias Mac Airt: sourced from the *Irish Times*, copyright untraceable

Ian Paisley: © Pacemaker Press International

Miami Showband: © Stephen Travers

Roy Mason: © PA Images/Alamy Stock Photo

Provisional IRA Conference: © Trinity Mirror/Mirrorpix/Alamy Stock Photo

Father Alec Reid giving last rites: © Shutterstock

'The conflict is over' note: courtesy of Niall Ó Dochartaigh

Gerry Adams, Albert Reynolds and John Hume: © Pacemaker Press International

Announcement by Gerry Adams and Martin McGuinness: © PA Images/Alamy Stock Photo

Gerry Adams and Bill Clinton: © William J. Clinton Presidential Library

Bertie Ahern, George Mitchell and Tony Blair: © Dan Chung/AP/ Shutterstock

Martin McGuinness and Queen Elizabeth II: © Paul Faith/WPA Pool/ Getty Images

Peter Taylor and Brendan Duddy: courtesy of the Duddy family

Brendan Duddy's Funeral: © PA Images/Alamy Stock Photo

Introduction

'Operation Chiffon' was the top-secret intelligence operation whose roots and antecedents go back to the bloodiest years of the conflict in the early 1970s, involving officers from MI6 (the Secret Intelligence Service, or SIS) and latterly from MI5 (the Security Service). Its aim was to get the IRA to call a ceasefire, end violence and enter talks. 'Chiffon' finally succeeded, leading to the historic IRA ceasefire of 1994, the Good Friday Agreement of 1998 and the fragile post-Brexit peace that exists today.

Its eventual success was largely due to the courage and determination of three remarkable men. One was a former senior MI6 officer now working for MI5, operating under three aliases and known simply as Robert – and to the IRA as 'Fred'. Robert tells his story here for the first time. On his retirement one of his senior MI5 colleagues commended him.

> The case ['Operation Chiffon'] has been an exceptional one and I believe the progress made is due to a significant extent to your skill and experience. I wish you well for the future and hope that if we do eventually achieve the desired result [peace], you will sit in your garden content in the knowledge that you played a significant role in its achievement.[1]

The second remarkable man was the MI6 officer Michael Oatley, whom the IRA knew by the codename 'The Mountain Climber'. It was his groundwork for 'Operation Chiffon' in the seventies, eighties and early nineties, which I have chronicled in my books and television documentaries, that in the end made 'Operation Chiffon' possible.

Jonathan Powell, Prime Minister Tony Blair's Chief of Staff, who was instrumental in helping Blair achieve peace through the Good Friday Agreement, described Oatley's contribution.

> Michael Oakley was crucial. No one else could have done that. If
> you look around the world it's nearly always the intelligence services
> that do open up these channels because it's dangerous, it has to be
> deniable and can't be official. The intelligence agencies played a
> critical role in making peace in Northern Ireland possible.[2]

The third remarkable person, through whom Robert and Michael Oatley both worked, was the Derry/Londonderry businessman Brendan Duddy. Their remarkable achievements would not have been possible without him. He was initially codenamed 'Soon' but when 'Operation Chiffon' came on stream he was given another codename. Brendan remained anonymous for thirty-five years because of the top-secret nature of his work, operating a clandestine back channel to the leadership of the IRA throughout the darkest days of the Troubles. Jonathan Powell later recognised his groundwork in the lead-up to the ceasefire and the Good Friday Agreement.

> Brendan Duddy's role was absolutely fundamental. If you
> hadn't had this channel opening up from the early 70s right the
> way through, you'd have had no way of communicating. The
> Government would have been caught in a Catch 22: they could
> never find out if the IRA was prepared to go on to a ceasefire and
> negotiate; and the IRA would never go on to a ceasefire unless they
> saw that there was a political way forward. If you hadn't had that
> channel created by Brendan Duddy there really would have been no
> way to get to the ceasefire.[3]

Brendan Duddy finally allowed me to reveal his identity in my BBC2 television documentary *The Secret Peacemaker* in 2008. I write about him in much greater detail here as he repeatedly put his life on the line for peace, narrowly surviving three terrifying IRA interrogations when he was suspected of being a British spy.

It is a truly astonishing story, told in full for the first time in this book in all its complexity and drama, from the summer of 1972 when

Michael Oatley's MI6 predecessor, Frank Steele, first met Gerry Adams to arrange secret talks with the IRA to the moment in 1993 when Robert met Martin McGuinness and, without authorisation, spoke the words the IRA had been waiting twenty years to hear, Ireland 'will be as one'.

Robert appears at the critical moment of 'Operation Chiffon'. To free the logjam blocking efforts to end the conflict, he broke the rules, disobeyed orders and against all the odds, helped bring about the ceasefire that eventually, with the Good Friday Agreement, led to the end of the conflict that had claimed more than 3,600 lives. Robert was not the first to disobey orders. Michael Oatley had done the same by maintaining contact with the IRA over many years against strict ministerial instructions.

Until now, Robert – a modest and private man – has never spoken about his work, remaining an unidentified, unsung hero in the shadows, and his true identity has never been before revealed. Despite the passing of many years, he has to remain anonymous due to the draconian restrictions of the Official Secrets Act. But in this book he has at last broken his silence. After more than twenty years of trying to track him down, I was finally able to secure an interview with him in which he told me the extraordinary inside story of what really happened, step by precarious step, on the fraught and dangerous road to peace. Like Brendan Duddy and Michael Oatley, Robert put his life on the line, always aware of the possibility of kidnap by the IRA, interrogation, torture and 'execution' as a spy. Robert, a modest and private man, has never spoken before and his true identity has never been revealed. Now in this book he at last has broken his silence. His interview is a historically important document, the final element in the complex jigsaw of peace. 'I'd like what I did to be remembered,' he told me. 'I did think I'd brought peace to Northern Ireland.' Officials and others involved in 'Operation Chiffon' and its predecessors were honoured with knighthoods. Robert and Brendan Duddy received nothing. Peace would probably not have happened without them.

PART I

I

Finding Robert

Robert's role in breaking the roadblock on the road to peace in Ireland came down to less than a dozen words, recorded in Sinn Féin's minutes, that he addressed to the IRA leader, Martin McGuinness, in a secret and unauthorised face-to-face meeting in Derry in March 1993. They were explosive:

> The final solution is union... This island will be as one.

If these words were intended to reflect unspoken, long-term Government policy, they were diametrically opposed to the British Government's oft-repeated and consistent public position that Irish unity could only be achieved with the consent of the majority, and historically the majority in Northern Ireland had been Protestant and unionist.

When I read those words in Sinn Féin's minutes of the 1993 Derry meeting, I could not believe they had been spoken by Robert in his capacity as 'the British Government Representative', words that would have been taken by the IRA to indicate British Government policy. Is that what Robert really did say, or was it wishful thinking on the part of the republican movement (the IRA and Sinn Féin), or was it simply IRA propaganda?[1] I knew that the only way to find out the truth was to track down Robert and confront him. The problem was finding him. Nobody, apart from MI5 and MI6, for whom Robert had originally worked, and Her Majesty's Government, knew who Robert was, and no arm of the state was likely to provide the information in keeping with its policy of 'Neither Confirm Nor Deny', the standard response to all queries from journalists and others about the secret intelligence agencies.

Finding Robert and establishing whether he had really said those words became a tantalising twenty-year search for the truth. I had one slender clue to go on. When Robert finally said goodbye to Brendan Duddy, his secret back-channel link to the IRA, he gave him a farewell present, Robert Kee's *The Laurel and the Ivy*, the biography of the controversial late nineteenth-century Irish nationalist Charles Stewart Parnell. Brendan admired Parnell as a politician who believed in trying to solve the Irish problem through peaceful and constitutional means and not through violence.

Robert signed the book with a Latin quote from the Roman poet Virgil's epic poem on the escape from Troy and the founding of Rome, the *Aeneid*, named after its eponymous hero, Aeneas: *Forsan et haec olim meminisse iuvabit*. Aeneas, in search of a new home after the sack of Troy and undergoing a series of hair-raising adventures on the high seas, tells his exhausted crew, on first reaching dry land, 'Perhaps one day it will be good to remember even these things.'[2] Virgil provided the clue that many years later finally led me to Robert.

The quote suggested that Robert may have had a classical education, possibly at Oxford or Cambridge. It was a stab in the dark, a needle in the Oxbridge haystack of final examination results. It was around 2000 when, with producer Sam Collyns and team, I was making the documentary *Brits: The War Against the IRA*, the third part of our TV trilogy, preceded by *Provos: The IRA and Sinn Féin* and *Loyalists*. The trilogy and accompanying books explored the three parties to the Irish conflict. We estimated Robert's likely age and our indefatigable researcher, Julia Hannis, trawled through endless 'Tripos' lists in the Cambridge University Library and before going on to Oxford to check 'Mods' results, scrutinised old Diplomatic Records in the BBC library. It was there that she finally came up with the name Robert. I omit his surname because for security reasons we always kept that secret. Julia then managed to establish the address where he lived.

Producer Sam Collyns and I took the train and alighted at the station closest to Robert's house, but still many miles away. I had rented a car and having studied a map (there were no satnavs in those days) drove over hill and dale to the location we'd identified on the map. It turned out to be a farm but it looked very empty. And it was. It seemed we had come all that way for nothing.

I had brought with me a copy of *Provos: The IRA and Sinn Féin* that I intended to give to Robert as my calling card. There was a cottage close by the farm. I knocked at the door and asked the woman who answered if I could leave a book and a note for her neighbour Robert. She explained he was away with his wife on a cruise around Greece. She promised to deliver the book when he returned in two or three weeks' time. I went back to London with an empty feeling in the pit of my stomach. Robert had not been at home to receive visitors.

Three weeks later I made the same journey again. Once more, I boarded the train, headed out of London and, for a second time, fastened my seat belt in the rented car, fearing it might be another abortive journey. The weather was foul. The heavens opened just as I left the station, with the wipers in overdrive, sweeping rivers of rain from the windscreen.

I finally arrived at the remote farm with the rain still hammering down. I parked the car, pulled on my anorak and nervously made my way to the farmyard where I'd seen someone. Could this be Robert? I swallowed hard, took a deep breath and walked towards the lone figure. He reacted with a look of astonishment, suddenly face to face with a stranger with a hood pulled over his head to ward off the rain.

I introduced myself, for the first time mentioning the BBC, and pushed back the hood in the hope of appearing less threatening. I asked him if he was who I thought he was – Robert. I mentioned his surname. He never flinched, looked me straight in the eye and said, 'Sorry, you've got the wrong man.' I mentioned Brendan Duddy in Derry. Surely he knew him? He said he'd never heard of him. I pressed him again. 'Are you sure?' 'Absolutely,' he replied. Standing there, still in the midst of the torrential downpour, I then asked if he had received the book I had left for him with his neighbour. He confirmed he had and, beckoning to the farmhouse, said he would let me have it back. I followed him to the doorstep where my recollection is that he left me standing, now totally drenched. A few minutes later, he returned with the book, handed it over and said goodbye. Crestfallen, I returned to the car and drove away, deeply depressed, the windscreen wipers still in overdrive. Robert had eluded me.

On the train journey back to London, which seemed even longer given the anti-climax and the feeling of deep disappointment, I tried to gather the thoughts racing round my head. Surely if he was indeed *not* Robert, as he appeared to be a gentleman of good manners, he would have invited me into the farmhouse to dry out, offered me a cup of tea and asked what this was all about. None of which happened. I then concluded that this was the giveaway, although it was no consolation. That was it, I thought. No interview. I had failed.

Some years later, I happened to be talking to a friend of a friend. In the course of our conversation, I mentioned my abortive excursion to see Robert. 'Yes, I know,' he said. 'He got in touch and said you had paid him a visit. He wanted to know if he should have talked to you.' 'Certainly not,' he was told. My spirits were lifted at the thought that at least I had got the right man, but I had still failed to put the crucial question to him: did he really say to Martin McGuinness, in the words that continued to haunt me, 'The final solution is union. This island will be as one'? But this is only the beginning of the story. There was a remarkable development.

In the summer of 2021 I returned from a short break in Devon with my partner Irene. It was time off after making my documentary *Ireland After Partition*, which had just been shown on BBC2. When I arrived home, there was the usual pile of unopened mail awaiting my attention. Among the items was a letter addressed in handwriting I didn't recognise. It was dated 16 June 2021. Irene remembers me opening it and then exclaiming, 'I don't believe it!' Astonishingly the letter was from Robert.

> Dear Peter.
>   You will no doubt be surprised to hear from me after so many years. I was stimulated by your recent programme. For a variety of reasons, I could now give you some background which might fill some gaps – were you so interested.

'Surprise' was an understatement. I was dumbfounded. The letter arrived more than twenty years after our rain-sodden meeting in the farmyard. I couldn't believe it. It felt as though I had won the lottery. The letter concluded:

> Two of the leading figures in my involvement have died [Martin McGuinness and Brendan Duddy]. The third, crucially for me, is my wife. It is her death which puts me in a position to contact you.

The letter was signed 'Robert'. There were two phone numbers at the top of the letter, a mobile and a landline, a suggestion that Robert was ready for me to make contact. After time for reflection and recovery from the shock of the letter, I picked up the telephone, with considerable apprehension, and rang Robert. He was surprisingly friendly and warm, unlike the man in the encounter in the farmyard whose reception was about as unwelcoming as the weather. I asked if he would be happy for me to come and see him. 'Yes,' he replied, but on certain conditions, the most important being that his identity and whereabouts remain a secret. I made the journey in much better spirits than on the previous fruitless occasion. Robert came to the door and greeted me with a smile, because now, unlike the last time when we met in the rain, I was an expected and welcome visitor. Over time as we got to know and trust each other, I made more visits and he finally agreed to an interview to fill in the gaps in my knowledge and give me the remarkable story of 'Operation Chiffon'.

It was this encounter with Robert that, above all, led me to write this book. It is the final piece in the complex jigsaw of peace put together over many long and violent years by Robert's predecessors, the MI6 officers Frank Steele and Michael Oatley, and the pivotal figure in the back channel to the IRA, Brendan Duddy.

2

Meeting Frank Steele

The story that eventually culminates in 'Operation Chiffon' begins in the early 1970s with the MI6 officer Frank Steele. I remember meeting him in the late 1990s at his flat in a Victorian mansion block in London. I had tracked him down through a process of elimination and clues from public records where his Foreign Office connections and record in the Colonial Service were listed, although without mentioning that he was an officer in Her Majesty's Secret Intelligence Service. He was lying in bed, seriously ill with terminal cancer and supported by a series of dedicated carers who looked after him around the clock. One of them showed me into his bedroom where he was propped up with pillows and obviously frail, his slippers by the bed. He was wearing striped pyjamas and had a round face and bright attentive eyes that seemed to belie his frailness and infirmity. I remember they were staring and wide. His voice was weak and slightly croaky, but he was clearly mentally alert. I said I recalled meeting him briefly in Belfast in the summer of June 1972 after the IRA ceasefire he had been instrumental in arranging came to an end. When we met then, I had not been aware that it was he who had set up the talks in Chelsea between the British Government and the IRA. To my surprise, he was happy to talk about what he had done in Northern Ireland as I suspected he would like it known, especially by future historians of the conflict. As a bonus, they would benefit from tasting the flavour of the man who was the antithesis of the often dry, soulless bureaucratic minutes of the period released – or in some cases not under the Official Secrets Act, even after thirty years.

After reflection, Frank agreed to do a television interview for the BBC TV documentary series I was making in 1997, *Provos. The IRA and Sinn Féin*. I never asked him if he had sought permission from SIS. I suspected he had not, perhaps because he knew he did not have long to live and he was unlikely to have been given it anyway. He did the interview brilliantly, full face to camera, given that he was 'old school' and had never been in front of a television lens before. He sat in his wheelchair in his darkened drawing room with the curtains drawn to accommodate the lighting, fascinated by the television paraphernalia and asking technical questions about the interview.

Frank passed away a few months after the interview. His obituary concluded, 'In the long years of his battle against cancer, Frank Steele showed the same courage he displayed through the many vicissitudes of his adventurous life. A big man in every sense.'[1] Part of Frank's legacy, thanks to his interview, was a remarkable first-hand account of dealing with the IRA face to face in an endeavour to facilitate peace in 1972, the most violent year of the conflict in which almost 500 people were killed. It was to be a quarter of a century before peace finally arrived with the Good Friday Agreement in 1998.

Frank Steele joined MI6 in 1951, after serving with the Royal Engineers in the Second World War and later in the Colonial Service in Uganda and Kenya (1948–50). According to his obituary, he was 'denied combat experience because of atomic bombs. Because of that he never avoided fraught, possibly dangerous situations in his later life.'[2] One such potentially dangerous situation was in Northern Ireland when he came face to face with the leadership of the Provisional IRA.

Northern Ireland was the last place Frank Steele expected to end up, after two decades of tours in the trouble spots of Cyprus, Lebanon, Libya, Jordan and Kenya, some of the overseas colonies and theatres in which his expertise and experience were rooted. Perhaps he shouldn't have been surprised as Northern Ireland was Britain's own 'trouble spot'. In 1971 he was back in London, 'awaiting posting which is a very dangerous thing to be'. He was anticipating another foreign assignment and hadn't done any particular preparation for his interview with MI6's Personnel Department, apart from reading the newspapers that morning on his way to the meeting at the then SIS Headquarters, Century House, a grey, anonymous building in Waterloo. Frank was hardly well prepared.

I was asked what did I know about Northern Ireland? Had I heard
of someone called 'Faulkner'? I happened to have read in *The
Times* that day that Faulkner was the Southern Ireland Minister of
Agriculture, so I thought I'd show off and say, 'Yes he's the Southern
Irish Minister of Agriculture.'

Steele got *nul points* for his answer. Faulkner was Brian Faulkner, the
Prime Minister of Northern Ireland.

In typical personnel fashion they said, 'Oh well, that means you've
got an untrammelled mind and you'll be unbiased, so you're just the
person to send there.'

If Steele had hardly passed his interview with flying colours, his card
had been marked by a distinguished member of the Foreign Office's
Diplomatic Service, Howard Smith, who had been a member of the
Bletchley Park code-breaking team during the Second World War.
Three decades later he rose to become Ambassador to Moscow (1976–8)
and Director General of MI5 (1978–81).

In 1971, Smith was heading for Belfast as the UK Government's
Representative at Stormont, the imposing seat of Northern Ireland's
parliament, a glistening white building set in leafy gardens and parkland,
five miles east of Belfast. The post was initially established in 1969 by
Labour's Prime Minister, Harold Wilson, and was designed to have
a British representative on the spot to keep a wary eye on Northern
Ireland's parliament. The alternative had been to abolish Stormont
once British troops had been committed to the province in August
1969 to avoid a potential civil war. Appointing a British Government
Representative was the less incendiary choice, and that post would play
a major role in the years ahead.

Howard Smith anticipated how much work would be involved in his
new position and decided that two British heads were better than one.
Frank Steele, he concluded, was just the man to act as his 'counsellor'
with his pedigree of working in conflict areas overseas. Not being one
to resist a challenge, Steele accepted the offer.

There had been allegations that I'd been sent to establish a line of
communication with the IRA but that is absolute rubbish. HMG

didn't want a line of communication with the IRA. HMG wanted
to beat the IRA. It was really that I had got considerable experience
of conflict situations in the Middle East and Africa – civil wars and
unrest and so on – that it was thought that my experience would be
useful in Northern Ireland as a general deputy to Howard Smith, if
I could get amongst the extremists on both sides as well as helping
him generally in relations with the Faulkner Government.[3]

Frank arrived in Belfast in October 1971 and soon found himself with
his feet under the desk in an office in a villa called Laneside in a leafy
and secluded suburb along the shore of Belfast Lough. Howard Smith
had overseen the acquisition of Laneside in 1971, just before Frank
arrived, with a view to having a secure, discrete and discreet base where
sensitive meetings with the province's political and paramilitary leaders
on all sides could be held, well out of the media spotlight. It was perfect
for Frank. Unofficially, Laneside was MI6's operational headquarters in
Northern Ireland, although under diplomatic cover because MI6 was
not supposed to operate on home ground within the United Kingdom.
At Laneside, Frank was rapidly brought up to speed on how and
why the conflict had evolved: how it had begun with the eruption of
the civil rights campaign in 1968, which challenged discrimination by
the unionist majority against the nationalist minority in matters of
housing, employment and voting.[4] Frank would also soon have become
familiar with the origins of the conflict lying deep in Irish history,
with the partition of Ireland – the division of the country – enacted in
1921, a temporary solution that was never intended to be permanent.
Reunification – Irish unity – was always the long-term intention of
the original legislation. The resulting state of Northern Ireland that
emerged from partition was gerrymandered to guarantee an inbuilt
unionist/Protestant majority. There was good reason why its parliament
at Stormont became known as 'a Protestant Parliament for a Protestant
People'. That was the whole point. Frank found little to raise his spirits
as he familiarised himself with the history with which he would have
to grapple and the words he would have to use to make friends and
avoid losing them: to say 'Londonderry' in Protestant/unionist/loyalist
company and 'Derry' in Catholic/nationalist/republican circles. Such
was the semantic minefield that Frank and other visiting 'Brits' had to
navigate. Frank was shocked by what he found.

When I arrived the place was a shambles. The community which at the foundation of the state [in 1921] was 30 per cent Catholic to 70 per cent Protestant was, when I arrived, 40 per cent Catholic to 60 per cent Protestant but the Protestants still continued to try and treat the Catholics as second-class citizens. The Catholics would no longer have this, and the civil rights movement became more and more violent as protests intensified. As they put it, they were being repressed by the security authorities and, as the security authorities put it, the IRA was infiltrating the civil rights movement. By the time I arrived in October 1971, the place was almost in a state of civil war. The Royal Ulster Constabulary [RUC] couldn't cope and British troops, with long experience of dealing with civil unrest in the colonies, had no experience of dealing with violent protests on home ground.

The army had been deployed in August 1969 to restore order after loyalist mobs had invaded nationalist areas and torched some of them, triggering a mass exodus of thousands of Catholics fleeing across the border to seek safety and sanctuary in the South. The troops were initially told they would be home by Christmas. They were not told specifically which Christmas their officers had in mind. They were to remain there, with all the consequences, for the next thirty-seven years, the longest single deployment in the British army's history, known as 'Operation Banner'.

When Frank Steele arrived in Northern Ireland and unpacked his bags at Laneside in October 1971, the conflict had already entered a critical stage. Internment without trial had been introduced two months earlier, on 9 August, when 342 nationalists and republicans had been detained without charge in a military operation codenamed 'Operation Demetrius'. Not one loyalist was lifted.

The mass arrests were supported at Westminster by the Conservative Prime Minister, Edward Heath, and accepted as the draconian response to insistent unionist demands, led by Stormont's Prime Minister, Brian Faulkner, for a tough security crackdown to smash the IRA. Many of those detained were subsequently incarcerated in compounds surrounded by high wire fences, known to those locked inside them as 'cages'. The whole internment camp was situated at Long Kesh, a former RAF base ten miles south of Belfast where detainees were housed behind the wire in Nissen huts, reminiscent of the Second World War. The image only served to confirm the inmates' insistence that they were prisoners of war and not the criminals the Government insisted they were throughout most of the conflict. Frank Steele had no illusions about internment and its impact.

> The theory of internment was knowing the infrastructure and command structure of the IRA. You lifted these people and you left a headless chicken behind, often consisting of young and inexperienced people who could be picked off at leisure. Well, the theory was fine. You take away the intelligence officers, the quartermasters, the training officers and so on but the practice was just a joke. Not one Protestant was interned. It did enormous damage to the credibility of the RUC and its Special Branch because a lot of the people who were interned were not a threat in any way at all. Although it did do some damage to the IRA's command structure, it didn't do all that much. The counter to it was a great flood of recruits to the IRA and of money and weapons. It showed up how poor RUC intelligence was and that it was directed at the Catholic community. A lot of the people picked up were just ordinary civil rights people. They weren't terrorists. Internment was a farce and a disaster.

The statistics bear out his assessment. For Frank, it was a baptism of fire. In the five months between the introduction of internment in August 1971 and the end of that year, 146 people were killed – 47 members of the security forces (army and RUC) and 99 civilians. In addition, there were 729 explosions and 437 shooting incidents.[5]

Internment also produced a human disaster that for decades went largely unrecognised and surprisingly unreported given its enormity and scale. In the days of rioting that followed the arrests in the Catholic Ballymurphy estate in West Belfast, British paratroopers shot dead at least nine civilians. At the inquest, nearly fifty years later, the coroner, Mrs Justice Keegan, concluded that all those killed were innocent, none of the victims was armed and none posed any threat. For many Catholics who only two years earlier had welcomed British soldiers as saviours, Ballymurphy destroyed the hearts and minds that had been won by tea, buns and bacon sandwiches when the troops arrived. I remember interviewing Ballymurphy's Briege Doyle whose mother Joan was shot dead by paratroopers as she broke cover to help a young man who'd just been shot. Briege was fourteen at the time. She is a tragic illustration of how and why attitudes changed so swiftly and disastrously.

> As far as my mummy was concerned the army was here to save us because the Protestant people were burning the Catholics out of [nationalist] areas like Bombay Street and the Falls Road or anywhere they could. She and the neighbour next door used to make them tea and sandwiches and she thought it was just the best thing. They were a lovely Regiment because they used to come in the house and sit down as well. My sister actually had met a soldier the year and a half before mummy died and she married him. And my mummy was quite happy with that. We all were. The Paras moved in and that's when everything changed.[6]

Alienation of sections of the nationalist community had begun a year before the Ballymurphy killings. In July 1970 the army had locked down and placed under curfew 3,000 homes along the length of the Falls Road, the main artery running through nationalist West Belfast. The purpose of the operation was to search for arms in the hope of dealing the IRA a major blow and nipping its campaign in the bud as it had been intensifying day by day. For thirty-six hours, no one was allowed to leave their home. The soldiers carrying out the searches weren't wearing carpet slippers and some homes were trashed as floorboards were ripped up in the hope of discovering hidden weapons. In the lower part of the Falls Road, an IRA stronghold, there were fierce gun battles. Four civilians were killed by the army and more than seventy wounded. Eighteen soldiers were also wounded and large quantities of weapons and ammunition were seized. More than 330 arrests were made. The Falls Road curfew marked a turning point in the relationship between Catholics and the army. A year later, internment and Ballymurphy sealed the alienation of large sections of the nationalist community, in Belfast, Derry and beyond. Frank Steele understood why soldiers' attitudes changed too.

> On occasions the soldiers helped destroy what had originally been friendly relations with the Catholic community. Soldiers were

being shot at and shouted at and screamed at and stoned from
the Catholic side rather than the Protestant side so they naturally
tended to look on the Catholics as hostile.

Frank was also concerned about what the army did in the weeks
following internment. He was shocked when it emerged that fourteen
'high value' detainees had been singled out and subjected to in-depth
interrogation using the so-called 'Five Techniques' that the army had
used to gather intelligence from insurgents in colonial situations in
the years before. These consisted of sleep deprivation, lack of food and
drink, hooding and forcing detainees to stand against a wall for long
periods in stress positions, resting on fingertips, and being subjected to
a loud, interminable and disorientating hissing sound known as 'white
noise'. The hope was that these extreme interrogation techniques would
elicit the detailed intelligence that 'Operation Demetrius' had failed
to produce. As an intelligence officer, Frank was appalled. 'It was just
damned stupid as well as morally wrong. I just thought it was counter-
productive and it does enormous damage internationally. And what
intelligence does it get you? Not very much.'

When Frank arrived in Northern Ireland there were two separate
IRAs. The 'Official' IRA was the linear descendant of the 'old' IRA
whose origins lay in the Easter Rising in Dublin centred around the
General Post Office in 1916. The 'old' IRA had remained largely dormant
since its previous military campaign along the border with the republic
from 1956 to 1962 and had now largely put its guns aside to concentrate
on building a Marxist-based political party and contesting elections.
Lacking arms and organisation, it was therefore only in a position to
mount a desultory response to the loyalist attacks on nationalist areas in
Belfast in 1969, the IRA's traditional responsibility being to protect such
areas. Graffiti appeared on walls in its heartland with the slogan 'IRA.
I Ran Away'. Its failure to defend nationalists was to have momentous
long-term consequences for the future of the republican movement.

December 1969 saw the birth of the 'Provisional' IRA, four months
after the deployment of British troops, founded by disillusioned
members of the 'old' IRA, such as the veteran Belfast republicans, Joe
Cahill and Billy McKee. Cahill and those around him who had no time
for constitutional politics, Marxist or otherwise, had one single-minded
aim. I remember him telling me in those early days, 'The main purpose

of the IRA and Sinn Féin, as far as I was concerned, was to break the connection with England, to get rid of the Brits from Ireland.'[7] At this stage for the Provisionals, or 'Provos' as they became colloquially known, it was about the gun, the bomb and 'armed struggle', not about contesting elections and recognising the political institutions of Dublin. The ballot box, North and South, would have to wait another decade and more.

3

'Bloody Sunday' and Beyond

Internment was the trigger for much of the violence that followed, leading to a chain of events that nearly six months later, on 30 January 1972, resulted in the day that forever became notorious as 'Bloody Sunday'. It was the day that soldiers of the Parachute Regiment's 1st Battalion, some of whom had been present at the Ballymurphy killings six months earlier, shot dead thirteen innocent civil rights marchers in Derry who had been protesting against internment and the alleged torture of detainees. The march had been banned by the Stormont Government but the ban was ignored. The Paras had been deployed from their base in Belfast, where they had achieved a fearsome reputation for dealing with rioters and removing barricades. In Derry, the rioters were referred to by the army's resident battalion as 'the Derry Young Hooligans' and were expected, with good reason, to cause trouble during Sunday's march, stoning soldiers who were blocking roads to protect the city centre. Lieutenant-Colonel Derek Wilford, the Paras' Commanding Officer, told me that his soldiers were not going to be passive.

> I wasn't pleased at all that British soldiers could line up behind
> plastic shields and just stand there and let people throw rocks
> at them and do nothing whatsoever about it. We thought it was
> a peculiar way for soldiers to behave. They just stood there in
> the road like Aunt Sallies and never went forward. It was quite
> horrifying. I actually said publicly that my soldiers were not going
> to act as Aunt Sallies. Ever! We did not carry shields. We did not
> wear cricket pads. As far as I was concerned, it was not a game of

cricket that we were indulging in. In my view this was a war. When
we moved on the streets, we moved as if we were moving against
a well-armed, well-trained army. I wanted my soldiers to stay alive
and I actually said to them, 'you will not get killed'.[1]

Senior army officers based in the City and the RUC's Chief
Superintendent, Frank Lagan, one of the few Catholics promoted to
the RUC's upper ranks, strongly advised against bringing in the Paras,
fearing the worst. Their fears were tragically fulfilled. On the day of
the march, all thirteen innocent civilians were killed within the space
of barely thirty minutes, between 4 and 4.30 p.m. on an icy cold but
sunny Sunday afternoon. I first set foot in Derry late that evening as a
young journalist. I'd never been to Ireland before and was shamefully
ill-informed about the conflict.

Colonel Wilford insisted at the time that his men had come under
fire from the IRA and told me when I interviewed him many years
later that it was something he would believe 'until the end of my days'.
The conclusion reached in the epic judicial inquiry conducted by Lord
Saville, which lasted twelve years and cost almost £200 million, was
that none of those shot was carrying a firearm, none was posing any
threat and no warning was given before the soldiers opened fire. It was
a conclusion similar to that of the Ballymurphy coroner, Mrs Justice
Keegan, nearly eleven years earlier. That Sunday afternoon Frank Steele
was with Howard Smith at Laneside waiting to hear the outcome of
the march. Both feared violence in the wake of a clash between anti-
internment marchers and the Paras the weekend before, as the protesters
attempted to reach another internment camp at Magilligan Point, at
the mouth of Lough Foyle, forty miles east of Derry. Frank remembers
the moment he first heard the news about 'Bloody Sunday'.

We knew, of course, that although the parade was banned the civil
rights demonstration was going to go ahead. Howard [Smith] and
I were sitting in his office at Laneside waiting for reports to come
in. We just found it very difficult to believe. When we got to three
deaths, five deaths and then seven deaths, Howard and I looked
at each other and said, 'Right, that means Direct Rule.' And,
of course, when it came to thirteen deaths, Direct Rule became
inevitable. [Direct Rule meant the suspension of the Stormont

parliament and Westminster taking over the running of the province.] The Labour Government Home Secretary James Callaghan had looked at the option before only to rule it out on the grounds that the time wasn't right. In any case we humble Brits were not the people to understand these complex problems in Northern Ireland and the Northern Ireland problems were best left to the Northern Irish to solve. Our ministers were pretty reluctant, but they realised that it had to be done.

Like internment and Ballymurphy, 'Bloody Sunday' was a disaster but one of an even greater magnitude, as Frank recognised.

It built up the IRA. Catholics were saying we need the IRA to defend us against the British army. And it led to a flood of volunteers, money and weapons going to the IRA. The only good thing that came out of it was that it enabled Direct Rule to be brought in two months later. Brian Faulkner was summoned to London and there was a big meeting with Prime Minister Ted Heath and Faulkner. Faulkner was told that Stormont would be disbanded and that HMG would be taking over responsibility for security affairs. Faulkner said, 'Well, there's no point in my being Prime Minister if I don't have powers over security.' And we were saying, 'Well, we want the powers over security because we can't allow our army to be used by a unionist government in this way.' So Faulkner was told that Friday, 'It's going to be Direct Rule.'

Barely two months after 'Bloody Sunday', on 28 March 1972, the Stormont parliament was suspended and Direct Rule from Westminster was introduced. William Whitelaw became the first Secretary of State for Northern Ireland. Frank developed huge admiration for 'Willie', as he was affectionately known both at Westminster and in the media. A former officer in the Scots Guards, he was a Tory grandee of the old school, a man of integrity, honour and principle.

There was a divergence of opinion in London about what should happen after Direct Rule, in order to try to end, or at least attenuate, the conflict. Frank was intimately involved in the debate. Some of the military top brass believed that the IRA could be beaten, while others, like General Sir Harry Tuzo, the army's top soldier in Northern Ireland

and one of the more far-sighted, who had thought internment was a bad idea, were of the view that military means would not achieve the defeat of the IRA and that only political initiatives would help provide a solution to the Irish problem. Frank was one of those others. He believed that the Government had to engage with the IRA to see under what circumstances it would be prepared to end its campaign and enter politics – which twenty years later turned out to be the purpose of 'Operation Chiffon'. Frank had no scruples about talking to 'terrorists' with blood on their hands if that held the key to peace. And he had form in dealing with 'terrorists', experienced in the course of his previous posting in Kenya and his dealings with President Jomo Kenyatta, the former leader of the notorious 'Mau Mau' insurgents who terrorised British settlers in Kenya's fight for independence during the 1950s.*

> We'd interned Kenyatta because of his links with the Mau Mau whose obscene rituals made the IRA look like a Sunday School picnic. A British governor at the time described Kenyatta as 'a leader until darkness and death'. If you're prepared to talk to someone like that in Kenya, to people like me it seemed just pragmatic to talk to the IRA. Ministers realised that, if word leaked out, there would be uproar in the unionist party. What were we doing shaking the bloody hands of terrorists when we should be fighting them? But we pointed out to ministers that they would score genuine Brownie points from the Catholic community by saying that in their determination to try and find a peaceful solution to Northern Ireland they were prepared even to talk to terrorists.

Not that all Catholics regarded the IRA as 'terrorists'.

On the face of it, Willie Whitelaw was the last person you would have expected to be prepared to meet the IRA leadership, but he was finally convinced, with great difficulty by Frank Steele, to take the risk on the grounds that peace, if that was the outcome, was a risk worth taking. 'There was a lot of heart searching and soul searching,' Frank

---

*'Mau Mau' was the Kikuyu name for the Kenyan nationalist movement. To the British 'Mau Mau' meant 'terrorists'. Thousands were detained in internment camps. In the eight-year emergency, thirty-two white settlers were killed – a fraction compared to the killing of more than 1,800 Africans.

said. 'Anyway, the long and the short was that Willie said, "OK, I'll talk."' Whitelaw later told me that he had found it extremely distasteful to talk to those who may have been responsible for killing British soldiers and described it as 'the greatest mistake of my political career'.[2]

The Provisional IRA, who at the time believed it was winning – 'One more push and the Brits are out' was the mantra – offered a ceasefire in return for a meeting with the British. On 13 June 1972 at a press conference in Derry, the Provisional IRA's Chief of Staff, Seán Mac Stíofáin, invited Mr Whitelaw to come to Derry for talks. Mac Stíofáin was flanked by the young Martin McGuinness, who, in the wake of 'Bloody Sunday', had just taken over as Officer Commanding the IRA's Derry Brigade, David O'Connell, the IRA's political strategist and dovish member of its all-powerful seven-man Provisional Army Council, and Seamus Twomey, the hard-line commander of the IRA's Belfast Brigade.

Some senior Provisionals were convinced that it was only a matter of time before the British threw in the towel, packed their bags and boarded the boats – as they had done in December 1921 after signing the Treaty that gave two-thirds of Ireland a large degree of independence at the end of the IRA's so-called 'War of Independence' in which atrocities were committed by both sides. Martin Meehan, a notorious IRA gunman from Belfast's Ardoyne area, put it succinctly. 'We actually believed we could drive the British army into the sea,' he told me. 'We believed without a doubt we had the capability of doing it.'[3] In fact, nothing could have been further from the truth. But Frank wasn't the only one advocating that Whitelaw should take the plunge. After the IRA's press conference, John Hume and Paddy Devlin, both prominent members of the moderate and mainly Catholic Social Democratic and Labour Party (SDLP), also spent several days urging a reluctant Whitelaw to take the IRA up on its offer. He finally agreed – but not to come to Derry. Throughout his life John Hume remained a tireless worker for peace.

One of the IRA's conditions for the meeting with Whitelaw was that the Government should grant 'political status' to the IRA's convicted prisoners. The pressure to meet the demand was coming from the IRA leader, Billy McKee, who was on hunger strike in the Crumlin Road jail in a campaign for 'political status'; several of his comrades later joined the protest. This status would allow prisoners to wear their own clothes in place of the prison uniforms that they believed branded them as common criminals. They pointed out the anomaly that their comrades interned in the compounds of Long Kesh were allowed to wear their own clothes. Fearing violent demonstrations now that McKee was rumoured to be dangerously close to death, Whitelaw gave way and agreed to the hunger strikers' demands and granted Special Category Status. The term was less provocative than 'political status' but amounted to much the same thing. Sentenced prisoners were now allowed to wear their own clothes. It was a symbolic but, as events were to show, a hugely important concession that ultimately was to have monumental consequences for the conflict. The issue was not much remarked upon at the time but almost a decade later was to explode in the conflict-changing hunger strikes of 1980 and 1981 in the Maze prison, as the Long Kesh internment camp would come to be known.

4

Face to Face with the IRA

With Whitelaw now in principle on board, it was up to Frank Steele to sound out the IRA and arrange the logistics for the meeting. The notion of Whitelaw coming to Derry to meet the IRA was a non-starter, but that didn't rule out other venues. Frank's first and potentially dangerous task was to venture close to the border, a few miles outside Derry, on the edge of enemy territory from where the IRA would plan and launch attacks. This he did a week after Mac Stíofáin's invitation to Whitelaw and in the company of a senior British civil servant, Philip Woodfield, now attached to the new Northern Ireland Office (NIO), established as a result of Direct Rule. But first the Government had to agree to another of the IRA's demands: Gerry Adams, then a young Provisional leader from Ballymurphy, had to be released from the Long Kesh internment camp. Frank and his colleagues were aware of Adams's standing in the republican movement. Frank told me about meeting Adams for the first time.

> What intrigued us was that the man chosen to represent the whole
> of the Northern IRA was Gerry Adams and that they wanted him so
> badly that we had to arrange for him to be released from internment
> and given a special pass. So he was released. We had our meeting
> at a neutral place in the small area between the north of Derry and
> the Donegal border. I was intrigued to see what Gerry Adams was
> going to be like having been told he'd been commander of the IRA's
> Ballymurphy battalion which had been very efficient in blowing
> up and murdering people. He then held a senior position in the

Belfast Brigade which also had been very efficient in blowing up and murdering people. I had expected an aggressive, streetwise, arrogant young thug and I was very pleasantly surprised when the man who appeared was not like that at all. He was very personable, pleasant, intelligent, lucid and persuasive. He hid his ruthlessness and the powers of manipulation that he possesses to a great degree, otherwise he would never have got to where he was. It's this combination that makes Adams so effective and dangerous. They would not have chosen him unless he was a member of the IRA. [Mr Adams has repeatedly denied that he was ever a member of the IRA.][1]

At 3 p.m. on 20 June 1972, Frank Steele and Philip Woodfield secretly met Gerry Adams and David O'Connell at a country house close to the Donegal border near Derry called Ballyarnett House, where they were to discuss the modalities for the unprecedented meeting with Whitelaw. Over time, Frank got to know O'Connell, who, when not an active IRA volunteer (euphemistically known as an 'active republican'), was a building and woodwork teacher at a college in Donegal. O'Connell joined the IRA in his late teens and was wounded in the IRA's border campaign (1956–62).[2] I remember meeting him in a safe house in Dublin in 1974 when he struck me not as an IRA gunman but as a thoughtful, articulate person who was anxious to achieve a political solution – but by no means on any terms. O'Connell was the 'dove' in the Provisionals' leadership. Frank's view was that he was a 'very quiet, self-contained, self-disciplined man' but still 'a bloodthirsty terrorist'. Frank wasn't fazed by meeting Adams and O'Connell.

Was I nervous? We did think of arming ourselves. They were interested in preliminary talks. They didn't want to kidnap us. It was all rather sweet. They wanted to represent themselves as representing an army and not a bunch of terrorists. We all had to have letters of authority. They had them and we had them, ours signed by a minister or Willie. I thought at the time, 'This is simply ridiculous.' We hadn't just wandered in off the street to chat. We were obviously representing HMG and they the IRA.[3]

Fascinated to discover that Adams was the antithesis of what he had imagined, Frank continued the conversation once the business was over.

I said, 'You don't want to spend the rest of your life on the run from us British. What do you want to do?' He said, 'I want to go to university to get a degree.' I said, 'Well, we're not stopping you. All you've got to do is renounce violence and you can go to university and get a degree.' He grinned and said, 'I've got to get rid of you British first.'[4]

The Government's top-secret minute of the encounter, presumably written by Frank and his NIO colleague, Philip Woodfield, records:

> There is no doubt whatever that these two at least [O'Connell and Adams] genuinely want a ceasefire and a permanent end to violence. Whatever pressures in Northern Ireland have brought them to this frame of mind there is also little doubt that now that the prospect of peace is there, they have a strong personal incentive to try and get it ... Their appearance and manner were respectable and respectful ... Their behaviour and attitude appeared to bear no relation to the indiscriminate campaigns of bombing and shooting in which they have both been prominent leaders.[5]

This is where the seeds of 'Operation Chiffon' were first sown, the recognition that the IRA might be persuaded to end its campaign and talk peace. The question that remained was how to get there. The meeting was businesslike and polite without polemics or animosity. The two sides agreed the details of the ceasefire that would be the prerequisite of talks. The IRA would cease operations; the army was to leave IRA suspects alone and cease operations and raids in nationalist areas. A telephone hotline was to be established between David O'Connell in the South and Frank Steele at Laneside in the North to deal with the inevitable problems that would arise. Steele remembers with a degree of affection the relationship he established with O'Connell over the hotline: 'He had the endearing habit of ending all his conversations with "good luck, good luck". Everything was "good luck". I know it's an unfashionable thing to say but I liked him. I could do business with him.'[6]

With surprisingly cordial relationships now established, despite the fact that the IRA was still killing British soldiers and policemen, the modalities of the historic meeting between the British Government and the IRA were agreed. The first step, as it was the official prerequisite for talks in all subsequent negotiations over the more than two decades ahead, was for the IRA to declare a cessation of offensive operations – in shorthand, a ceasefire. This was due to begin at midnight on Monday 26 June 1972 in the hope that there would be 'meaningful talks between the major parties in the conflict'. In a pattern that was to become grimly familiar in the lead-up to ceasefires in the years ahead, the IRA carried on killing right up to the appointed time for the guns and bombs to fall silent. On this occasion it killed three soldiers in a landmine explosion the previous Saturday and two more on the Monday afternoon before the ceasefire was scheduled to begin.

It was to be the first such face-to-face meeting between the British Government and the IRA since Michael Collins, the IRA's chief military and political strategist in the IRA's 'War of Independence', met the British Prime Minister, David Lloyd George, in Downing Street in 1921. The negotiations resulted in the Anglo-Irish Treaty, which gave the primarily Catholic/nationalist Twenty-Six Counties of the South, now partitioned, a degree of independence from Britain, although remaining under the Crown in a form of Home Rule. The new political entity became known as the Irish Free State (Eire). The primarily Protestant/unionist Six Counties of the North continued as the state of Northern Ireland with an inbuilt Protestant majority, umbilically joined to the rest of the United Kingdom.

A week after Frank Steele and Philip Woodfield met Gerry Adams and David O'Connell, the IRA declared a 'suspension of offensive operations' that would make it politically possible for the British Government to be involved in a meeting with the enemy, although the meeting was to be kept a closely guarded secret. The Government was relieved that the ceasefire was in place, as were many IRA volunteers who had been involved in fighting the war for two years. Brendan Hughes, the IRA's commander in the Lower Falls Road and republican legend, summed up what he told me was the widespread feeling:

Most people never lived beyond the next month, never mind the next year. There was no long-term strategy to fight the war. And when the British troops were taken off the streets in 1972 because of the IRA ceasefire, obviously people thought, 'This is it.' No one before had fought the British Government to a position where they were negotiating with the IRA [except, of course, at the end of the

IRA's 'War of Independence' in 1921]. There were expectations that
the war was over. I think there was a need to believe it, a wish to
believe it and a desire for it to happen. Most people involved had
been on the run, and being 'on the run' means living from hand to
mouth and depending on people to feed you. It means not seeing
your kids, it means not seeing your wife and it can be a very, very
difficult situation to be in. People wanted it to end then. They
wanted to get back to their wives and back to their kids.[7]

The unlikely venue for the meeting with the IRA leadership that
Frank Steele had organised was the home of Whitelaw's number two,
Paul Channon, in Chelsea's exclusive Cheyne Walk. It was scheduled
for Friday 7 July 1972. The logistics were not easy to manage. Given the
complexities, the whole operation from Seán Mac Stíofáin's invitation
to Whitelaw to the IRA and British Government delegations sitting
down in the elegant surroundings of Paul Channon's house, with
its grandstand view of the Thames, had taken just over a month – a
remarkably short space of time given the enormous sensitivities of the
enterprise. But now, with everything in place and the reality of meeting
the IRA getting ever closer, Frank had one more thing to do as he feared
the Northern Ireland Secretary was getting understandably wobbly:

persuading Willie to actually go ahead with the talks because,
having agreed, he started having doubts. But he courageously made
it his decision. It's all right for we officials to say, 'You should do
this. You should do that,' but in the end the political can rests with
Willie and he took the decision and said, 'Ok, we'll go ahead.'

Brendan Hughes told me that prior to the meeting the IRA delegation
had even thought about what to wear.

I remember a discussion taking place and I remember Ivor Bell
[Operations Officer of the IRA's Belfast Brigade and veteran of the
IRA's border campaign] saying that he wasn't going to wear a suit
and tie. He was going to dress as a combatant as he always dressed.
He said history had taught him that British politicians would try
to make the Irish feel at ease. He was going to wear this gear to put
them ill at ease.[8]

In the end, Bell was overruled on the dress code and jackets and ties were the order of the day, not combat fatigues. Frank would have approved. Keeping his fingers tightly crossed, he was now ready to put the plan into operation. It wasn't the most auspicious of starts.

> One bright morning on Friday 7 July [1972], I find myself with an army captain and minibus where there's this very small area between Derry and the Donegal frontier which made it easier for the IRA to get to. There was a ceasefire on as well so they weren't going to be arrested. There was I and this army officer, in civvies, and a minibus waiting for the IRA to turn up but unfortunately there was no sign of them. I thought, 'Oh my God, they're not going to come!' All the business of persuading ministers and Whitelaw persuading himself that he must go ahead with the meeting, talk to them, and then all the complicated arrangements to get the IRA to the talks, all this would be wasted. So we waited and waited and then suddenly up drove a car at a rate of knots, absolutely bulging with IRA. They explained that they'd set off in two cars but they had had trouble with the second car and they hadn't been able to repair the thing. It was a puncture or something. After trying for a bit they then all bundled into this one car. There were six of them. They then got into the minibus with a look of utter disgust on the driver's face, a very taciturn army officer, who I think obviously disapproved of the whole proceeding. We then drove off to the field where the helicopter was going to come down and pick us up and take us to Aldergrove airport outside Belfast.[9]

But that wasn't the end of Frank's logistical problems.

> As we drove along this narrow country lane, what should happen but a herd of cows floods out from a field on the right and some of them take up station ahead of the minibus and some of them take up station behind the minibus. They were escorted by a stolid Northern Irish farmer who wasn't going to get a move on for anyone and Seán Mac Stíofáin, whom I never think of as being a funny man, must have made one of the few funny remarks of his life when he said, 'I do think the British army could have given us a better escort!' Anyway, the cows, thank God, peeled off into a

field on the left and we finally reached the field where the helicopter
came swooping down. We got in and were flown to the RAF side of
Aldergrove airport where we got into an RAF Andover.

The RAF had sent what they call 'a meet and greeter' for VIPs.
We were met by an RAF officer who was standing to attention and
doing all the courtesies with his jaw hanging open at the sight of six
IRA men. He wouldn't have recognised them all but he would have
recognised enough of them to realise that he was shepherding an
IRA delegation.

The delegation was then flown to RAF Benson, roughly halfway between
Oxford and Henley on Thames, the epitome of middle England, for
most of whose residents the conflict in Ireland would seem a million
miles away. 'At Benson, we got into two waiting Special Branch cars,
with a third back-up car. There were seven of us altogether – six IRA
and me. I was in the front car with three IRA in the back. The other
Special Branch driver and Special Branch officer were in the second car
with the other three IRA.'

This astonishing convoy, consisting of six of the most wanted IRA
men in the kingdom, then drove to London on the final leg of their
journey on what Frank remembers was 'a glorious summer day'.

As we drove through Henley I remember thinking here's this lovely
English country town full of women going about their shopping
and here is this IRA delegation, four of whom [Adams, Cahill, Bell
and McGuinness] come from those grim, mean terraced-house
backstreets of Belfast and Derry, I thought, 'God, what have they
got in common?'

By the roundabout on the approach into Henley, they passed a small
grocer's shop with its produce on display outside in the bright summer
sunshine. Frank thought his charges might be hungry as they'd had a
very early start and a long and eventful journey; although the RAF may
have provided some refreshments, it was unlikely to have been a full
English. Frank got out and bought a bag of apples.

I got back in the car and handed the bag into the back seat to the
IRA passengers. They all looked at each other and I thought, 'My

God, they think they're drugged!' So I took one of them at random and took a great bite out of it and handed the bag to the Special Branch driver so he could have one. I then handed it over to the back. Then I think they were satisfied. It was typical of this sort of conspiracy theory. We wanted talks, not to drug them in the back of the car.

In addition to Adams, McGuinness, O'Connell and Seán Mac Stíofáin, the other two members of the delegation were Seamus Twomey, Commander of the Belfast Brigade, 'very tough', and Ivor Bell, Twomey's Deputy, also 'very tough', hence his insistence on combat fatigues.

A contemporary minute of the meeting, marked 'Secret and Personal' and written by the Cabinet Secretary, Sir Robert Armstrong, for the attention of the Conservative Prime Minister, Edward Heath, provides a unique insight into how Willie Whitelaw, Philip Woodfield, Sir Robert and, of course, Frank Steele, whose identity as an MI6 officer was not revealed in the minute, viewed the talks. The minutes of the meeting held in Paul Channon's spacious drawing room in Cheyne Walk were very formal, like the meeting itself, with the IRA delegation being introduced as 'The Provisionals represented by: Mr. Seán Mac Stíofáin, Mr. O'Connell, Mr. McGuinness, Mr. Adams, Mr. Twomey and Mr. Bell'. The minute notes that 'Mr. Seán Mac Stíofáin was very much in charge.'

I asked Frank how Whitelaw had reacted to meeting the IRA leadership, given his profound reservations about going ahead with the encounter.

I must pay tribute to Willie. He was absolutely first class, he walked over to Seán Mac Stíofáin and said, 'How do you do, Mr Mac Stíofáin,' and pronounced him by his Irish name, not his English name, John Stephenson. [Mac Stíofáin was born in Leytonstone, London.] He shook him by the hand and then said a few words of welcome. He then said, 'Perhaps you would now like to talk,' and that's where it all started going wrong.

Sir Robert Armstrong's minute to Prime Minister Heath quotes Mac Stíofáin's opening statement.[10] It was a conciliatory beginning: 'The Leadership of the IRA welcomed the discussions with the Secretary of State which they hoped would lead to a settlement of the problems of Ireland.' Frank became less impressed as Mac Stíofáin got into his stride.

> It was appalling, far worse than I thought it was going to be.
> I did at least think they'd say, 'Well, we're all in a very difficult situation. Fighting each other is getting us nowhere. Let's see what we can do by talking and if it doesn't work, OK we'll go back to fighting.' But it was nothing like that. He proceeded to read out his demands. He behaved like the representative of an army who had fought the British to a standstill and that we British wanted out. He behaved like Montgomery at Lüneburg Heath, telling the German generals what they should and shouldn't do if they wanted peace. He said the future of Ireland must be decided by the whole of the Irish people looking at Ireland as a unit, as a whole. The British army must leave Ireland by January 1975. Then there were lesser requests like 'political status' and ending internment. Then he said these talks are secret and therefore what's agreed at them can't be made public, but what we'd like is sort of Heads of Agreement and both sides would sign this in the presence of a high-level person, for example the Secretary General of the United Nations. It was cloud cuckoo land. We wanted the talks to continue so Whitelaw made sort of noises that he had to consult his Cabinet colleagues.

In his note to the Prime Minister, Sir Robert summed up the three main demands that underlined the IRA's peace plan:

(1) the British Government should recognise publicly that it is the right of the whole of the people of Ireland acting as a unit to decide the future of Ireland. [Sir Robert had added a handwritten note at the side that said, 'This is the declaration of intent.']
(2) the British Government should undertake to withdraw the British Army from Ireland by 1975.
(3) the expected conditions on internment and amnesties [that is, an end to internment and amnesty for IRA prisoners and volunteers].

Sir Robert added, 'Mr Mac Stíofáin made it clear that the crucial item was the "Declaration of Intent". If that was got right, the rest would follow: so it was only worth talking about that. The Secretary of State said that the British Government was statutorily committed to a pledge not to change the status of Northern Ireland except with the will of the majority of the people of Northern Ireland.' This addendum, which became known as the 'guarantee' to unionists, was the Government's red line and remained so up to – and including – the Good Friday Agreement of 1998. It was the insurmountable hurdle at which all subsequent attempts at reaching a political agreement with the republican movement would falter.

At the end of the meeting, according to Sir Robert's summary, the British delegation was realistic. 'If they could not get what they wanted,' Woodfield thought, 'they would either resume violence or simply disengage and wait for a better opportunity.' Prime Minister Heath was informed that the talks had been recorded (presumably in secret) and that a transcript would be available as soon as possible. Sir Robert signed off on a personal note: 'The Secretary of State admitted to being emotionally exhausted by the afternoon's work. He was clearly depressed at the outcome of the meeting, and had found the experience of meeting and talking to Mr Mac Stíofáin very unpleasant.'

On the flight back to Northern Ireland, Frank held an impromptu debriefing with the IRA leaders. He didn't mince his words.

> I was so appalled at their naivety and lack of understanding of
> political realities with HMG and the unionists that I opened up
> by saying, 'I hope you're not going to start your bloody stupid
> campaign of violence again.' I explained that if they really wanted
> a united Ireland, instead of enjoying themselves blowing up things,
> they were wasting their time shooting at British soldiers and
> bombing Northern Ireland into an industrial and social slum. They
> should be trying to persuade the Protestants, the unionists, that
> they would have some sort of satisfactory life, jobs with housing
> and so on, in some sort of linkage with the South. Their basic
> line was, 'As long as you're there, we'll never come to a sensible
> agreement with the unionists. They will always shelter behind
> HMG and the British army. Therefore, in order to come to a
> sensible agreement with the unionists, we've got to get rid of you

British and the way to get rid of you British, that has been proved
all over your empire, is violence.'

Frank hit several nails on the head. He was convinced that the
conversation on the plane back to Northern Ireland registered with
Gerry Adams, who had said little during the flight, perhaps deep in
thought, taking in the implications of all that he had heard from the
'Brits'. 'I think that strengthened his belief that military operations
weren't enough and it was essential to have a political dimension to what
you were doing.' Although Frank recognised that both communities
welcomed the ceasefire, he was never convinced that it had sufficient
support from all the other elements necessary to make it work.

> The unionists didn't want it. They wanted the British army to go
> on knocking hell out of the IRA and the Catholic community.
> The RUC didn't want it. They wanted to be able to fight with the
> British army against the IRA and restore some of their credibility
> and morale which had taken such a knock over internment. The
> Protestant paramilitaries didn't want it. They saw themselves
> fighting alongside the British army against the IRA. The IRA didn't
> want it. Part of the British army didn't want it. They reckoned the
> IRA could still be beaten militarily. And although this sounds a
> callous thing to say, I don't think either community had suffered
> enough to want peace and make it an absolute imperative. And so
> we settled down to twenty-five years of waste and murder.

The story of the following twenty years is how Frank Steele's
successors – MI6's Michael Oatley and latterly MI5's Robert – tried
to persuade the IRA, with the Derry businessman Brendan Duddy
acting as the secret intermediary, to end its campaign, enter talks and
become part of a political settlement to end the war, while recognising
the unionist guarantee. This was the endgame of 'Operation Chiffon'.

5

Back to the War

The 1972 ceasefire did not last. Either by design or by accident, most likely a combination of the two, it ended on the afternoon of Sunday 9 July, two days after the Cheyne Walk meeting. I remember it well as I was in Belfast over that pivotal weekend. I was filming a *This Week* documentary for ITV about the increasingly sectarian and separate nature of the sprawling housing estates across the city and how the few remaining mixed areas of Catholics and Protestants were systematically being cleared of residents of the unwelcome religion through blatant intimidation. Protestants were being driven out of Catholic areas and Catholics were being driven out of Protestant areas. It was mutual ethnic cleansing. Graffiti on the walls of loyalist areas warned 'Taigs Out' or 'No Taigs Here'[1] or, more sacrilegiously, 'Fuck the Pope'. The pattern was depressingly familiar. A large van or truck would arrive on a housing estate. The family would then load their furniture and worldly possessions on board and head for an estate where most of their own religion lived. I followed one displaced Catholic family, intimidated out of Rathcoole, a hard-line loyalist area on the fringe of the east of the city, to Lenadoon Avenue, the Catholic/nationalist area of Andersonstown in West Belfast. Andersonstown had become an IRA stronghold. I had no idea that Sunday in July 1972 that two days earlier Whitelaw had met the IRA leadership in London. All I knew was that there was a ceasefire in place and from what I saw walking up and down Lenadoon Avenue it was becoming increasingly fragile.

Lenadoon had become a flashpoint as homeless Catholic families arrived from outside the area to take possession of the handful of

Protestant houses at the bottom end of the Lenadoon Avenue whose
occupants had fled to the safety of the loyalist Suffolk housing estate on
the other side of the Andersonstown Road, the dividing line between
the nationalist and loyalist areas in the west of the city. The now
homeless families had been given permission by the City's Housing
Executive to move into the vacated Protestant houses. The militant
loyalist Ulster Defence Association (UDA) was having none of it and
was ominously gathering, ready to stop Catholic families moving into
what they regarded as 'their' houses in 'their' territory. Confrontation
seemed inevitable. The army moved in and blocked Lenadoon Avenue
around the midway point with a Saracen armoured car to cut off access
to the empty Protestant houses.

I remember standing at the midpoint of the Avenue watching
a large truck laden with household possessions, accompanied by a
crowd of supporters, making its way down the hill from the top end
of Lenadoon Avenue towards the soldiers now blocking access to the
truck's intended destination – the empty Protestant houses at the
bottom. Towards the front of the crowd I saw the unmistakable figure
of Seamus Twomey, the Commander of the IRA's Belfast Brigade.
I didn't know he had just arrived fresh from London after meeting
Secretary of State William Whitelaw as a member of the IRA leadership
delegation. Tension had been building throughout the weekend. By
Sunday as I watched the convoy heading down the hill to confront
the soldiers and the Saracen blocking its way, it was clear the ceasefire
was on a knife-edge and it was only a matter of time before it ended
with shots being fired. Frank Steele, who had also just arrived back
from London, had the same feeling. It was not the peaceful weekend
he had been expecting.

> On Saturday the whole thing was building up. The Catholics were
> saying we've got to move these families in. The Protestant mob of
> the UDA were saying, 'If they move in, we'll burn them out.' Dave
> O'Connell got on to me on the hotline on the Sunday. I get wary
> of people doing things to the British on Sundays. They think they're
> going to catch us on the hop, that we're all lying round stupefied
> after a lunch of Yorkshire pud and roast beef, burgundy and port.
> O'Connell said, 'Look, Lenadoon is getting really serious and unless
> your army backs off and allows this Catholic family to take up the

housing they've been allocated, the ceasefire could end.' So I said to him, 'Well, I'll look into it.'

I rang the army and, of course, it looks very different from their point of view. Here was the IRA trying to railroad a family in, and here was the Protestant mob of the UDA saying, 'If they do there'll be all hell let loose and we'll burn them out.' The poor old army, as usual, was stuck in the middle, trying to keep the peace. I explained all this to O'Connell on the hotline and said he must get Seamus Twomey to back off. O'Connell rang back again later saying the situation's getting worse. I said, 'All we're doing and all the army's doing is following policy laid down by Whitelaw. We're not going to let the IRA railroad this family into what had been a Protestant house. There'd be hell to pay. There'd be local mayhem. You must get Twomey to back off.' Twomey has a notoriously short fuse and I think he just got fed up and told the lorry with the Catholic family's furniture on board to move forward.[2]

The inevitable then happened as it was clear that the IRA, with Seamus Twomey leading from the front, was not going to back down and abandon the homeless Catholic family whose worldly possessions were loaded on the back of the truck. It was like watching a slow-motion car-crash movie. The truck rammed the Saracen. The army fired rubber bullets. Shots were heard, fired by IRA snipers hidden in flats at the top end of Lenadoon Avenue. The army fired back. The ceasefire was over. Twomey had never been an enthusiast for it anyway. Our crew, at the bottom of Lenadoon Avenue, watching events unfurl, was attacked by a group of loyalists who took our camera. I narrowly avoided a headache. (See photo section.)

Frank had done all he could to bring about the ceasefire that he hoped would be the beginning of the breakthrough to peace, but as he reluctantly and sadly admitted, history at this stage was not on his side. He died in November 1997 aged seventy-four, five months before the Good Friday Agreement that heralded the peace he had hoped for and worked for and that came so painfully and slowly.

On Monday 10 July 1972, the day after the confrontation in Lenadoon Avenue and the end of the two-week ceasefire, Whitelaw came clean and announced that he'd met the IRA in London in an attempt to end the violence and reach a political solution. He explained his reason for doing so, saying, 'I decided that if I were to see these people personally I might be able to do something to save lives.'[3] Significantly, the account of that morning's regular security meeting at Stormont Castle, marked 'Secret', noted 'the Government's intention to carry on the war with the IRA with the utmost vigour'. The conflict was now unofficially a 'war', although it was never publicly referred to as such. To do so risked giving the IRA the combatant status it sought.

Prophetically, on the day before the ending of the ceasefire, Sir Harry Tuzo, the General Officer Commanding (GOC) the army in Northern Ireland, had written to William Whitelaw enclosing a paper outlining 'possible action in the event of a renewed IRA campaign'. It was prescient:

> The emphasis will be on vigorous action and speed. The aim will
> be to swamp the IRA strongholds with troops; to achieve complete
> domination and demoralisation; to force the IRA to fight; and to
> exert such pressure on them that they have little opportunity to
> carry out their own offensive operations. For example it is envisaged
> that two battalions would occupy Andersonstown/Suffolk until
> such time as the local IRA units are neutralised or dispersed.[4]

The ceasefire over, the IRA's Belfast Brigade was making plans too. Seamus Twomey was never enthusiastic about the pause in hostilities, still believing, like many of the hard-liners on the Army Council, that only the language of force, not dialogue, would register with the 'Brits' and lead to a change in policy. I remember meeting Twomey a few days after the ceasefire ended, at his council house in West Belfast. It was an incongruous scene, with Twomey sitting by the fireside, wearing carpet slippers. He made it clear that the talking was over and it was now back to the war. The result, twelve days after Twomey had led the confrontation in Lenadoon Avenue, marked one of the worst atrocities of the conflict, carried out by the Belfast IRA. Again I remember, while looking for a contact in West Belfast, going into a school where I'd been told the person might be, and stumbling upon a meeting of senior Provisionals, some of whom I recognised. There appeared to be no security involved. I made my excuses and left. I later wondered whether it was a planning meeting for the atrocity that was about to follow.

On Friday 21 July 1972, the Provisional IRA planted twenty-two bombs across Belfast city centre, killing nine people and injuring about 130, many of them shoppers with young children. The day became notorious as 'Bloody Friday'. Frank Steele was bemused that the IRA could contemplate such an atrocity, risking so many civilian casualties within a fortnight of the high point in its still nascent campaign, negotiating with Whitelaw at Cheyne Walk.

> The IRA get ahead and then they go and do something like 'Bloody Friday'. Within an hour and a half, in the centre of Belfast, they let off twenty-two bombs. I remember because my daughter was in the city centre. We wondered whether we'd ever see her in one piece again. The IRA say, 'You British deliberately ignored some of these warnings. We warned about each bomb. We telephoned in a warning about it. And you British deliberately didn't do anything about the two worst bombs, where there were the most casualties.' But it wasn't like that at all. A city the size of Belfast and its services can't cope with twenty-two bombs in an hour and a half. The RUC couldn't cope with clearing the areas concerned. You just couldn't get the place into action to cope with all those bombs in an hour and a half.[5]

There were warnings but they were hopelessly inadequate. To make matters worse, there were also hoax calls to confuse the army and police. With bombs going off all over the city, people were terrified and confused, not knowing where the next bomb would explode. At 2.42 p.m. there was a telephone warning of a car bomb at Oxford Street bus station. It exploded twenty minutes later, ripping through the station, killing two soldiers, who had come to defuse it, and four civilians, two of them teenagers aged fifteen and eighteen. More than a hundred people were injured in that blast. There were horrific and indelible television images of body parts, like lumps of black jelly, being shovelled into bin bags. Viewers were spared the worst of the graphic images. A police officer near the scene later told me what he saw. The memories still haunt him.

> At first there was almost like a silence. Then you could hear people screaming and crying and moaning almost as if they were winded.

The first thing that caught my eye was a torso of a human being
lying in the middle of the street. It was recognisable as a torso
because the clothes had been blown off and you could actually
see parts of the human anatomy. One of the victims was a soldier
I knew personally. He'd had his arms and legs blown off and some
of his body had been blown through the railings. One of the most
horrendous memories for me was seeing a head stuck to a wall.
A couple of days later, we found vertebrae and a rib cage on the
roof of a nearby building. The reason we found it was because the
seagulls were diving on to it.[6]

The army, police and emergency services had never had to deal with
an attack on this scale before and simply could not cope. The IRA
accepted responsibility, claiming it had given adequate warnings and
blaming the 'Brits' for incompetence. Even some of the most hardened
IRA leaders, like Brendan Hughes, told me they were shocked.

What happened on Bloody Friday was a disaster. It was largely
the fault of the IRA. I think they overestimated the British army's
capabilities of clearing that particular area that day and it resulted
in that disaster. The IRA put warnings into the town. They gave
warnings. To my knowledge there was never an attempt at any
time to kill people with the car bomb because the people who were
putting the car bombs there had their own families shopping there
as well.[7]

I doubt if the IRA ever deliberately intended to kill civilians, many of
whom inevitably would have been from its own community, although
clearly it must have known the risk of widespread casualties and
potential deaths in planning such a massive attack on the city centre
with multiple car bombs. Its aim was more likely to be to cause panic
and economic disruption. 'Bloody Friday', like the bomb attack on the
Enniskillen Remembrance Day parade fifteen years later, was one of the
IRA's blackest days. Gerry Adams later wrote:

It is a moot point whether the IRA operations just stretched the
British too far for them to be able to cope with the situation, or
whether they deliberately failed to act in relation to two of the

bombs, but it is clear the IRA made a mistake in putting out so many bombs and civilians were killed who should not have been killed. This was the IRA's responsibility and a matter of deep regret.[8]

'Bloody Friday' gave Whitelaw and the army the opportunity they had been waiting for to clear the IRA's 'No Go' areas in Belfast and Derry and other urban areas, in particular in Derry where the nationalist Bogside and Creggan estates had become an IRA stronghold, blocked by formidable barricades which had remained after 'Bloody Sunday' and beyond which the army had not penetrated. The Paras' Commander, Lieutenant-Colonel Derek Wilford, had come close to doing so on 'Bloody Sunday'; as he told me, 'I owned the Bogside,'[9] but he was ordered not to penetrate further into the IRA-controlled areas. Unionists had long been demanding that the army smash the IRA's barricades and reclaim the areas for the 'Brits' and the Crown. After the atrocity of 'Bloody Friday', nationalists were likely to take a more sympathetic view of troops invading and reclaiming the 'No Go' areas that harboured the IRA. The offensive was codenamed 'Operation Motorman'. It was the biggest army operation since the Suez crisis in 1956. Thirty thousand troops were involved, including two armoured regiments.[10] The GOC, General Sir Harry Tuzo, was putting his words into practice – but in Derry not in Belfast. The IRA was tipped off by an intermediary about what was going to happen. They didn't want to take on the assembled might of the British army and the army didn't want to run the risk of triggering another 'Bloody Sunday'.

To minimise the risk of another nightmare scenario, Frank Steele and the RUC's senior officer in Derry, Superintendent Frank Lagan, were involved in trying to get the IRA to remove its weapons from the Bogside and Creggan. The person they approached in the hope of bringing this about was the local Derry businessman Brendan Duddy. The chain of communication ran from Steele to Lagan to Duddy. The chain had worked in the lead-up to 'Bloody Sunday' six months earlier when Duddy had helped effect the removal of the IRA's arms from the Bogside. Tragically it made no difference as it was the Paras who had done all the shooting, not the IRA, with the exception of the two rounds fired towards the end of the march by a single gunman left behind by the Official IRA for 'defensive purposes'.

Frank Lagan approached Brendan once again with a similar request –
to help get the IRA's guns out of the Bogside and Creggan areas – with
the warning that the army was coming in 'with all the heavy stuff',
with tanks, bulldozers and thousands of men. Brendan was highly
sceptical given the experience of 'Bloody Sunday' but Lagan convinced
him that this was different. Brendan hesitatingly agreed. He says he
went to Dublin to see Seamus Twomey and told him what was about
to happen, warning him that the IRA would face overwhelming force
and the loss of life would potentially be great. He explained that the
British had no objection to the IRA removing its weapons, presumably
across the border into the Irish Republic, where the IRA could hang
on to them. Shortly afterwards Brendan says he received a message
from a 'mysterious' visitor who told him that the weapons were ready
for removal. Having carried out the mission as instructed by Frank
Lagan, Brendan remained concerned that some of the weapons might
have been used to kill people and might be so used again once he had
been instrumental in their removal. He was to face many more such
agonising dilemmas. 'I had two choices,' he said. 'Either do it or not do
it.' Brendan decided to do it.[11]

By the time the formidable military force moved into Derry's Bogside
and Creggan in the dead of night, the IRA had vanished, having 'got
offside', some over the border, to avoid taking on the might of the
British army, and were now ready to fight another day. Casualties
were remarkably light, with only two people being killed, both in
controversial circumstances. One of them, Seamus Bradley (aged
nineteen), reported to be an IRA member, was shot in the Creggan
estate, and the other, Daniel Hegarty (sixteen), was killed by a soldier
in contentious circumstances. His father said his son was not a member
of any illegal organisation. The coroner expressed sympathy for the
relatives.[12]

Frank Steele left Northern Ireland in May 1973 and after his
retirement from SIS in 1975 went on to lead a far less stressful and more
lucrative existence working for the investment bank Kleinwort Benson
in London. He left 1972 behind him, the bloodiest year of the conflict,
with 479 people killed, including 130 British soldiers, and 4,876 people
injured. He had done all he could to try and engineer peace but it was
now left, in the years ahead, to his MI6 colleague Michael Oatley and
later Robert in MI5 to see if they could prevail as the IRA's campaign

became ever bloodier. Crucially, Oatley and Robert could not have done what they did without their indispensable secret partnership with Brendan Duddy, which Frank Steele had helped initiate with Michael Oatley. In the years to come, Duddy was to become the Government's vital intermediary with Martin McGuinness and the IRA.

6

Meeting Brendan Duddy

For years, Brendan Duddy's identity was a closely guarded secret, known only to MI6 and later to MI5. He was variously referred to as the 'Link' or the 'Contact' by the media as journalists gradually became aware that there was a secret intermediary with the IRA, but no one knew who it was or its connection with the British Government. It was to be many years before I finally discovered the intermediary's name. One of the first public mentions of his role, but not his name, was in an *Observer* article in 1993 in which he was referred to as one of a chain of contacts to the IRA.[1]

His name was first mentioned to me when I was having dinner with a clergyman in Northern Ireland, who had become a good friend and with whom I had come to share a mutual trust developed over many years. It was just after the signing of the 1998 Good Friday Agreement. We were discussing each other's work and the challenges we would both face when the overt and covert workings of the peace process had finally made the Good Friday Agreement possible. I mentioned the mysterious 'Link' or 'Contact'. My friend then volunteered his name without my even having to ask. To my surprise, he had no hesitation in doing so. 'His name is Brendan Duddy,' he said, 'a businessman in Derry.' I went to bed, thinking about the name of the no-longer anonymous person and wondering how I was going to approach him.

The following day, having decided to ring Brendan Duddy, and after finding the phone number of the business enterprise that bore his name, I went into the Richmond Mall, Derry's main shopping centre. I opted to use a public telephone fixed to a wall inside the

Mall. Mobile phones were not a universal accessory at the time. I had
prepared myself by gathering a small mountain of coins to feed the
phone, not knowing how long or short – I feared the latter – the call
would be. I pressed the coins into the slot, each one dropping with
the unmistakable clunk. I held my breath as I heard the ringing tone.
A woman finally answered. I had decided in advance to be upfront.
I gave my name, said I worked for the BBC and asked if it was possible
to speak to Mr Brendan Duddy. I waited nervously on the line while she
put me through. To my relief a voice said, 'Brendan Duddy speaking,'
and then, adding to my astonishment, 'I've been waiting to hear from
you.' I could hardly believe it. He said he was familiar with my work
in Northern Ireland over many years. I didn't go into any detail about
what I was doing and why I was calling, except to say that I would
very much like to meet him. He asked, 'When?' I said, 'How about
tonight?' He said, 'Fine. Come to my restaurant, it's called Rafters.' He
gave me the address. He told me to find a table, sit down and 'someone
will come and get you'. I remember Rafters as a cavernous, barnlike
steak house on the edge of the city, close to the border with Donegal
and the Irish Republic.

I sat down at a table, started looking at the menu and waited for
something to happen. Before I had the time to order, a man came up,
introduced himself as one of Brendan's sons, and asked me to come and
meet his father who was entertaining someone downstairs. His guest
turned out to be an Irish banker from Dublin. It was the first time I had
set eyes on Brendan. He was sitting at the head of the table, discussing
finance with the Irish banker and other guests, along with his wife,
Margo. He greeted me with a handshake and a warm smile as if he had
known me for years and introduced me to his wife, the banker and the
others around the table. He said he'd almost finished his business and
suggested we repair to his home a short drive away in order to have a
private conversation.

Having set foot in the hall of Brendan's house, I was immediately
met by Tara, a Great Dane of Baskervillian dimensions, and then
invited to join Brendan in what he called his 'wee room'. It was a small
and cosy parlour with a sofa and an armchair in the corner. There was
a smouldering peat fire in the grate above which was a plaque with the
inscription 'Angels Live Here'. Margo brought us tea and biscuits. It was
the beginning of one of the most remarkable nights of my working life,

opening the door on to the secret world that might ultimately result in the illusory prize of peace.

Brendan settled in the armchair and began to talk, a facility, I was soon to learn, he had in abundance. From time to time, he would get up and pace around the confined space of the 'wee room' to make his point. I began by saying that anything he told me would be in the strictest confidence and I would never write or broadcast anything he said until he gave me the green light. It was a promise to which I stuck. I had decided not to take any notes, aware that writing things down might make Brendan more cautious and inhibit his narrative. At some stage a bottle of Irish whiskey was produced to lubricate proceedings, not that Brendan needed any lubrication. I don't normally drink whiskey (or its Scottish equivalent, whisky), but under the circumstances it seemed both impolite and impolitic to refuse.

Brendan talked about facilitating the removal of IRA weapons from the Bogside in advance of 'Bloody Sunday' and 'Operation Motorman'; of knowing Martin McGuinness for thirty years, whose daughter, he told me, worked in his dress shop in the city; of senior IRA leaders being secretly smuggled across the border, with the connivance of his friend and fellow Catholic Superintendent Frank Lagan, to meet the MI6 officer Michael Oatley and discuss a possible way forward for peace. Brendan's 'wee room' deserved a blue plaque on the door. He told me how things actually worked.

> This is where it all happened, hard as it is to believe. There's a
> notion that big things happen in the Oval Office in Washington
> or the Grand Hall in the Kremlin, but it doesn't happen that way.
> It happens less formally and more simply. And when you get a
> situation where eventually someone is dying for a cup of tea and he
> says, 'I'll make a cup of tea' and you have to ask somebody who you
> are not very happy about, 'Would you like tea?', it breaks down.
> And then of course somebody says, 'When you're there, would you
> get a bucket of coal?[2]

Such were the Duddy dynamics of peacemaking. We talked, with Brendan doing most of it, until around three or four o'clock in the morning. It must have been a mammoth six- to seven-hour session. Dawn was almost breaking when I left. By then, after several whiskeys and hours of intense concentration, I was not in the best state to drive back to my hotel. Brendan kindly said his son would take me and I could pick up my car from his house later that day. He also said I should meet some of his family and his confidant, neighbour and accomplice in the secret contacts, Bernadette 'Bernie' Mount, who lived close by, so I could get the full picture.

I woke up the following morning, not surprisingly with a headache, and wondering at first if, like Bottom in *A Midsummer Night's Dream*, what I had heard the previous night was all the stuff of a dream. I then set about making copious notes of all that I could remember.

Without Brendan Duddy, the peace process might never have happened, as those most intimately involved later testified. On the face of it Brendan was a most unlikely secret peacemaker, which was one of his great advantages. His family was sworn to secrecy and none of them ever breathed a word. Not even his closest friends suspected what he was doing. The writer Nell McCafferty, a Derry legend and one of his oldest and closest friends, told me she was 'stunned' when she discovered 'what he'd been up to'. She'd had no idea. And when she finally found out, she said, 'I was proud of him.'

No one would have suspected that the successful Derry businessman, a keen marathon runner with an extensive portfolio of restaurants, shops and hotels, would have had such a crucial role to play in the shadows: gaining the confidence of Martin McGuinness and his IRA predecessors, although there were many difficult and dangerous moments; winning the trust of MI6 and MI5, and there were many nail-biting moments there too; and ultimately earning the trust of successive British Governments, spanning the frequently turbulent premierships of Harold Wilson, Edward Heath, James Callaghan, Margaret Thatcher, John Major and Tony Blair. Throughout those long and difficult years, Brendan was constantly aware of the danger: 'My life was under threat all the time. All the time. There were people dying everywhere. People were being blown up everywhere. People were living on the very edge. I think there would have been no tolerance for someone who was saying, "let's talk".'

The threat to Brendan's life was always likely to come from the Protestant paramilitaries of the Ulster Defence Association (UDA) or the Ulster Volunteer Force (UVF) or one of their militant offshoots like the Ulster Freedom Fighters (UFF), the UDA's 'killer' wing. All shared the widely held loyalist view that talking to the IRA was treachery, the first step on the road to a united Ireland and a British 'sell-out'. Or the threat might come from sceptical and dangerous members of the IRA who suspected Brendan was really a spy using peacemaking as a convenient cover to penetrate the republican movement. Brendan was never a spy in the accepted sense of the word. I once asked him directly, after knowing him for many years, if he was an MI6 or MI5 agent. His reply was as direct as my question: 'I'm glad you asked me that. I am my own person in my own right. I didn't have to be MI6 or MI5 – and never was. They never even came close to trying to recruit me. The notion of joining them was not my job.' Brendan was what the intelligence services would call an 'agent of influence', someone who would help facilitate the common aim of MI6 and MI5, in this case the aim being to get the IRA to abandon its 'armed struggle' and take part in the political process. That was what 'Operation Chiffon' ultimately came to be about.

What drove Brendan was his abhorrence of violence and the tragic human consequences of it. He traces it back to his early days and an experience for which he felt undying shame, the result of a .22 rifle that was a present from his uncle. He loved to go up into the hills a mile or so from his home and go hunting. Anything that moved, he shot. He still lives with the memory of what happened one winter's day. He first told me about it during that long night in his 'wee room' with the whiskey when he became quite emotional.

> The weather was frosty and sharp and the top of the heather was crisp. I was a good shot. I had no feeling whatsoever for what I was doing. Then about fifty metres in front of me arises this big hare, which was wonderful for me. I'm here and he's there. Bang! One shot! I ran up and looked. I said to myself, 'What the hell are you doing?' I'd taken its life and the blood was trickling down on top of the frosty heather. And it changed my life. I took the hare and placed it on a cairn of stones, came down from the hills and handed in my rifle to the local RUC barracks.

Brendan was also uniquely placed to understand both sides of the Irish Question. He was educated at St Columb's College in Derry, a grammar school run by secular diocesan priests ordained to serve the local community, who imbued their students with Irish history of the greenest hue. Its famous alumni included John Hume MP, Bishop Edward Daly, who waved the bloodstained white handkerchief in front of the dying Jackie Duddy on 'Bloody Sunday', the poet Seamus Heaney, the playwright Brian Friel, the musician Phil Coulter, who composed Derry's unofficial anthem 'The Town I Loved So Well', and the singer, songwriter and musician Paul Brady, who wrote 'The Hills of Donegal'. Brendan Duddy would now be added to the list of St Columb's distinguished alumni.

His understanding of Irish nationalism and republicanism would also have been deepened when he attended Irish-language classes run by the veteran republican Sean Keenan, who had been interned during the IRA campaigns of the 1940s, 1950s and early 1970s. (His son, Sean Keenan Jnr, is believed to be the unidentified person in the foreground of the jacket cover of this book.) But what set Brendan apart was his parallel understanding of England and the English, which was vital when he was endeavouring to make peace between two conflicting traditions and histories. His understanding began when he left to live and work in London in the early 1960s because there were no jobs in Derry. As a young man, the height of his ambition had been to drive a bin lorry like one of the friends with whom he went running. 'I hoped that one day I would get a job as his assistant.' But that was not to happen. 'There was serious discrimination against Catholics. I was desperate,' he told me. 'It was the feeling of being boxed in. No chance of work. No house and no houses being built. Basically, Ulster unionism at its very worst.' There was no job, not even on a bin lorry, and so, given the absence of work, Brendan, like many Derry men before him, journeyed to England to find it.

> I got a job in the Bush television factory, putting little knobs on TV sets. I earned £11 a week. I sent £8 back to Margo in Derry and the rest went on board and lodging. When it came to the lead-up to Christmas, Bush was paying overtime. I remember four men coming in and an English guy saying, 'We're on overtime!' I said, 'I'll not be getting it.' I had that distinct feeling because I was Irish and an Irish Catholic. He just said, 'By alphabetical order. Duddy, you're first.' It was a different world. Different people. Different to everything I had thought. I had met a group of people who were honest, easy to get on with and fair with me.

To Brendan, one-to-one relationships with his English co-workers were a revelation. He may have been born into a sectarian state but he had been brought up in a non-sectarian mixed area of Derry where many of his mates were Protestants; he regarded them as friends not enemies and respected the fact that they came from a different tradition. As a young boy, he even helped his Protestant neighbours build their 12 July bonfire, celebrating the Protestant King William's iconic victory over the Catholic King James at the Battle of the Boyne in 1690. The experience, living with Protestants as neighbours, helped him later understand Protestant and unionist fears about the loss of their identity and their deep concerns about and antipathy towards the idea of a united Ireland. He understood the importance of the British Government's long-standing and constantly reinforced guarantee that there would be no constitutional change in Northern Ireland without the consent of the majority, a majority which traditionally had always been Protestant and unionist and whose preservation had been the original intention of carving out the Northern Ireland state.

His confidence and his faith in human nature restored, Brendan returned to Derry only to witness the beginnings of the civil rights movement and the violence that ensued as the RUC and its paramilitary wing, the 'B' Specials, clashed with marchers and rioters. He went into business and set up a fish and chip shop on the edge of the Bogside with the money he had managed to save from working in London. Brendan's 'chippie' proved increasingly popular.

I began to cook fish and chips and loved every second of it. I was the best – and still am. I understand potatoes. I understand chips. Every day was busier than the day before. It was a turnaround from earning £11 a week in London to lifting £10 one night and £12 the next and £14 the night after that. It was a wonderful time. We had a little alcove at the back where John Hume, Eamon McCann and leaders of the civil rights movement would talk until three or four in the morning. There were big, big arguments about the rights and wrongs of various courses of actions. Hume was the boss, although everybody argued about what he had to say.

Bernie Mount managed the chip shop for Brendan, and his wife Margo helped out behind the counter. It became the Bogside's political salon.

Bernie loved it. 'They were all socialists and they all talked like socialists. The craic [conversation] was good. Every night was different.' But there was one person absent from Brendan's salon and its heated political debates. Brendan remembers the young Martin McGuinness.

> He was always an innocent, handsome young boy, always around but never in a leadership role. He worked in the butcher's shop across the street and would deliver the box of hamburgers to the chip shop. Martin would bring the box in and chat up the girls. And I'd say, 'Come on, Martin, we've got work to do here.' He was polite, innocent and non-aggressive. Not the later stereotype of Martin. He had absolutely no interest in politics. None. Just none.

Many years later, Martin McGuinness went on to play a vital role with Michael Oatley's MI5 successor Robert at a critical moment in 'Operation Chiffon'.

7

Meeting Martin McGuinness

I first met McGuinness in Derry in 1972 shortly after 'Bloody Sunday'.
I was watching a torchlight procession winding its way from the Bogside
up the hill to the Creggan estate and to St Mary's Church where the
coffins of the thirteen victims were laid out in front of the altar. I was
watching the procession, standing next to John Hume, whom I had
met shortly beforehand, and remember him saying to me, 'If you want
to find out what's going on here, he's the man you need to talk to.' He
pointed out the young Martin McGuinness, who was among the long
line of mourners, head bowed and walking slowly. Although I didn't
know it then, he was at the time of 'Bloody Sunday' the second in
command of the IRA's Derry Brigade. He was soon to take over as its
leader.

On a subsequent visit to Derry some months later, I took John Hume
up on his suggestion, asked around and was told I would probably find
Martin McGuinness in the vicinity of the disused gasworks, beyond
the flyover at the far end of the Bogside. The 'Provos' appeared to have
made the gasworks their headquarters, conveniently obscured by the
flyover from the line of sight and line of fire of British soldiers stationed
high on Derry's ancient city walls.

To my surprise, McGuinness was friendly, charming and chatty and
seemed to show no resentment towards me as a 'Brit' whose paratroopers
had recently shot dead thirteen of his fellow Derry neighbours on
'Bloody Sunday'. He told me he would much rather be washing the
car and mowing the grass on a Sunday than doing what he was doing.
He didn't elaborate on what that was, nor did I press him further. I felt

slightly guilty for believing him. I distinctly remember from that first meeting how he looked you straight in the eye with eyes that could be warm and welcoming but, as I later discovered, could switch to being hard as iron.

He later told me that he'd joined the Provisional IRA in 1970, a few months after it was formed at the end of 1969. He never told his parents. The first they knew was when his mother found black gloves, a sign of IRA membership, in his bedroom. He remembers how upset she was and how she admonished him. 'I think it was a moment in time and she was obviously annoyed at the prospect that all of our lives were changing and maybe mine more dramatically than anyone else's.' McGuinness did not remain at liberty for long. After 'Operation Motorman', he took refuge across the border in Donegal and on 30 December 1972 was arrested and charged with possession of 250lb of gelignite and nearly 5,000 rounds of .303 ammunition, which were found in a Ford Cortina that had been abandoned as it approached a Garda Síochána checkpoint. McGuinness appeared in the Special Criminal Court in Dublin and was given six months for IRA membership. He told the court:

> For over two years I was an officer in the Derry Brigade of the
> IRA. We have fought against the killing of our people. Many of
> my comrades have been arrested and tortured and some were
> shot unarmed by British troops ... I am a member of Óglaigh
> na hÉireann* [the IRA] and very, very proud of it ... We firmly
> believed we were doing our duty as Irishmen.[1]

McGuinness avoided extradition to Northern Ireland by claiming the political offence exemption in the Irish constitution, which forbids extradition if the offence concerned is political.[2] Other IRA fugitives claimed the same exemption and thus avoided being returned to Northern Ireland to face justice.

In its Christmas message of 1972, the British army was bullish, announcing that it had arrested 200 Provisional IRA officers since 'Operation Motorman'

---

*'Óglaigh na hÉireann' translates to 'the young men of Ireland' and is used idiomatically to mean 'young soldiers' or 'young volunteers'. It came to refer to the IRA, the Irish Republican Army.

the previous summer, including Chief of Staff Seán Mac Stíofáin. The arrest of McGuinness across the border only a few days after the message was a bonus. The IRA Army Council knew that the tougher security of the 'Brits' in the North and the crackdown by the Irish police, An Garda Síochána, in the South was hurting. After much discussion within the Army Council, the decision was made to bomb England, a strategy last used during the IRA's campaign in the Second World War. Billy McKee, who had been released from Crumlin Road jail in 1974 having won the concession of Special Category Status as the result of his hunger strike, was now a member of the Army Council and a leading voice, as he told me, in the decision to take the campaign to England.

> There had been a discussion early on about bombing England.
> I thought we should wait until there was a crisis before we should
> start. I agreed with the strategy but I didn't agree with bombing
> civilians and pubs that were full of people. Blowing up the Houses
> of Parliament wouldn't have made any difference to me but not
> ordinary civilian people. Our people were suffering. The English
> people were telling us they knew nothing about the situation. It's
> time they were made to find out what was going on here [in the
> North] and not brush it under the carpet.[3]

The year 1973 marked the beginning of the IRA's England offensive which was to continue on and off throughout most of the following twenty-five years. An eleven-person team was selected to bomb London. It included Gerry Kelly, a rising figure within the Provisional leadership, and the Price sisters, Dolours and Marian, who had escorted Gerry Adams from Long Kesh when he was released for the Cheyne Walk negotiations with Secretary of State William Whitelaw. Paul Holmes, another member of the team, had just been released from internment but had no hesitation in signing up for the London attacks, despite running the risk of being sent to jail for even longer. He echoed Billy McKee's sentiments: 'The fact that bombs were going off in England was bringing home to British people what was happening in the North – the fact that there is a war going on here and that there's more than one participant that's going to have to suffer.'[4]

In the middle of February 1973, four cars were hijacked in Belfast, resprayed and driven to Dublin where their number plates were changed and the bombs loaded. The team crossed on the ferry and drove the cars to London where they were parked overnight in a garage in Dolphin Square. The Price sisters had gone ahead earlier and selected four targets including New Scotland Yard in Victoria and the Old Bailey, the Central Criminal Court, in the City of London. The bombs were timed to go off at 3 p.m. An hour's warning was to be given. But the Metropolitan Police were several steps ahead of the IRA. They'd received intelligence, presumably from the army or the RUC Special Branch in Belfast, that an IRA attack might be under way. With eleven IRA volunteers involved in planning and carrying out the attack, the risk of a leak from informers and telephone intercepts was high.

At an early-morning briefing, officers of the Metropolitan Police's Special Patrol Group (SPG) were told to look out for suspicious-looking vehicles. Out on the ground later that morning, one eagle-eyed SPG officer, Constable Stanley Conley, patrolling the area around Scotland Yard with a colleague, noticed a green Ford Corsair with no tax disc. He also registered that it was a 1968 model with a 1971 number plate, drilled in place on the chassis with four holes instead of two. He opened the boot, to discover that although the car was green, the inside of the boot was black. He also saw a couple of wires going up to the back seat. At the end of the wire, under the seat, was 175 lb of fertiliser-based explosives. The Corsair was the first car bomb to be discovered in England and the first to be defused. Scotland Yard immediately gave the order to 'Close England' to make sure none of the bombers could make it back to Belfast. An hour's warning about the other bombs was phoned to the police. The bomb outside the offices of the British Forces' Broadcasting Service in Dean Stanley Street, near Smith Square, Westminster, was defused. The two other bombs, outside the Army Recruiting Centre in Whitehall and the Old Bailey in the City of London, were not defused in time and exploded just before 3 p.m. The police had not had time to clear the areas. One hundred and eighty people were injured and one man subsequently died of a heart attack. By this time, England had been 'closed' and ten of the bombing team were arrested at Heathrow, waiting to get an evening flight back to Belfast. The attack produced massive headlines and media coverage, 'armed propaganda', which was no doubt one of the IRA's main intentions, to wake up the British public and its politicians to the war in Ireland.

The bombers were tried and sentenced on 14 September 1973. Eight of them got life. Three of them became the longest-serving prisoners of the conflict. One of them was Roy Walsh. He told me the only regret he had was getting caught. 'For actually doing what I did, I've no regrets.'[5] Meanwhile throughout 1973 the IRA's campaign continued remorselessly in the North, killing sixty soldiers and twelve RUC officers in gun and bomb attacks.[6] Media coverage in England of the killing of seventy-two members of the security forces in Northern Ireland was dwarfed by the massive coverage of the Old Bailey and London bombs. It was the point that Billy McKee and the IRA intended to make.

8

Enter 'The Mountain Climber'

Nineteen-seventy-three was the year that was to change Brendan Duddy's life utterly, and it was the year when the early seeds of 'Operation Chiffon' began to germinate. Brendan says he got a phone call from his friend RUC Superintendent Frank Lagan who had prevailed upon him on two previous occasions, prompted by Frank Steele, to help facilitate the removal of weapons from areas dominated by the IRA, which Brendan had helped accomplish. Lagan said there was someone whom he would like Brendan to meet. Intrigued, Brendan said to bring him along. Brendan says it was then that Michael Oatley walked into his 'wee room' and into his life. Michael Oatley's recollection, however, is somewhat different. He says it was Frank Steele who first put him on to Brendan, suggesting that he (Brendan) would be somebody Michael would find worth talking to at some point. Michael says he then set up a meeting with Brendan through another of Frank Steele's contacts, James Docherty, and it was at his house that Oatley's first meeting with Brendan took place. Brendan knew that Michael was Frank Steele's successor but did not know that he was working for MI6. He accepted that they were both political advisers on the staff of the Secretary of State. Given all that Michael and Brendan were to share together, it's not surprising Michael describes their relationship as being 'closer than brothers'.

Brendan was indeed fundamental and no one else could have played the part so well. He was an arch manipulator. But it is not true to say that we could not have got there without him. He was the most promising of several potential lines of communication. No one did more or risked more for peace.[1]

Michael Oatley's successor, Robert, shared that view of the importance of Brendan's role.

> Brendan was absolutely crucial, right from the beginning of the Troubles. Without him, nothing would have happened. There would have been no contact with the IRA at various stages.[2]

Oatley disagrees with Robert, saying that he would have got there in the end via his other contacts, but the fact remains that it was Brendan who did the business.

Brendan remembered his impressions when he first met Michael Oatley.

> In comes this six-foot, handsome man, beautifully spoken, in a grey suit and tie. He was like a film star. I felt he was just a very articulate British diplomat who knew everything. He was the educator. I needed him and he needed me. He could listen for hours, drinking tea without once going to the toilet. Michael and I talked for the rest of the day and we had so much to talk about. It was so easy. We just gelled. There was never a dishonourable moment, never a hidden question about a gunman or something to do with bombs. I did not want to be part of that. I did not want to be involved.[3]

Bernie Mount also later met Michael Oatley and was bowled over: 'Good looking. Tall, thin, perfectly dressed. He was just a James Bond kind of person. Completely relaxed. He made you feel that everything was fine.'[4]

Brendan's first meeting with Michael at James Docherty's house was exploratory and relatively short compared to the second meeting when they got down to business at what Michael says was another safe house in the Derry area. That was a seven-hour epic, starting around 3 p.m. and finishing around 10 p.m. Michael instilled confidence in Brendan and Brendan instilled confidence in Michael. It was the beginning of a relationship that was to last, on and off, for twenty years. Both suited the other's purpose. Brendan wanted to stop the violence he abhorred and Michael's mission was to find a way of doing so. Both were of the same view that the only way to do so was to talk to the IRA. Michael soon realised that Brendan was the key to the mechanism.

I'd never heard of Michael Oatley until his name appeared in *The Times* on 28 November 1993. In the article, headlined 'MI6 man was IRA go-between', he was described as 'The Mountain Climber', the MI6 officer who had been in touch with the IRA, attempting to scale the mountain of peace. It also mentioned that, since retiring, he had been working as 'a senior director for the corporate intelligence specialists, Kroll Associates'. The origin of his sobriquet was when Brendan first mentioned Michael's existence to his IRA interlocutors by using a series of codenames. 'The Mountain Climber' was one of them. Other codenames included 'The Man from Jerusalem' and 'The Donkey Rider'. When Michael later asked Brendan what the latter meant, he replied, 'Simple. The Prince of Peace.' Brendan later also publicly claimed ownership of the 'Mountain Climber' codename as he believed it was he who was climbing the mountain. In truth both had a right to claim ownership as both were climbing the same mountain. But it was Michael to whom 'The Mountain Climber' stuck.

I remember reading the *Times* article that autumn morning in 1993 while having a coffee at Heathrow, waiting to catch a flight to Belfast. I had arrived at the airport in plenty of time to make sure I wasn't delayed by the heavy rush-hour traffic. Instinctively I drained my coffee and made for the nearest telephone. I dialled 192 for Directory Enquiries and found the number for Kroll Associates, which *The Times* had mentioned as the company for which Oatley was working. I rang the number and was put through to Oatley. I expected him to put down the receiver or say he was not in a position to talk but, on the contrary, he was quite friendly in his response and, to my surprise, agreed to meet. That was the beginning of a relationship that many years later finally led to his agreeing to do an interview. He says he initially agreed to meet to find out what I knew and then much later agreed to an interview when I told him I had seen and read the IRA's minutes of the 1975 ceasefire negotiation in which he, Michael, had been intimately involved. He said he had wanted to assess how accurate they were. I remember him later saying with a flicker of a smile, raising one of his luxuriant eyebrows, 'Peter, you seduced me!'

Michael Oatley arrived in Northern Ireland in 1973 by the same route as his predecessor, Frank Steele. Having served overseas in East and West Africa, he was now on a home posting, in Hampshire, training new recruits to the Secret Intelligence Service on the course that he had redesigned. Most of the course took place in London and less than half at Fort Monckton, a fortification built in 1790 at the beginning of the American War of Independence to protect Portsmouth harbour from enemy attack. He was awaiting his next assignment, having been promised a more exciting job by the Personnel Department once he had finished tutoring the new young recruits in the basics of being an MI6 officer.

But Personnel's promise was never delivered. 'They didn't know what to do with me,' he remembers, but he solved Personnel's problem for them. He had friends in the military who were serving in Northern Ireland and they were having 'a very exciting time'. He'd heard that a post was becoming free in the province as Frank Steele would soon be leaving. Oatley suggested he might just be the man for the job. Personnel admitted they had thought about that possibility too but had decided that he probably wouldn't be interested as he was married with a family. He told Personnel his wife wasn't a shrinking violet and on the contrary he was interested. And so he went. He was given no instructions to develop contacts with the IRA, in fact he was given no instructions at all. He thought his brief, such as it was, was to go there and make himself useful. He was driven by the belief that the 'awfulness' had to stop and he hoped he might be able to make a contribution to that end, which he believed might involve trying to influence the IRA's leadership.[5] His stance was entirely at odds with Government thinking at the time. After the abortive Cheyne Walk meeting, further contact with the IRA was unthinkable, which is why Frank Steele told Michael little about his dealings with the IRA that had led to its leaders meeting Willie Whitelaw.

Michael had no contact at this stage with Northern Ireland's civil servants but he was aware of what they were going through. For the last five years they had been desperately trying to put their fingers in the dyke to stem the rising tide of anarchy. They were further disconcerted by the suspension of 'their' parliament at Stormont and the introduction of Direct Rule from London – it being 'their' parliament because the vast majority of civil servants, like the vast majority of police and prison officers in the province, were Protestant and unionist.

With Direct Rule came a small cadre of Whitehall civil servants flown in from London, sitting in Stormont Castle, the seat of Northern Ireland's Government, located below Stormont's iconic Parliament Buildings, issuing directions to Northern Ireland's officials. The latter were rarely invited to attend the meetings from which the decisions, authorised by the Secretary of State, Willie Whitelaw, emanated. Oatley sympathised with them and respected their probity and diligence, but he regretted that they did not all possess those qualities. Many of these local officials were English, whom he believed had been indoctrinated to work for what he regarded as a hopelessly bigoted and discriminatory regime. He could well understand the resentment they felt at the suspension of Stormont and the invasion of 'Brits' from Whitehall. Sensitive documents, marked 'UK Eyes Only', were largely kept from them, which only served to exacerbate the feeling of alienation. After all, Northern Ireland was an integral part of the UK. Michael was acutely aware of the gulf.

> They were decent people who had got to the end of the line
> in trying to handle a situation that had got out of control and
> therefore we were obliged to rely on our own judgement. It was
> very much 'us' and 'them'. I'm afraid we did see them as the natives,
> part of the whole society that had broken down.

For the new arrivals from London, excursions to the more convivial parts of night-time Belfast were out of the question because bombs were going off every night. They were effectively in 'lockdown'. As a divertissement in a light-hearted moment, one of the senior officials from Whitehall devised a shield with a crest, a series of hooks and a motto to reflect statements by the Secretary of State that were frequently made and subsequently withdrawn, only to be superseded by yet more statements that were to suffer the same fate. The motto was 'And it seemed like a good idea at the time'. The root of the problem was that, like Michael Oatley, the *nouveaux arrivés* knew little about Northern Ireland and had no familiarity with the place and its people, which made devising policy and reacting to events an inexact and precarious science.

Oatley and his Foreign Office colleague James Allan and their two
secretaries settled into the Laneside villa, a location handy for Stormont
and good for the soul, calmed by the proximity of the woods and the
sylvan shoreline of Belfast Lough. With the arrival of Direct Rule in
1972, Laneside became the office of the Political Adviser to the Secretary
of State, formerly Frank Steele and now James Allan, with Oatley as his
notional assistant, crucially with carte blanche to operate independently.
This enabled Oatley to travel around the province to test the mood in
nationalist and republican communities, which was where IRA violence
was coming from. He visited loyalist and unionist communities, too,
to get the full picture. He also made important and extensive contacts
with the army's area and battalion commanders to discuss strategy and
learn about the situation on the ground. He found the quality of the
officers mainly very high.

One of the wonderful things I had going for me was that I had
complete freedom – I didn't have a daily desk job to deal with – to
go around the province and to understand as much as I could of
what was happening. And I did that largely by getting people in
the various parts of the country, like Eugene O'Hare, a pharmacist
in Derry, and Joe Mulvenna, a communications officer in Belfast
[as important to Oatley in the early stages as Brendan was later].
They were among those who took me round and introduced
me to people who were close to loyalist extremism or close to
republican extremism or were simply members of the community
which was suffering from the effects of violence. And in the
nationalist areas, I did discover the extent to which, at that stage,
IRA activity was tolerated by a lot of people, although they might
not approve of it.

It was to me quite a surprise that the quality of the young people
joining the IRA was very impressive and you could go to a street
in a staunchly republican area in Derry and find that everybody's
favourite son had joined the IRA, however much their mothers
might disapprove of what they were doing. I came to deduce that
if so many young people were going to do this then there must be
social and political reasons, more complex than I had understood,
propelling them in that direction and that the quality of the IRA
leadership was quite interesting and would be worth studying.

Michael was shocked by the fact that some sixty British soldiers and twelve members of the RUC had been killed by the IRA during 1973, his first year in the province.

I was very conscious of the attrition rate against the British army. I remember one day picking up a copy of the *Observer* colour supplement which had a two-page spread of photos of all the soldiers, most of them very young, who had been killed in the previous twelve months – or perhaps even longer – and thinking that if I was going to spend two years or longer in Northern Ireland, I ought perhaps to try to concentrate on seeing whether my particular skills and background could enable me to find a way to influence the leadership of the IRA or to make some kind of contact through which they could be influenced. And I think that did become my main preoccupation after about six months in Northern Ireland.

Oatley wasn't starry-eyed about the IRA but understood the reality on the ground and the reasons why, given recent sectarian history, it had support in the nationalist community.

I wasn't lacking in hostility towards what the IRA was doing. I had merely developed, at a fairly early stage, the thought that there must be some interesting people running it and that quite a lot of people in the nationalist community, while they rejected the violence, understood and to some extent sympathised with why the IRA was there. And then, of course, one learned more about what had gone on in 1969 and the fact that the Irish army had considered mobilising in order to come across the border to help people in the nationalist communities who were being burned out of their houses by loyalist mobs. So one developed, rather belatedly, an understanding of where the modern IRA had developed its strength.

The problem for Oatley in his desire to pursue his 'studies' and what he referred to as his 'Bogside Ramblings' was that the Secretary of State, Willie Whitelaw, had been left red-faced when word of the Cheyne Walk meeting was leaked to the newspapers, presumably via the IRA.

Whitelaw had understood that the meeting would be kept a closely guarded secret and assumed that his interlocutors would be men of their word, as indeed he was. The IRA probably felt that it had nothing to lose as the ceasefire was over two days after the meeting and it now believed the 'Brits' were not in the business of serious negotiation. Causing Whitelaw maximum embarrassment was a bonus. The result was that Oatley's desire to find out more about the enemy was hampered by an edict from the Government, in the wake of the revelation of the Cheyne Walk talks, that no British official was to have any contact, either direct or indirect, with the IRA. But Oatley, being an experienced and adaptable intelligence officer, found a way of bending the rules. In the handover, Frank Steele inadvertently helped him find a way of doing so. During his time in Northern Ireland, Steele had established a network of contacts which he passed on to Oatley in the hope that some of them might bear fruit. One of them, indirectly, was Brendan Duddy. Duddy was to deliver the fruit in basketfuls.

At some stage during his negotiations with the IRA to get weapons removed from the Bogside and Creggan in advance of 'Bloody Sunday' and 'Operation Motorman', Duddy had met Ruairí Ó Brádaigh, who had been the IRA's Chief of Staff in its border campaign, and who in 1973, when Oatley began his fact-finding missions, was President of Sinn Féin. After Oatley's epic seven-hour meeting with Duddy, Duddy agreed to act as secret intermediary between Oatley and the IRA leadership. Oatley became known to the IRA in his official capacity as 'the British Government Representative'. He admits bending the rules on not communicating with the IRA, 'just a little bit'.

> I had developed what you might think of as a hollow bamboo pipe
> between me and someone significant on the republican side down
> which nothing was being said but if one sort of blew down it gently
> the person at the other end could feel the pressure and blow back.
> We had got hold of part of the leadership, got its attention and
> it was clear it wanted to establish some kind of connection with
> us. Very, very few people knew about it. And it was quite a nice
> bamboo pipe.

Oatley would metaphorically blow down the pipe at one end, in the middle Brendan Duddy would metaphorically hold it to his ear and then, again metaphorically, blow down it again to pass on any message to Ruairí Ó Brádaigh at the receiving end. Oatley's pipe was intended to be a work in progress, the long-term aim being to see whether, via the imaginary bamboo pipe, there might be some possibility of a ceasefire and perhaps a longer cessation of hostilities as a prelude to political dialogue and a possible political solution. The hollow bamboo pipe had its place in the foothills of 'the Mountain Climber's early ascent as a mechanism to sound out Ruairí Ó Brádaigh, who was genuinely interested in trying to reach a political solution with the 'Brits' along with other 'doves' on the Army Council like David O'Connell. Seamus Twomey was one of the hard men, the 'hawks'. As Oatley recalled:

> This seemed to me to be not much more than a slight bending of
> the Secretary of State's rules. I went back to Frank Cooper [the
> Permanent Under Secretary at the Northern Ireland Office, the
> senior British official, at Stormont] and told him what I had been
> up to. I said I have not broken the rules too badly. I haven't talked
> to Ó Brádaigh directly. It is more as if I had a bamboo pipe which
> is held by my friend [Brendan] and it reaches Ó Brádaigh. If I puff
> down it, he can feel that and puff back. It's quite a nice pipe so may
> we now perhaps put some bits and pieces of material down it to
> develop the situation?

Frank Cooper, a former Spitfire pilot, was not averse to taking risks. In 1944 he had been shot down and captured by German troops but managed to escape and rejoin his unit. Cooper gave Oatley the green light but kept a tight rein on what messages he was permitted to send down the pipeline. Cooper told Harold Wilson, Prime Minister again since 1974, what was going on. Wilson was prepared to go along with the initiative and said, 'Keep me informed, Frank, but don't tell Merlyn, it will only worry him.' Merlyn Rees was Northern Ireland Secretary at the time. As far as Oatley and Cooper's political masters were concerned, there was no question of reconstituting political talks with the IRA, although Wilson, the ultimate political master, was clearly interested in exploring the possibility. Official Government policy was to intensify military pressure, given the belief in some, though not all, of the upper echelons of the Ministry of Defence that the IRA could be defeated. But Oatley became increasingly concerned that the initiative was being compromised by the paucity of meaningful 'material' that was being put down the pipe. 'It was rather like a hot air balloon with insufficient gas in the cylinder.'

> So then, over the next few months we found very, very minor things to talk about down this tube and it developed into an exercise which enabled Ruairí Ó Brádaigh and, to some extent David O'Connell, to feel that they were in contact with a part of the British Government which might, at some stage, help them to move in a political direction.

Any such approaches were also being circumscribed by the ongoing violence in Northern Ireland and in particular by the extension of the IRA's campaign to England. It was no coincidence that it began at the height of the British General Election campaign in October 1974 when the Labour leader, Harold Wilson, sought to improve on Labour's performance in the General Election the previous February, which had resulted in a hung parliament with Labour forming a minority government. Wilson then called another General Election for 10 October in the hope of winning an overall majority. Ireland was not an issue in the campaign – it seldom was in British elections – despite the fact that in Northern Ireland the loyalist Ulster Workers Council had led a devastating strike the previous May that paralysed the province. The protest was against a political settlement agreed at the Sunningdale conference in December 1973, consisting of an embryo power-sharing executive at Stormont and a cross-border Council of Ireland. Sharing power with Catholics and closer relations with Dublin were anathema to the vast majority of loyalists. As ever, Ian Paisley, the Protestant fundamentalist cleric, was Sunningdale's most vociferous opponent. He excoriated it as 'Ulster's Munich betrayal paper'.[6]

The IRA was determined to make Ireland an electoral issue. On 5 October 1974, five days before polling day, the IRA struck at what it claimed were 'military' targets, planting bombs in two pubs in Guildford, the Horse and Groom and the Seven Stars. Both were frequented by off-duty soldiers from nearby army training camps. No warnings were given. At 8.50 p.m. the bomb in the Horse and Groom killed four soldiers, two of them women, who had been sitting in the alcove where the nitroglycerine bomb had been placed. A civilian sitting nearby also died and fifty-seven people were injured.[7] A soldier who survived gave a vivid description of what happened.

> I had just leaned forward to buy my round when there was a bang. I must have gone straight through the window because I was lying outside with my hair and clothes on fire. Some people tore off my jacket and shirt to save me from serious burns. My two mates were killed outright and another was critically injured.[8]

Half an hour later, at 9.25 p.m., the second bomb in the nearby Seven Stars pub exploded but only eight people were injured, mainly staff, because the manager had cleared the bar after the explosion in the Horse and Groom.[9]

Harold Wilson won the General Election but with a slender majority of three seats. That was when Merlyn Rees, an MP from a mining family in South Wales, became Northern Ireland Secretary. Ireland was in his family's blood. His father had served with the British army in Dublin during the Easter Rising of 1916.[10] Willie Whitelaw had left the Northern Ireland Office the previous year and had been moved by Prime Minister Edward Heath to become Secretary of State for Employment to deal with the ongoing miners' strike.

Merlyn Rees faced a baptism of fire. The following month, on 21 November 1974, IRA bombs exploded in two pubs in Birmingham, the Mulberry Bush and the Tavern in the Town. Nineteen people were killed and more than 160 were injured, many of them seriously. Many of the dead and injured were Irish. The first bomb exploded at 8.17 p.m., six minutes after a man with an Irish accent phoned the *Birmingham Post and Mail* warning of two bombs, mentioning the general location but not naming the pubs. The carnage was horrific. One barman described the scene: 'There was an almighty blast and there were screams and shouts from everywhere. The ceiling fell in and the bar blew back at me. It was just a screaming mass of people. I saw one man with the side of his head blown off.'[11] At the city's General Hospital, doctors and nurses worked through the night trying to save lives and deal with horrific injuries. One doctor said, 'You went to put drips on an arm and it isn't there. You look for a leg, and there isn't one.'[12]

The atrocity provoked a wave of anti-Irish feeling with attacks on Irish community centres, bars and businesses. Thirty Midlands factories

were hit by strikes in protest against the bombings. At Manchester and
Liverpool airports, workers refused to handle flights destined for Belfast
and Dublin.[13]

The newly re-elected Labour Government had to react in a way that
seemed commensurate with the outrage. Prime Minister Harold Wilson
looked to his Home Secretary, Roy Jenkins, for a swift and clear response.
Jenkins, one of the few British politicians with a deep knowledge of
Irish history, obliged, introducing the Prevention of Terrorism Act,
permitting detention without trial for seven days (to provide longer
time for interrogation) and authorising the deportation of suspects
back to Ireland, North and South, ironically in some cases deporting
UK citizens from one part of the United Kingdom (Britain) to another
(Northern Ireland). Jenkins admitted the powers were 'draconian' and
'unprecedented in peacetime but fully justified to meet the clear and
present danger'. In the frenzied climate of the time, grave judicial errors
were made – as they were in the wake of the Guildford bombs. Six men
were arrested and charged with the Birmingham bombings. All received
life sentences. They were convicted largely on statements allegedly made
to the West Midlands police, which they claimed had been beaten out of
them. The forensic evidence was later judged to be suspect and unreliable.
The Birmingham Six were eventually freed in March 1991 after spending
sixteen years in jail. It remains an indelible stain on British justice.

Billy McKee, now Commander of the IRA's Belfast Brigade and
a member of the Army Council following his release from Crumlin
Road jail in September 1974, told me he had been genuinely shocked
by Birmingham. He said he had not been aware of the operation as
it had been planned in Dublin by the IRA's 'England Department'.
McKee had always supported attacks in England but, as we have seen,
had always insisted that civilian casualties should be avoided at all costs.

> I didn't mind our own people and the 'Brits' – the security forces –
> going down but I didn't agree with ordinary civilian people losing
> their lives. At the time there was no report coming in to us about
> who was responsible. I think it was about a month later that
> I found out it was our own people who had carried it out.[14]

I then asked him who bombed Birmingham. 'The IRA,' he answered.
He also said the Birmingham Six were 'completely innocent'.

Some of them weren't even known to the IRA. When their names came out, nobody seemed to know them, except the odd person from Belfast. They might have bought fundraising tickets or something like that for prisoners' dependants. I think one of them even said he wasn't a republican. I don't know if any of them were republicans or not.[15]

The British public were understandably shocked and outraged by the attacks, and talking again to the IRA was probably the last thing they ever imagined. The mood was to hit the enemy hard, not to engage with it. Oatley was phlegmatic: 'Rather grotesquely, there was no inconsistency between people in the IRA leadership being prepared to explore the possibility of political options while continuing a vigorous campaign. That's always been the position until they finally stop their campaign.' To the IRA, killing was not incompatible with talking – and that remained the case for the next twenty-five years. But despite the Guildford and Birmingham atrocities the early, tentative back-channel communications, through Oatley's bamboo pipe via Brendan Duddy to Ruairí Ó Brádaigh, were still continuing and at last seemed to have the potential to develop into something more substantial. In April 1974, Ruairí Ó Brádaigh had sent out a signal through a column in Sinn Féin's weekly newspaper, *Republican News*. 'We want a situation to come about where political advance can take the place of guerrilla warfare,' he wrote. 'What we see is an honourable accommodation with the British coupled with an honourable accommodation with the loyalists.'[16]

With the extension of the IRA's campaign to England and its so-called 'armed struggle' in Northern Ireland showing no sign of slowing down, the need to explore the possibility of some kind of dialogue appeared to Michael Oatley to be more important than ever. The time, he felt, was right.

I think by that stage we were fairly advanced in the signals that we were sending to each other. One of the circumstances which helped to move things towards real dialogue was pressure from the community. The nationalist community was getting extremely fed up with living under very severe military pressure. We had a situation where somebody living in the Bogside would have their son visiting from Liverpool on a fairly rare visit and as soon as the boy steps outside the door to go and buy a packet of cigarettes, he's up against a wall with a soldier feeling his softer parts. And after this has happened five times, he decides he doesn't want to stay on with his family visit and goes back to Liverpool. People were living under very serious pressure as a result of that sort of situation so there was great desire within the community to get rid of the campaign and the leadership of the IRA was, of course, very conscious of this. All sorts of attempted negotiations and peace moves were going on.

The general confusion worked to Oatley's and Duddy's advantage.

9

Sideshow

Talking to the IRA came as no shock to Wilson. He had done it once before, with Merlyn Rees, in March 1972 when he himself was Leader of the Opposition and Rees was shadow Northern Ireland Secretary. Their intervention seemed all the more urgent, not just in the aftermath of 'Bloody Sunday' but following a horrific IRA bomb attack on the Abercorn restaurant in Belfast city centre.

The explosion happened at teatime on 4 March 1972 on a busy Saturday afternoon when the area was crowded with shoppers and the Abercorn was packed. Two young Catholic women, Ann Frances Owens (aged twenty-two) and Janet Bereen (twenty-one), who were having a coffee in a break from shopping, were killed in the blast. They were sitting at a table close to where the 5lb gelignite bomb had been planted. They took the full force of the blast. An eyewitness in the restaurant said she had seen two young girls walk out of the restaurant, leaving a handbag behind, which she thought the girls had forgotten. She thought no more about it, assuming one of them would be back to collect it.[1] An anonymous 999 call, later traced to a pub on the Falls Road, warned that a bomb was due to go off in five minutes. The general area, but no precise location, was given.[2] Around seventy people were injured, many horrifically mutilated, among them two sisters, Jennifer and Rosaleen McNern. Jennifer lost both legs, and Rosaleen, a bride-to-be, lost her legs, her right arm and one of her eyes. In the grim litany of the worst atrocities of the Troubles, the Abercorn is high on the list. Both the Provisional and the Official IRA denied responsibility. The Provisionals were the main suspects. The need to sound out the IRA on the circumstances under which it would end its campaign seemed more urgent than ever.

The arrangement for Wilson's clandestine visit to Dublin was made through a series of intermediaries, one of them a Labour MP in the Irish parliament, Dr John O'Connell. At this stage neither Brendan Duddy nor Michael Oatley was in the picture. Brendan was running his chip shop in the Bogside and Michael was teaching SIS recruits. Perhaps in response to the Abercorn atrocity and perhaps to help facilitate Rees and Wilson's visit, the IRA announced a three-day ceasefire on 10 March 1972, making it clear that for it to last the 'Brits' would have to withdraw their forces from the North, grant amnesty to their prisoners and abolish the Stormont parliament.

Three days later, the last day of the ceasefire, Rees and Wilson flew to Dublin for a secret meeting with the IRA. As a courtesy, they had informed Prime Minister Edward Heath of their intention and no objection was raised as it was essentially a fact-finding mission.[3] Four months earlier, on 25 November 1971, Wilson had made his views on a united Ireland clear in the House of Commons, rooted in the long-term intention of Partition in 1921, that the division of the island was never intended to be permanent.

> I believe that the situation has now gone so far that it is impossible to conceive of an effective long-term solution in which the agenda at least does not include consideration of, and which is not in some way directed to finding a means of achieving, the aspirations envisaged half a century ago, of progress towards a united Ireland … A substantial term of years will be required before any concept of unification could become a reality, but the dream must be there. If men of moderation have nothing to hope for, men of violence will have something to shoot for.[4]

The meeting took place in Dr O'Connell's house in Phoenix Park, Dublin. It lasted from dusk until midnight, the ceasefire deadline. Rees and Wilson were understandably apprehensive, as Rees told me: 'We went up the steps and one of Harold's staff said to me, "Harold would like you to go in first," and I thought, "I bet he does." And they said, "Harold doesn't want to shake hands with them." '[5]

The IRA delegation consisted of three of the Provisionals' top leaders, two from the North – Joe Cahill, the Belfast Brigade Commander, John Kelly, a founding member of the Provisionals – and David O'Connell from the South. Cahill later reflected on the mood of the meeting.

> We met in the sitting room and it was informal. No names were used. There were no introductions. Wilson referred to us as 'friends of friends'. The first thing that Dr John O'Connell did was to bring out glasses and a bottle of whiskey. We didn't drink. Wilson seemed to be disappointed that none of us took a drink. He was sort of surprised at this. Tea and biscuits were then brought in. Wilson was interested in a [longer] ceasefire. He said we needed to have peace to have talks. The atmosphere was quite cordial and friendly, although Rees struck me as being a nervous sort of person and appeared to be jittery, ill at ease.[6]

John Kelly told me he remembers Wilson asking a pointed question:

> He puffed on his pipe, in the way that he did, and asked what the republican movement's intention would be to a bombing campaign on the British mainland, in the event of there being no resolution to the conflict. We gave him a non-committal answer and said that was not for us to answer that question.[7]

The meeting was inconclusive. At this stage, the two sides were too far apart and remained just as far apart as at the Cheyne Walk meeting four months later. Rees told me he knew the chances of success were slim. 'What Harold was trying to get was a [longer] ceasefire. That was the whole point of it. And I think it was Kelly who said it's too late anyway because, looking at his watch, it's started again.'[8]

The following day, the IRA exploded a 200lb bomb in the centre of Belfast. The three-day ceasefire was over. It was back to the war again. Towards the end of 1974, with the horrors of the Birmingham and Guildford bombs still fresh in the minds of the Government and the public, Merlyn Rees recognised that the only way to end the violence was to try to engineer a political solution in which the republican movement and the loyalist paramilitaries were involved. With this in mind he legalised Sinn Féin and the loyalist Ulster Volunteer Force (UVF) in the hope that they would be encouraged to engage in a political solution. The UDA had never been banned. The next stage was to try and engage the IRA leadership for a third time, the previous two attempts being Wilson and Rees' visit to Dublin and the IRA's meeting with Whitelaw in Cheyne Walk. Frank Cooper, the Permanent Under Secretary at the NIO, was in favour of trying again for a third time through Michael Oatley, who worked under Cooper's supervision and with his strong support, and Brendan Duddy. Cooper told me there was no military solution.

> I didn't think the IRA could absolutely be beaten because there had to be a political settlement of one kind or another at the end of whatever period it took to achieve it. In the meanwhile, I thought it could be contained. My own view is that if you're dealing with a terrorist organisation you always ought to have a dialogue going because the basic problem about terrorism is that it's very difficult to snuff out. You've got, in the end, to find some way of stopping terrorism. We can't go around shooting everybody we think is a terrorist, which is certainly one possible way of doing it. Nobody in this country would have stood for that. But if a political solution made it possible, one should never discount the need to have a dialogue, although one should be extremely careful and extremely clear about what you were trying to do if you did.[9]

Merlyn Rees was aware that there was some sort of communication with the IRA but didn't know the details, which were deliberately kept from him. Harold Wilson told Frank Cooper that he was in favour of making an approach to the IRA via the back channel but, as we know, gave instructions that Rees be kept out of the loop. Harold Wilson was kept informed of what Oatley was up to because Oatley briefed Cooper who, in a few succinct sentences, briefed the Cabinet Secretary, Sir John Hunt, who in turn briefed Prime Minister Wilson. Oatley was present when the notes were being dictated for Wilson, and Cooper would check with him that what was being reported was correct. During the 1975 ceasefire that was to follow, the negotiations were formal and the desire to try and reach a political solution was genuine.

At this stage, towards the end of 1974, Michael Oatley's bamboo pipe wasn't the only game in town – although only a handful of people knew about it. There were other channels too. On 10 December there was a secret meeting between clergymen of all denominations, North and South, and prominent members of the IRA's Army Council, including Ruairí Ó Brádaigh. It took place in a room in Smyth's Village Hotel in Feakle, County Clare, roughly 140 miles across the border. Other members of the high-level IRA delegation included Billy McKee, newly released from Crumlin Road jail, Seamus Twomey, who had been instrumental in ending the ceasefire after Cheyne Walk, and David O'Connell, Kevin Mallon and J. B. O'Hagan. Twomey, Mallon and O'Hagan had made a spectacular escape the previous year from the exercise yard in Dublin's Mountjoy prison, on board a hijacked Alouette helicopter. They were now on the run and had become the most wanted men in Ireland.[10]

The meeting at Smyth's Hotel inevitably became public when the sleepy village was suddenly invaded by Special Branch officers from Ireland's Garda Síochána, acting on a tip-off that IRA leaders, including the three Mountjoy escapees, were expected at the meeting with the clergymen. The raid could hardly have been kept quiet. But the IRA leaders had also received a tip-off and managed to escape before the police burst in, only to find a group of astonished and bemused clergymen. One of them, Dr Arthur Butler, the Anglican Bishop of Connor, having recovered from the shock, said the meeting with the IRA leaders had gone well: 'We were all most impressed with their attitude, with their fair-mindedness, and we were so pleased to find that they were talking seriously and deeply and with great conviction and had listened very carefully with what we had to say.'[11] Billy McKee agreed. 'I think they [the clergymen] were expecting men coming in with trench coats and rifles over their shoulders and bayonets by their sides. But it wasn't like that. It was a very cordial meeting and very, very good.'[12]

The Garda Síochána's Special Branch officers, having arrived to find the birds had flown, departed empty handed and acutely embarrassed, having missed the golden opportunity to cut off the head of the Provisional IRA leadership by arresting many of its most prominent figures North and South of the border. Feakle however operated in Michael Oatley's favour. When news of the secret meeting between the clergymen and the IRA hit the headlines, Oatley calculated that should word of his indirect contacts with the IRA leak out, the sting of public anger would have been drawn by Feakle, not least because it involved senior clergymen of both denominations and from both sides of the border. It appears the IRA was happy to go along with the convenient fiction that it was Feakle and not Michael Oatley and Brendan Duddy that was responsible for putting in place the ceasefire and talks with the IRA leadership – Ó Brádaigh, McKee and later Twomey. Feakle was a convenient sideshow and a politically convenient diversion that could later be used to mask the fact that the British, and not just the clergymen, were talking to the IRA. Oatley welcomed the sideshow: 'Feakle became a convenient concealment device because the Feakle clergy were quite sure that they had achieved a negotiated cessation of hostilities. It was a very helpful coincidence.'

All that mattered was that there was a ceasefire. The public would not be unduly concerned about how it had come about.

10

The Bamboo Pipe in Action

Around the same time, the noises that Brendan Duddy was hearing down the pipeline were becoming increasingly optimistic, much to Duddy's relief – and Michael Oatley's too.

> By the end of '74 we felt that we'd established a situation where there was going to be more direct discussion about how we could reach an agreement for a ceasefire and that the situation would hold over Christmas. The IRA was going to declare a ceasefire and we felt that the opportunity to talk more directly would be available after Christmas. So everybody packed their bags and went off to London feeling that the sorts of noises we'd been hearing down our channel over the previous weeks suggested that now the communication which had been at a very low level could perhaps become really significant and we had an opportunity to do something quite important.[1]

Brendan Duddy informed Oatley that he'd received a message down the back channel that the IRA was planning to declare a Christmas ceasefire to create a climate in which 'a more meaningful dialogue might be pursued'. On 20 December 1974, the IRA gave substance to the message by ordering a ten-day 'suspension of operations' to last from midnight two days later, on 22 December, until midnight on Thursday 2 January 1975, in order to give the British Government an opportunity 'to consider the proposals for a permanent ceasefire'. A 'permanent ceasefire' were the words the British wanted to hear.

Michael Oatley was now home in England looking forward to a few days' relaxation and peace, reassured by the fact that the ceasefire was about to be in place. All seemed to be going well until on Christmas Eve he got an urgent phone call from Brendan, in the middle of the night as was Brendan's wont, saying that the ceasefire was breaking down and the IRA was planning to go back to war on 2 January. Brendan told Oatley that the imminent crisis was because the IRA had received no reciprocal gesture from the British Government in response to its ceasefire. He was frustrated and angry, concerned that the trust that had been slowly established with Ruairí Ó Brádaigh over the previous year, and in the face of the Guildford and Birmingham atrocities, was in danger of being destroyed by the lack of any reciprocal response from the British. Brendan made it clear to Oatley that they needed to concoct a reassuring and positive message from the British Government for him to convey to the IRA. And it was urgent.

Oatley knew he had to act swiftly to stop the imminent slide back into violence. So much for a peaceful Christmas. He went to see Cooper at his home in London, explained the problem and showed him what he and Brendan thought would be a suitable message. Cooper left the room and went off to make a call, presumably to the PM, and got authority for the message to be sent. Bearing in mind Frank Cooper's caveat about not sticking his neck out too far, Oatley knew he now had Cooper's agreement, authorised by the Prime Minister, to send an encouraging message to the IRA, suggesting what might be on the agenda should talks take place. The enticing words in the message that Oatley conveyed to Brendan was that the British were prepared to discuss 'structures of disengagement'. The resonant phrase was entirely Oatley's idea. Taken at its face value, that would seem to imply the modalities of British withdrawal from Northern Ireland, which is what the IRA was fighting for and what it wanted to hear. That's certainly how I interpreted the phrase when I first heard of it, although it seemed incredible at this stage that the British would consider such a departure from long-established Government policy. Brendan had no doubt what the phrase was meant to imply and what the British were prepared to discuss. 'Michael would always say, "an end of violence and we can then discuss the various areas". He would be very careful but basically was he prepared to talk about British withdrawal? And the answer to that was, on his terms, yes.'[2]

Brendan scribbled notes of his conversation with Michael on a piece of paper, highlighting the key phrase, 'structures of disengagement'. As Oatley later confirmed, the phrase was suitably ambiguous but enough to encourage the IRA into talks, while making it clear that the Government's ability to consider withdrawing from Northern Ireland was entirely dependent on the will of the majority. Oatley had always emphasised there was no question of unilateral withdrawal of British rule as a result of negotiations with the republican movement.

> I always made it clear that when asked what I was prepared to discuss, I said, 'I am prepared to discuss anything you like.' 'Structures of Disengagement' could mean a reduction of security force pressure or it could mean looking forward to the next century and seeing if there would still be British rule in Northern Ireland. I think that the ambiguity was recognised by both sides so that each could make of it what it wanted. Ambiguous phrases were very much the currency we were involved with. They wanted some encouragement, I think, that republican aspirations could in some way be accommodated. You have to bear in mind that we're dealing with Irishmen who have a wonderful facility for language and subtlety. Marvellous poets and lawyers, so everything was open for discussion.[3]

Brendan had no time to lose. He knew as a matter of urgency he had to go and see Ruairí Ó Brádaigh at his home in Roscommon in the middle of Ireland, a three-hour drive from Derry. Rising early on Christmas morning he climbed into his battered Datsun – although a successful businessman, he was never one for status symbols – to begin his journey, only to realise that he was low on petrol and that, as it was Christmas Day, all the local petrol stations were shut. However, as he knew one of the owners, he persuaded him to open up and fill his tank, stressing the urgency of his need, but without spelling out the precise reasons for it. The owner, suspecting something might be afoot given the IRA ceasefire that was still in place, obliged and refused to take any money. 'People suspected that something that might alter their lives was happening,' Brendan reflected.[4]

It was a nightmare journey to Roscommon in heavy snow that made the narrow, winding roads even more treacherous – not that there would have been much traffic on Christmas Day morning in a blizzard. Brendan remembers the car 'sliding from side to side' at heart-stopping moments on the journey. He arrived at Ruairí Ó Brádaigh's house just as the family was sitting down to Christmas lunch. He tapped on the window. Brendan Duddy was the last person Ó Brádaigh expected to see, as a face at the window on Christmas Day. Another place was set at the table to accommodate the unexpected but welcome guest. Over Christmas lunch, Brendan, grateful for the invitation, grew increasingly frustrated as the conversation consisted of interminable observations about the weather. Ruairí, like Brendan, could talk for Ireland. With the ceasefire due to end at midnight in two days' time, the weather was the last thing Brendan wanted to discuss. He was bursting to give Ó Brádaigh the news.

Lunch over, Ruairí and Brendan adjourned to the privacy of the Ó Brádaighs' small, neat front sitting room where, to Brendan's relief, he felt free to talk and deliver the message. He produced the paper on which he had scribbled notes of his telephone conversation with Michael Oatley the night before and told his host that Oatley had said the British were prepared to discuss 'structures of disengagement from Ireland'. Everything that the IRA wanted to talk about was on the table. Ó Brádaigh was excited by the news but pointed out that he could not make a decision on such a potentially historic message on his own. He said that a decision to agree to a face-to-face meeting with the 'Brits' could only come from members of the Army Council itself. The best way to achieve that, he suggested, was for Brendan to meet them and convince them, as being the primary source, that the offer was genuine and it wasn't a trap. The notion of 'Perfidious Albion' always loomed in the background. Ó Brádaigh reasoned that the Army Council would want to see the whites of Brendan Duddy's eyes.

Brendan then drove back to Derry with much to think about, with the prospect of making his case to the most wanted men in Ireland. Ó Brádaigh then set about exploring the logistics. A week later, after more discussions, everything was in place. On New Year's Eve 1974, Brendan drove south again, met up once more with Ó Brádaigh and was driven to the secret location where the Provisionals' Army Council was meeting. Brendan had his own rules for survival. He didn't want to know where he was being taken. He didn't look out of the car window. He didn't look at the road signs and didn't ask any questions.

He judged it better not to know the details of his journey were he to be interrogated by the intelligence services on the British or Irish sides of the border about the end destination and the route he had taken to get there. He was naturally apprehensive but said he 'saw it as a job'. He was confident he could pull it off, having carefully rehearsed the pitch he was going to make to the Provisionals' Army Council (PAC). He was going to make his case and then say, 'You guys make up your mind.' The final destination was not what Brendan had expected, but a big country house. 'It was the most enormous house I'd ever seen, almost a castle.' Brendan was occasionally prone to a degree of exaggeration. He assumed it must have been owned by a rich businessman sympathetic to the republican cause.

He was shown into a huge drawing room, an incongruous setting for a meeting of the Army Council. 'They were sitting round this big table, just like a board of directors. Everyone was very polite,' Brendan remembers. Ó Brádaigh introduced Brendan and then adjourned to the wings, as it wasn't normal for the President of Sinn Féin to attend an Army Council meeting, unless invited as an *ex officio* member in his political capacity. The intimidating figure of Seamus Twomey was in the chair, still on the run in the South after his dramatic helicopter escape from Mountjoy prison and his further escape after the secret talks with the clergymen at Feakle were busted. Billy McKee, obviously not apprised of Brendan Duddy's appearance, told me of his surprise when Duddy walked in. (Perhaps Ó Brádaigh had not cleared his visit with all members of the Army Council in case it was vetoed.)

> We were just finishing up an Army Council meeting. He [Twomey] looked bloody surprised when he [Duddy] came into that room. I'd never seen Brendan Duddy before, and I was amazed because it isn't on the books to bring anybody [from outside] to an Army Council meeting. There was nobody at these meetings except Army Council men.[5]

Ó Brádaigh remembers that Brendan faced a gruelling interrogation and wasn't given an easy time. Brendan says that the question of him being a British spy never arose as it had been established by Ó Brádaigh that he was the channel down which messages from HMG had been conveyed over many months and the channel was 'totally reliable'.[6] Looking the members of the Army Council in the eye, Brendan explained that he'd been talking to Michael Oatley, whom he described as the British Government Representative, who had delivered a message that the British Government was prepared to engage in talks with an open agenda, in which anything that the IRA wished to be discussed could be discussed. He said that Billy McKee was the only person that the British Government Representative wished to meet. McKee was taken aback and instantly suspicious, suspecting that the man who wished to meet him was a 'spook', sensing that he might be walking into a trap laid by MI5 or MI6. 'I said I wasn't going to meet any British agent on my own,' he warned his fellow members on the Army Council. 'I want a witness to hear what's going on.' Twomey agreed and decided that McKee should go to meet Oatley. McKee consented, but wanted a companion to go with him.

During an adjournment, Brendan was sent to an upstairs room so the Army Council could talk in private. Brendan says he overheard a chilling exchange through the floorboards. Was Duddy an asset who could be used by the IRA or was he a British spy who should be shot? Duddy was enormously relieved when he got the thumbs-up.

The preliminary meeting between the IRA and Michael Oatley took place on 7 January 1975 in Brendan's 'wee room' at his house in Derry. The witness the Army Council selected to accompany Billy McKee, for whom Oatley later admitted a grudging admiration, was McKee's former adjutant and IRA veteran, Proinsias Mac Airt (Francis Card in English). They had been arrested together in 1971 in charge of a firearm and spent time together in Crumlin Road jail when McKee was leading his hunger strike in 1972. Mac Airt, like McKee, had recently been released from the jail. Oatley, wanting to avoid meeting an active IRA man face to face, had never heard of Mac Airt, so he did not pose a problem, not having been identified as an IRA commander. And McKee, whose IRA history was familiar, was now a free man. It was not known at the time that McKee was now a member of the Army Council. At the preliminary meeting, McKee was anxious to nail down what the 'Brits' were prepared to talk about.

I asked Oatley what was on the agenda and he said, 'Withdrawal.' That was the word used during the whole of the negotiations with Oatley and others. They [the British] said that's what they wanted and they needed the IRA to help them so there wouldn't be a bloodbath. They said they wanted us to meet the loyalists and they said that could be arranged all right. I can tell you, if they hadn't mentioned withdrawal, there'd have been no ceasefire and no truce at that time.[7]

The preliminaries were agreed and plans for a full meeting confirmed. The IRA then extended its ceasefire for another two weeks, until 16 January 1975, thus allowing time for the full meeting to happen. It was also agreed that Seamus Twomey would follow at a later stage should the negotiations prove encouraging and if his presence was felt to be necessary to put the seal on any agreement that might be reached. Oatley was concerned about who might be the participants he was likely to face at the full meeting.

My only trepidation was that I might be confronted with somebody of such a high profile, who is so obviously known to be a leading terrorist in British political terms as to cause potential embarrassment to the Secretary of State. I didn't want to meet anybody who looked like a publicly recognised terrorist and I didn't particularly want to know whether the people I was meeting were members of the Army Council or not.[8]

For the first full meeting, held on 20 January 1975, the IRA broadened its team. Ruairí Ó Brádaigh, a former IRA Chief of Staff (1958–62) and President of Sinn Féin since 1970, was lead negotiator along with Billy McKee and Joe McCallion, a Derry IRA commander, who replaced Proinsias Mac Airt. McCallion was a close colleague of Martin McGuinness and had been arrested with him on 29 January 1973 in County Donegal and charged with the same explosives offence. During their trial at Dublin's Special Criminal Court the charges were dropped. McCallion, like McGuinness, refused to recognise the court, admitted IRA membership and, again like McGuinness, was sentenced to six months.

Arriving at Brendan's house and seeing that McCallion was part of the IRA delegation, Oatley was concerned that if word leaked out that he had met an IRA commander like McCallion there would be serious political repercussions and trouble. Brendan, sensing the meeting might be about to fall apart, says he intervened and persuaded Oatley to stay, fearing that the whole back-channel enterprise might be on the brink of collapse. Oatley says he has no recollection of Brendan's intervention, citing what he regarded as Brendan's sometimes tenuous relationship with the truth. At the meeting, Oatley made one thing clear:

I said at the outset that, while I was happy to discuss anything including the future of Ireland, we all knew that British ministers could not divest themselves of responsibility for Northern Ireland without the consent of the majority. This was tacitly agreed. No comment was forthcoming from either of the three.

During the talks, a senior army officer, a lieutenant-colonel armed with a pistol, sat outside the 'wee room' for many long hours so that should an army patrol on routine duties happen to come along to search the house, the officer, being superior to all of them, except their Brigadier, could order them to go away and find another house to search.

Making the meeting possible in the first place involved a complex logistical operation smuggling IRA leaders across the border. Brendan arranged the logistics of transport, security and accommodation but recognised that he could not carry everything on his own. His family knew of his comings and goings but never asked any questions about the details or got involved in what he was doing. 'They were coming here for peace talks so that is all I knew,' his wife Margo told me. 'I never asked anything about the meetings, what happened during them or what they talked about. I didn't want to know, for my own sake.'[9] The family knew Brendan's mission was secret and that it had to be kept that way. His son, Brendan Junior, felt the same. 'We didn't know. We weren't told. At the same time, you saw the "boys" on TV so you knew who they were and the people who were here. And then there was a ceasefire, so you figure what was going on.'[10]

Not wishing to involve any member of the family, Brendan looked to his close friend, confidante and neighbour Bernie Mount, who besides being manager of his chip shop was vital to the logistics of the operation.

She drove Brendan's visitors across the border and provided B&B for them at her house a few hundred yards from Brendan's. Brendan and Bernie also ran marathons together and therefore had the stamina necessary for the long haul. Feisty, quick-witted and discreet – not to mention courageous – Bernie was the perfect smuggling companion for Brendan in his high-risk endeavour. She knew the general picture of what he was trying to achieve, although not the specific details, and became familiar with the people involved, several of whom she would pick up in the South and then drive across the border to Brendan's house. She had absolute faith in Brendan.

> I did it because of Brendan. He kept saying things will have to change. People need to talk. Every time somebody was shot or the violence was getting out of hand, he kept saying there has to be a solution. There has to be dialogue, there has to be talk. It was very, very hard and very lengthy and it took a long, long time. You can't bomb people into peace. Slowly, bit by bit, it was coming together but it was hard going. Every single day I opened my eyes in the morning and put on the radio to hear what had happened on the night before. You felt something had to change which meant keeping at it and not giving up. There were so many knock-backs. I knew that unless we talk to these people [the IRA] and try to work it out, it's the only way we're going to achieve a better life for all of us living in this country.[11]

Bernie knew she was running great risks and preferred not to think of what would happen should she be arrested in a car with a senior leader of the republican movement sitting beside her. Although she may not have been aware of it, RUC Superintendent Frank Lagan, who two years earlier had liaised with Brendan over the removal of IRA weapons from the Bogside and Creggan, was one of only a handful of people who knew about the existence of the back channel, Bernie's involvement and Brendan's pivotal role in it. Lagan was even reported to have used his official car to help.

> Brendan assured me that it would be OK because it was known that this was being done at that time by the British Government. He said if you get into any bother, we'll get it sorted out. So I was quite

happy that if anything did happen and I was arrested, at the end of
the day, it would be OK. But it was nerve-racking. I was nervous
because I wanted to do the job and do it right.[12]

Bernie had some close calls. There was a heart-stopping moment
when she first collected Ruairí Ó Brádaigh to drive him across the
border. They were held at a roadblock and questioned by soldiers
who clearly did not recognise Bernie's passenger. Ó Brádaigh, having
imagined the likelihood of this happening, had briefed Bernie on what
to do: to take the papers he had prepared for the meeting and stuff
them up her jumper. Bernie duly obliged. Ó Brádaigh admired Bernie's
sangfroid under pressure. 'She would be very polite and nice to them.
I think they appreciated that too. She was a good-looking girl.'

Driving 'terrorists' across the border was only Bernie's first step.
She then had to accommodate them at home, occasionally presiding
over the odd musical evening to relax her visitors after an intense day
of discussions in Brendan's house. She remembers Seamus Twomey,
her house guest when the negotiations were getting critical, being in
good voice, 'singing a wee song', and Ruairí Ó Brádaigh emerging
from the bathroom in paisley pyjamas. She took a photo and teased
him by threatening to send it to Dr Paisley to show that Ruairí
thought about him every night when he went to bed. Ó Brádaigh
took it in good part. But there were few moments of levity in the
negotiations that went on at intervals during the first few months
of 1975 after the IRA had gone on to declare its indefinite ceasefire.
As Frank Cooper, who had given his imprimatur to the talks, told
me, Ruairí Ó Brádaigh described the enterprise as 'the most exciting
thing that had ever happened to me'.[13] 'There was no doubt at all that
they [the IRA] were delighted to be involved in what they saw as a
political dialogue.'

Inevitably there were highs and lows during the talks. At one stage
there was a serious impasse when neither side could agree the wording
of a particularly sensitive sentence. Oatley remembers leaving the room
with Ó Brádaigh to fill a bucket of peat to keep the 'wee room' warm
on a cold winter's night. 'We have to make this work,' he remembers Ó
Brádaigh saying with tears in his eyes. 'We have to make this work.' On
another occasion when a similar impasse was reached, Ó Brádaigh left
the room saying he needed a bathroom break. He knew Brendan would

be outside as he was not allowed to be present during the negotiations. He took Brendan to one side and told him the words that were causing the problem. Brendan suggested using different words to express the same thing. This was Brendan in his 'managerial' role. Ó Brádaigh returned to the 'wee room' relieved – whether having been to the bathroom or not. Brendan's 'managerial' role also occasionally involved calming things down when things became a little fraught. When, in the early stages of the talks, Joe McCallion became over-excited and disruptive, Brendan intervened and calmed him down with a mug of cocoa into which he had sprinkled some ground-up Valium pills.[14]

II

Negotiating with the IRA

I always found it difficult to believe that the phrase 'structures of disengagement' was really on the agenda of the talks. It just didn't seem in keeping with the Government's position. In the end, around 1996 and early 1997, in the lead-up to the Good Friday Agreement, I decided the best way of finding out was to try to get access to the minutes of those early ground-breaking meetings. I knew that Sinn Féin was assiduous in keeping a record of the proceedings for its own purposes and for posterity. It might have been in the republican movement's interest to give emphasis to certain sections that favoured its agenda but it was not in its interest to falsify what was said by either side – or seek to use the minutes as propaganda. Governments on both sides of the border take minutes and deposit them in state archives. The republican movement, which has always seen itself historically as the exiled Government of the Irish Republic declared during the 1916 Easter Rising, also keeps records and lodges them in archives, one of the recent repositories being the National University of Ireland, in Galway, where Brendan Duddy's archive is currently stored. I had no doubt that the minutes of the 1975 ceasefire talks existed; the question was how to find them and read them.

I started by going to visit Ruairí Ó Brádaigh at his home in Roscommon. I had got to know him during the early 1970s, when he was close to Joe Cahill (they were of the same generation), and had always found him helpful and obliging, and always ready to provide his correction to my knowledge of Irish history, by giving me a detailed dissertation on its finer points. He looked like, and spoke like, a university professor rather than any preconception of a former IRA chief of staff, and he knew Brendan Duddy well, having metaphorically held his ear to the receiving end of Oatley's bamboo pipe. I explained what I was doing and that I needed to see the minutes for myself. He told me he would do what he could to help. I was told to expect a phone call.

The call came and I was given my instructions: to drive to a location, many miles across the border, and wait in the car park of a certain pub in a certain village at a certain time. It was a long and uninspiring drive through the farming flatlands that stretch across the middle of Ireland. In those days before mobile phones and satnavs, old-fashioned maps were my guide. I found the pub and parked as instructed. Two men then emerged from another car, checked who I was and instructed me to follow them to their car and do exactly as I was told. I was unlikely to do otherwise. I assumed they were members of the IRA or Sinn Féin but it wasn't a question it would have been judicious to ask, nor did it matter. They were not masked.

I was told to get in the front seat and ordered to keep my eyes on the floor so as not to see where I was being driven. There was no conversation, no small talk and none of the drama of being blindfolded or curled up on the back seat and covered with a blanket as I was once ordered to do while being driven at night to a lonely cottage in the fastness of South Armagh to meet the IRA. After a drive of about half an hour we arrived at our destination. I was told I could now look up. We were parked outside a substantial house, not period but sizeable nevertheless. I was greeted in the hallway by a man and a woman who never gave their names. They were friendly and hospitable and set out the ground rules for my visit. They told me the minutes I had come in search of were on a desk in the study and I could spend as long as I liked reading them. There was no rush, no time pressure and no deadline. And there would be no minder to watch over me. The couple were happy for me to use a tape recorder which would make the process of taking notes much simpler and swifter. And would I like a cup of tea? I said I would love one.

The record of the minutes, with an account of what both sides were purported to have said, was neatly filed in a large red ring binder, the kind that will take a bite out of your fingers if you're not careful. I set about digesting and taking notes for the next five hours, sustained by cups of tea and home-made fruit cake. The minutes were very formal and, judging by the typeface, written on an elderly typewriter rather than on any fancy new electric Remington. In 1975, the year of the ceasefire negotiations, word processing and universal use of the internet were still a decade and more away.

I came to the minute of 2 April 1975 and it was remarkable. I knew that the British were represented by Michael Oatley, although his name is not mentioned in the minute, and James Allan, his NIO colleague at Laneside. Oatley did all the talking. Allan was effectively an observer to confirm that what Oatley was reporting back to Frank Cooper at Stormont was accurate and objective. Brendan Duddy was not in the room during the negotiations but was stage-managing things behind the scenes. The minute recording what the British were reported to have said lay before me in black and white as its representatives tried to reassure Sinn Féin's increasingly sceptical and restless negotiators.

> The acceptability of the republican movement as a respectable movement has greatly increased. It is now viewed as a serious political movement which should be listened to. This is an enormous gain. It would be lost if the republican movement goes back to war. There is no magic way forward. This is an extremely historic moment. It may never happen again for a long time. The alternative to going back to war is to accept a rate of progress which is slow but will increase as it goes along.[1]

Again the words about 'slow progress' were prophetic. The 'extremely historic moment' indeed took 'a long time' and finally arrived in 1998 with the Good Friday Agreement. The minute continued:

> If on the other hand the republican movement helps the Government to create circumstances under which the *structures of disengagement* [author's emphasis] can naturally grow, the pace quickens immensely once the groundwork is laid. The only way to develop is to get the groundwork right. HMG cannot say they are leaving Ireland because the reaction would prevent that happening. They cannot make a stark, definitive statement. If one looks at events, the tendency is towards eventual British disengagement ... but it will stop if the republican movement goes back to war.

At a follow-up meeting as negotiations progressed, now with Seamus Twomey monitoring developments from Bernie's house down the road, the British and the IRA reached a formal ten-point agreement on what would happen in the event of a longer cessation of military operations. It involved the following key paragraphs.

- If there is a genuine and sustained cessation of violence and hostilities, the army would gradually be reduced to peacetime levels and withdrawn to barracks.
- Discussion will continue between officials and representatives of Provisional Sinn Féin and will include the aim of securing a permanent peace.
- Once violence has come to a complete end, the rate of release will be speeded up with a view to releasing all detainees.

As far as the IRA negotiating team was concerned, the ten-point agreement was a treaty. As far as Michael Oatley, James Allan and London were concerned, it was a statement of the likely consequences of a cessation of violence. It was deliberately ambiguous so each side could take from it what they wanted. As at Cheyne Walk, the agreement fell far short of the republican movement's irreducible demands for a declaration of intent to withdraw and the right of self-determination for the Irish people, North and South, but it was enough to keep the dialogue going.

In the later stages of drafting the ten points, another stumbling block arose when the IRA demanded that after a settlement senior commanders on the run returning to the North from the Irish Republic should be free from arrest and allowed to carry guns for their protection. Oatley instantly knew that such a proposal, the return of armed IRA fugitives, was not something the Lord Chancellor was going to wear, but Brendan assured him that the IRA only wanted the carrying of weapons to be intended as a gesture. A compromise formula was devised whereby persons identified as responsible community leaders engaged in monitoring the ceasefire would be issued with identity cards which would make them immune from being searched in the unlikely event of their encountering members of the security forces, in the light of the progressive withdrawal of troops from nationalist areas. Nevertheless there was an understanding that if a gun were sticking out of a pocket, the owner would be arrested. When Oatley rehearsed this tortuous formula at the next meeting Ó Brádaigh said, 'We will take that as a "yes".' It was a reflection of the word games and ambiguities – phrases like 'structures of disengagement' and 'cessation of violence' instead of 'truce' – that both sides were playing to keep the process on track.

For the IRA, the most tangible element of the IRA truce – or cessation of violence – was the establishment of 'incident centres' across the province to be manned by Sinn Féin to avoid a confrontation such as the one in Lenadoon Avenue that ended the 1972 ceasefire. In the event of any dangerously imminent clash, Sinn Féin officials would use a hotline, initially to Laneside and ultimately, if necessary, to officials at Stormont Castle, the heart of Direct Rule, with access to the Secretary of State himself. Oatley had no role in monitoring the ceasefire and was about to leave the province. These incident centres were to mark the first stage in the incremental rise of the IRA's political wing, Sinn Féin, giving it a base and a degree of credibility within the broad nationalist community, only a limited amount of which it had enjoyed before. It also resulted in a lessening of support for the IRA as nationalists saw the advantages of peace, however fragile it was.

12

Tit for Tat

The IRA having a direct hotline to British ministers and their officials was more than loyalists and their paramilitaries, the UDA and the UVF, could stomach, convinced that the 'Brits' had done a deal with the IRA to pull out of the North and leave the road clear for a united Ireland. It seemed like the ultimate betrayal, the loyalists' abiding fear, reflected in the savagery of the paramilitaries' response. In 1975 they lashed out with unbridled ferocity, brutally murdering 120 Catholics, the vast majority innocent civilians.[1] There was a calculated strategy behind the slaughter: to provoke the IRA into retaliation that would trigger the end of the ceasefire. The UVF was responsible for 100 of those deaths,[2] the most horrific being a bomb and gun attack on the Strand Bar in Belfast on 12 April 1975 in which four women and two men were killed. The bomb exploded at 8.12 p.m. just as the evening was getting under way. The pub was situated on the edge of a small Catholic/nationalist enclave in East Belfast known as Short Strand, a nationalist island in a loyalist sea and always vulnerable to loyalist attack. To block the escape route from the carnage, one of the bombers jammed the door handle with a piece of wood to stop customers getting out.[3]

But the attack that shocked Ireland to the core – North and South, Catholic and Protestant – came later, on the evening of 31 July that year, when the UVF targeted Ireland's phenomenally popular group, the Miami Showband. In England it would have been like targeting the Beatles. The Showband's charismatic lead singer was Fran O'Toole, with a fanatical fanbase, a cross between Paul McCartney and David Cassidy.

The band was heading back to Dublin in their minibus after a gig in Banbridge, south of Belfast, when their van was stopped at what appeared to be an army checkpoint between Banbridge and Newry. The band's bass guitarist, Stephen Travers, later told me what happened. 'The soldiers came up to us and said the usual, "Goodnight, fellas. How are things? Can you step out of the van for a few minutes and we'll just do a check."'

The checkpoint was bogus. The 'soldiers' were in fact members of a mid-Ulster UVF gang, two of whom, Lance Corporal Thomas Crozier and Sergeant James McDowell, were also serving soldiers in the Ulster Defence Regiment (UDR), an infantry regiment of the British army formed in 1970 to replace the 'B' Specials, the auxiliary arm of the RUC. The UVF's plan was to plant a bomb secretly in the van, timed to explode shortly afterwards, giving the impression that the members of the Miami Showband were in fact terrorists with a bomb on board. As Stephen Travers later told me, 'If the bomb had gone off, nobody would have known about the bogus checkpoint. The van would have blown up and the whole world would have said, "Well, who can you trust? The Miami Showband are carrying bombs."' As two 'soldiers' were closing the van's back door, the bomb exploded prematurely, killing both of them. Stephen described later seeing a photograph of one. 'Just a black torso, no head, legs or arms which reminded me vividly of what could have happened to me but for the grace of God.'

As the bomb exploded, the other UVF gunmen opened fire, killing Fran O'Toole. Stephen remembers Fran crying, 'Please don't shoot, don't kill me!' 'Then I heard the gunfire as they killed him.' Fran was reported to have been shot twenty-two times, including bullets in the face that adorned the walls of tens of thousands of young fans throughout Ireland. Two other band members were also killed in the gunfire. Stephen himself was hit by an explosive dum-dum bullet but miraculously survived. 'It exploded inside me in about 13 pieces.'[4] Lance Corporal Thomas Crozier and Sergeant James McDowell were later arrested and sentenced to life imprisonment.[5] The fact that Crozier and McDowell were serving members of the British army's UDR seemed to confirm, without concrete evidence, the suspicions of many nationalists that collusion was involved in the attack.

A fortnight later, the IRA retaliated. After such loyalist atrocities, it could not afford not to, given the IRA's historic remit to protect the nationalist community from loyalist attack, which it had singularly failed to do in August 1969. By this time, the summer of 1975, the ceasefire was becoming increasingly shaky. The talks with the British, as they appeared to the IRA, were not making the progress its leadership had hoped for. Suspicions were growing that the 'Brits' were playing a double game, seeming to talk to the IRA while in effect weakening it through its forced inactivity during the ceasefire.

In the face of the sectarian slaughter, to some elements of the IRA it was now an 'eye for an eye', despite its profession that it did not target innocent civilians. The ensuing attacks by the IRA on loyalist targets gave the lie to the claim. On 13 August 1975, three of its members launched a bomb and gun attack on the Bayardo Bar in the heart of the loyalist Shankill Road as a sing-song was in progress. One opened up with an Armalite automatic rifle while another threw a bomb in a duffle bag through an open door. Five Protestants were killed. Although the bar was thought to have UVF customers, which was no surprise given its location, none of the dead was believed to have any connection with any paramilitary organisation.[6] Up to sixty people were injured, many in the rubble from the blast. One of them, a seventeen-year-old Protestant girl, Linda Boyle, died later from her injuries. In the aftermath of the widespread horror and public outrage at what was seen to be a purely sectarian attack, the IRA's Army Council tried to cloak its embarrassment and justify the attack by issuing new ceasefire orders. It now allowed its units to open fire in 'retaliatory and defensive actions' and, seemingly justifying the operation, warned of the 'sectarian killers who operate from Orange [loyalist] strongholds'. It was an attempt to turn the sectarian tables.

The three members of the IRA unit that carried out the attack were arrested and sentenced to life. One of them was Brendan 'Bik' McFarlane, who became a legendary figure among the IRA leadership, especially during the hunger strike when he briefly became IRA OC (Officer Commanding) – briefly because in 1983 he escaped from the Maze prison along with thirty-eight other republican prisoners in what went down in republican folklore as 'the Great Escape'. He later fled to Holland with another Maze escapee and IRA leader, Gerry Kelly, who had been a member of the IRA's Active Service Unit that bombed the Old Bailey and Scotland Yard in 1973.

The tit-for-tat killings continued through the autumn of 1975 as the ceasefire became increasingly flimsy. On 1 September, a fortnight after the IRA attack on the Bayardo Bar, masked republican gunmen walked into the Tullyvallen Orange Hall near Newtownhamilton in South Armagh and sprayed it with automatic rifle fire, killing five members of the Guiding Star Orange Lodge, two of them aged seventy and eighty, and wounding seven others. In a phone call to the BBC, responsibility was claimed by the hitherto unheard-of 'South Armagh Reaction Force'. The caller said the attack was retaliation for the 'assassinations of fellow Catholics'. The 'South Armagh Reaction Force' was believed to be a flag of convenience for the Provisional IRA, whose leadership needed to cover the IRA's tracks in the hope of preserving the ceasefire.[7] But not all senior IRA commanders, many now locked up in the compounds of Long Kesh, were happy at the increasingly sectarian focus of the IRA's response. So called 'flags of convenience' did not pull the wool over their eyes. Brendan Hughes, who had shared a 'cage' with Gerry Adams in Long Kesh, told me he was opposed to the apparent change in policy. Hughes was later transferred to the H Blocks of the Maze prison.

> In the 1975 period there was a great deal of disillusionment among a lot of people in the jail, including myself and Gerry Adams. When the ceasefire was on, the whole machine slipped into sectarianism and a lot of us were very, very unhappy with that situation. I didn't believe that Tullyvallen and other attacks were going to achieve anything. I believed they were counter-productive. Sectarian bombings and killings were doing nothing except destroying the whole struggle.[8]

A month later, on 2 October, loyalists connected to the UVF gunned down four Catholics during a robbery at Casey's wholesale wine and spirits warehouse, a Catholic-owned business between the bottom of the loyalist Shankill and nationalist Falls Roads. The victims were two sisters and two eighteen-year-old teenagers. One of the gunmen, Lennie Murphy, shot three of them in cold blood through the head and neck.[9] Murphy was the leader of the gang soon to become notorious as the 'Shankill Butchers' who tortured and carved up their Catholic victims with butchers' knives before finally putting them out of their agony by cutting their throats. Murphy was a psychopath. Over the years, eleven members of his gang murdered nineteen people, most of them Catholics. Murphy was arrested on 13 March 1976 and, after plea bargaining, sentenced to twelve years in the Maze prison, from where he continued to direct his gang. He was finally released in 1982. Four months later, two Provisional IRA gunmen, armed with a 9mm submachine gun and a .38 Special revolver, shot him dead as he was getting out of his car. He died instantly, riddled with twenty-six bullets to the head and body.[10] The UVF gave the Shankill's 'Master Butcher' a large paramilitary funeral with shots fired over the coffin as it left his mother's house. 'Here Lies a Soldier' is written across the top of his headstone. Few tears beyond his family and close comrades would have been shed at his demise.

The final end of the ceasefire was marked by tit-for-tat attacks as the new year began. The first came in the evening of Sunday 4 January 1976, when three masked UVF gunmen from Mid Ulster burst into the cottage in the village of Whitecross, County Armagh, where the Catholic Reavey family lived. They shot three brothers, John Martin (aged twenty-four), Brian (twenty-two) and Anthony (seventeen) as they were watching teatime television. The key had been left in the lock of the door and the killers simply walked in. John Martin and Brian died instantly. Anthony, who hid under the bed hoping for safety, was dragged out by the killers, shot again in the legs and died later in hospital. A detective described the brothers as 'totally innocent'.[11]

Ten minutes later, fifteen miles away, in an apparently coordinated UVF attack, three masked gunmen attacked the home of the Catholic O'Dowd family at Ballydugan near Gilford, as they were enjoying a post-New Year's Eve sing-song around the piano. Two brothers, Declan (nineteen) and Barry (twenty-four) and their uncle, Joe (sixty-one), were shot dead. Barry was playing the piano.

I was working in Northern Ireland at the time and remember attending the Reavey brothers' wake on a cold, dark January night in the family's whitewashed cottage while army helicopters hovered above, sweeping the ground with high-powered searchlights, perhaps in case loyalist assassins decided to make a return visit. I looked at the white faces of the two murdered brothers, John Martin and Brian, lying in their coffins, neatly dressed in suits and collars and ties, surrounded by little memory cards left by the family, mourners and friends. I was given one of them and I wondered when and if the killings would ever end. I didn't know about the attack on the O'Dowd family that same evening.

Around 5.30 p.m. the following day, 5 January 1976, an IRA unit, now under the cover name of the 'Republican Action Force', retaliated with an even more blatant sectarian attack when they waylaid a minibus taking home Protestant workers from a factory. A group of men with blackened faces and automatic rifles stopped the bus just outside the village of Kingsmills, County Armagh. The passengers thought it was a routine army checkpoint. Soldiers, in particular in South Armagh, invariably had blackened faces. The bogus soldiers ordered the passengers and driver out, lined them up and asked if there were any Catholics among them. The driver, a Catholic, owned up, not knowing whether he was going to be killed or spared. He was spared and told to 'run up the road'.[12] The other passengers, all Protestants, were then mowed down in cold blood. Ten died. One miraculously survived, despite being hit eighteen times. His name was Alan Black. It took me a long time to find him and a long time to persuade him to do an interview. He finally agreed to describe the terrifying experience. He remembered talk in the factory that day about the murder of the three Reavey brothers the night before. At first, he wasn't worried when the minibus was stopped as he thought it was the army – until the 'soldiers' opened up.

> The gunfire was deafening, like something you have in your worst nightmare. I could not believe it the first time I was hit. It was total unreality but the pain was real enough. When the shooting stopped there was not a sound. Just dead silence. I watched them [the gunmen] walk off down the road. They were wearing Doc Marten boots.[13]

Alan lay there, with the rain trickling down his face, in unbelievable pain, convinced he was going to die, putting his fingers in the bullet holes to try and stop the blood oozing out. He lay there by the roadside for around half an hour, semi-conscious, until an ambulance and the police finally arrived. He was rushed to hospital where he made a miraculous recovery. 'It was calculated, that's what made it so hard to take. Ten lads who wouldn't hurt a fly, just wiped out. They didn't mean to leave anyone alive. They knew what they were going to do. How could they live with themselves?'[14]

As a result of the Kingsmills massacre, Labour's Northern Ireland Secretary, Roy Mason, who had replaced Merlyn Rees in September 1976, sent the SAS into South Armagh, now with the moniker 'Bandit Country'. It was a step that was to transform the security situation over the following decade – and not without controversy.

Viewing the sectarian carnage from a distance, Michael Oatley lamented the way the guarded optimism with which he had left Northern Ireland had degenerated into sectarian savagery, leaving the ceasefire, for which he and Brendan Duddy had worked so hard, in tatters. The last formal meeting between Oatley's successors and the IRA took place on 10 February 1976, the first anniversary of the ceasefire. By this time, Oatley had been gone for almost a year, and was now abroad. With the ceasefire and the ten-point plan that he had negotiated in place, he had hoped his job was done, although he was never confident that the ceasefire was going to last. But it was now up to others to bring the principles outlined in the ten-point agreement to fruition. Oatley's bamboo pipe had served its purpose in getting the initial stages of the talks under way.

Before he left, sharing like Brendan a penchant for a piece of theatre, Michael presented Ruairí Ó Brádaigh, Billy McKee and Joe McCallion with rolled-gold Cross ballpoint pens to mark the end of a historic relationship and to symbolise the fact that a formal, written negotiation had been completed. McKee, noting that the pens were only rolled-gold and not 24 carat, is reported to have quipped, 'At least the Government could have presented us with the real thing.' Ó Brádaigh, embarrassed that he had nothing to give Oatley in return, presented him with a signed copy of his own personal work, Sinn Féin's manifesto, *Eire Nua*, outlining a federal Ireland based on its four ancient provinces. It was his envisaged solution to the Irish Question and he inscribed it 'with thanks for your efforts for Ireland'. When the ten-point agreement was reached, Michael Oatley remembers Brendan saying, 'They value it. They will protect it. They will want to come back to it.' Twenty years later, they did. The 1975 negotiated agreement provided a platform for the future.

Nor did the British side lack imagination. At one stage during the ceasefire talks it was anticipated that, should they prove fruitful, they might lead to a plenary session between Sir Frank Cooper on behalf of HMG and David O'Connell on behalf of the republican movement. The question then arose, should that stage be reached, in what neutral venue could it be held? I understand that a yacht moored in one of the beautiful Fermanagh lakes was suggested. With this in mind, a motor yacht was purchased at considerable expense but never brought into service, although it would have been difficult to imagine David O'Connell stepping on board a yacht controlled by the 'Brits'. But the talks never got to a plenary session. It's not known what happened to the yacht.

PART II

13

The Coup

After the ending of the ceasefire on 23 January 1976 and a return to full-scale hostilities, two highly significant changes occurred that were to dramatically affect the course of the conflict. The first was the ousting of the IRA's Southern leadership, represented by the old guard of Ruairí Ó Brádaigh and David O'Connell, and its replacement by the younger Northern leadership of Martin McGuinness and Gerry Adams and their close circle. The axis of control and direction of the war was now radically changed from the South to the North, where the war was being fought. It was a coup in all but name. To the new leadership of the republican movement, the 1975 ceasefire was the great betrayal, cleverly engineered by the British to entice the IRA into the trap of inactivity, thus weakening the organisation and blunting what McGuinness called the IRA's 'cutting edge'. To the British side, this was Britain's 'win/win' strategy in action. Michael Oatley had always recognised that this might be the outcome. If the ceasefire ended in a settlement, that was a win. If it ended with a weakened IRA going back to war, that was also a win as its effectiveness as a fighting force would have been seriously blunted.

The advantage for the new leadership was that Adams and McGuinness were both untainted by the ceasefire. Adams had first been interned in 1971 and released the following year to attend the Cheyne Walk talks with Willie Whitelaw. He then went on the run and was rearrested in 1973 and locked up in Long Kesh, the internment camp that later became the Maze prison, until his release in 1977. Adams was therefore 'behind the wire' and 'behind bars' during the genesis, implementation and ultimate collapse of the ceasefire.

Martin McGuinness was also out of action during the critical period of the negotiations that led to the ceasefire. He was arrested on 11 February 1974 for a second time across the border in Buncrana, five miles from Derry, and charged once more with IRA membership. He was sentenced to a year in jail in the Irish Republic, of which he served nine months. He was released on 13 December, slightly more than a fortnight before the ceasefire was declared. Neither Adams nor McGuinness was in the loop. Both were clean and free from the taint of the 1975 ceasefire, given its failed outcome.

There was also a change of leadership at the top of the British Government. On 16 March 1976 Harold Wilson made the bombshell announcement that he was resigning at the age of sixty after serving as Prime Minister, at various stages, for nearly eight years. With the talks with the IRA over and the chances of any settlement involving the IRA gone – he had supported Michael Oatley and his bamboo pipe – Wilson left it to his successor, James Callaghan, and a new team to deal with the Irish problem. Merlyn Rees, the Northern Ireland Secretary, still had another six months to serve before Prime Minister Callaghan replaced him. Before he left office, Rees introduced a major change in Government policy that was to have seismic, long-term repercussions. The new policy was called 'criminalisation'.

From 1 March 1976, Special Category Status, extracted in 1972 by Billy McKee from a reluctant Willie Whitelaw as a result of his hunger strike, was abolished. Republican and loyalist prisoners convicted of terrorist offences were now to be deprived of the privileges that Special Category Status afforded them, including the right to wear their own clothes, be spared prison work and be allowed extra visits and food parcels. Those privileges had amounted, in all but name, to the 'political' status that republican prisoners were demanding – a designation that the Northern Ireland Secretary, Willie Whitelaw, and successive Governments steadfastly refused to grant.

Sentenced prisoners were now to be locked up in newly constructed wings known as 'H Blocks', so called because of their shape, with each wing forming one of the four concrete legs of the 'H'. The 'blocks' were constructed on the same site as the compounds and 'cages' at Long Kesh used to house internees. Prisoners now incarcerated in the new H

Blocks were regarded as common criminals and forced to wear prison uniform. 'Criminalisation' was designed to normalise the conflict, thus stripping it of the political motivation that republicans insisted was the reason for their violence. Names were changed to underline the process. Long Kesh became the Maze prison.

On the security front, the RUC was given primacy over the army in the battle against the 'terrorists'. Suspects were to be arrested, interrogated and sentenced by due process of law, not before a jury that might be subject to intimidation, but before a single judge, which would minimise the risk of coercion. These trials took place in what were known as Diplock courts, named after the Appeal Court judge Lord Diplock who had recommended their introduction in 1972 as an alternative to internment. The courts became operative the following year.

In many cases the evidence was based on statements made by the accused during interrogation by RUC Special Branch officers at special 'holding centres' like Castlereagh in Belfast, Gough Barracks in Armagh and Strand Road in Derry. Not all the interrogators wore kid gloves and there were widespread allegations and indeed evidence of ill-treatment – and it was not all down to IRA propaganda or allegedly self-inflicted injuries. I interviewed republican and loyalist suspects and lawyers and doctors attached to the interrogation centres. All confirmed that the allegations of ill-treatment were based on fact. Diplock judges then had to determine whether the accused had been subjected to 'torture or to inhuman or degrading treatment' in breach of Article 3 of the European Convention on Human Rights. If that in the judge's view was the case, the accused was released. I also interviewed RUC interrogators. I still have a note of what one senior detective told me. He described the confessions extracted during interrogation as 'laxity of tongue control': 'Tails were up, the scent was clear and we were heading for home. Terrorists were vomiting confessions all over the place. It was like emptying buckets.'[1]

In 1977 more than 1,300 suspects were charged with terrorist offences, almost a thousand of them by detectives of the four Regional Crime Squads that the new RUC Chief Constable, Sir Kenneth Newman, had brought together.[2] Sir Kenneth, appointed in 1976, dismissed the allegations of ill-treatment as IRA propaganda and told me that, although there might be 'bad apples' in any organisation, some of the injuries were clearly self-inflicted. Newman made it clear to the public what he had set out to do:

Terrorism continues to bring death and destruction to Northern
Ireland ... I will not be satisfied until the shooting and the whole
squalid catalogue of criminality is brought to a finish ... Our
purpose is to put behind bars those criminals who up to now have
perhaps regarded themselves as being beyond the reach of the law
... The intention is that the law should be enforced even more
effectively for the good of all the people of Northern Ireland.[3]

I remember later going to see Sir Kenneth Newman at Bramshill Police
Staff College in Hampshire to discuss what had been happening at
Castlereagh and other RUC interrogation centres. He did not take
kindly to some of my questions and to my surprise produced from his
desk drawer a copy of *Index on Censorship* for which I had written an
article on 'Reporting Northern Ireland'; in this I had explained how
difficult it was to cover sensitive issues like interrogation and security
policy. I was taken aback when Sir Kenneth produced the magazine and
accused me of being a 'leftie'.[4] Sir Kenneth, aged ninety, died in 2017.

The 'criminalisation' policy introduced by Merlyn Rees was energeti-
cally pursued by his successor, Roy Mason, who on 10 September 1976
was transferred from the MOD, where he had been Secretary of State
for Defence, to the Northern Ireland Office, where he became Northern
Ireland Secretary. Rees and Mason could not have been more different.
Rees was a quiet conciliator, slightly shy but honest and straightforward.
Mason, a blunt and proud Yorkshireman – and like his former Prime
Minister, Harold Wilson, an inveterate pipe-smoker – began his
working life down a coal pit outside his home town of Barnsley, having
left school at the age of fourteen with no qualifications. He went on to
become a Member of Parliament sponsored by the National Union of
Mineworkers. He was not backwards in coming forwards. When he left
the MOD, his press officers sent his cuttings books to the Northern
Ireland Office with the advice that they keep them up to date to keep
their new boss happy. Unionists loved him as they saw him as a man of
action producing results. Above all Mason was determined to show the
IRA no quarter.

With the increasingly important role of the RUC, supported by
the necessary levels of Armed Forces, the forces of law and order
are now effectively putting behind bars many of the murderers and

terrorists … the RUC will gradually tighten the net around these gangsters.[5]

We are squeezing the terrorists like rolling up a toothpaste tube. We are squeezing them out of their safe havens. We are squeezing them away from their money supplies. We are squeezing them out of society and into prison.[6]

One of Mason's first acts was to shut down Laneside, which Michael Oatley, James Allan, Frank Steele and their colleagues had used as their congenial and useful base. There was to be no more hobnobbing with the enemy, no more bamboo pipes and secret talks with the IRA. The enemy was to be defeated, not indulged. The combination of the new Chief Constable, Sir Kenneth Newman, and the new Northern Ireland Secretary, Roy Mason, was devastating and hit the IRA hard. The two men fitted each other like a hand in a glove – albeit of the mailed-fist variety. Roy Mason, aged ninety-one, died in 2015.

Unionist politicians and RUC detectives were delighted and relieved that at last the forces of law and order were taking the fight to the enemy. It was what they had been demanding for years. One anonymous Special Branch officer bluntly summed it up for me.

It showed a willingness to actually defeat the problem of terrorism as opposed to appeasing it. Roy Mason spoke to the lads who were involved and congratulated them. We felt we were actually achieving something. We were arresting, interviewing and charging people for terrorist crimes. They went to court and were convicted. We were fighting a war, but it seemed up until then only one side was fighting a war. We were going after them [the IRA] and it was working. I think it brought them to their knees at that particular period.

I asked him about the ill-treatment of terrorist suspects.

I can't deny in the light of events [that is, subsequent inquiries like the Bennett and Amnesty Reports] that people were abused. But the bottom line was we were dealing with murderers, we were dealing with people who were prepared to shoot and kill innocent

civilians. We were arresting and charging and convicting people
who were putting bombs in shops, killing innocent civilians, killing
children. We've had to look into the eyes of people we know are
murderers and killers. I had no compunction about making them
uncomfortable, through long interviews and letting them know
how we felt about them in no uncertain terms.[7]

I interviewed several IRA suspects who claimed they had been ill-
treated during interrogation. One of them was twenty-five-year-old
Tommy McKearney from the village of Moy (or The Moy, as it is known
colloquially) in Mid Ulster. He was arrested on 19 October 1977 and
charged with the murder of an off-duty part-time Ulster Defence Regiment
(UDR) soldier, Stanley Adams, who was working as a postman delivering
letters. McKearney was taken to Castlereagh and interrogated for seven
days under the Prevention of Terrorism Act, introduced by Labour's Home
Secretary, Roy Jenkins, after the Birmingham pub bombings in 1974.

> For the best part of the seven days I was subjected to physical
> torture. I had several Special Branch officers holding and bending
> my wrists. One would hold the elbow, the other would bend the
> wrist – both wrists. It's a particularly painful experience. So painful
> I recall very clearly it was the first time I ever fainted – it may have
> been on the third or the fourth day. The most traumatic piece of
> torture came towards the end of the seven days. They brought in
> four to six hefty policemen in civilian clothing. They pressed me to
> the floor, brought in a bin liner, put it over my head and started to
> tighten it around me so that I couldn't breathe. It was through that
> that I sustained several injuries, notably a black eye which was the
> most obvious sign.[8]

I also interviewed the police surgeon, Dr Robert 'Bertie' Irwin, who
examined McKearney after his interrogation. Dr Irwin, and his
colleague at Gough Barracks in Armagh, Dr Denis Elliott, became
courageous whistle-blowers about ill-treatment during protracted
RUC interrogations. Dr Irwin had no doubt that McKearney had been
abused. He also said that at first McKearney was reluctant to talk about
what he had endured and in the end he had to drag the information
out of him.

He was pale, nervous and exhausted. He had a black eye that looked
fairly recent and bruises whose colour suggested they were five to six
days old. His forehead was swollen and many muscles at the back
of his neck, forearm and abdomen were swollen and tender. His
fingers were trembling.[9]

There was no doubt that the 'criminalisation' policy and the tougher
security regime implemented by Newman and Mason, in particular the
extension of the interrogation period to seven days, were hurting the
IRA badly. Heightened cross-border security was producing results too.
On 3 December 1977 the IRA's former Chief of Staff, Seamus Twomey,
was arrested in the centre of Dublin by the Garda Síochána after a
high-speed car chase. He'd been on the run since being helicoptered
out of Dublin's Mountjoy jail in October 1973 and narrowly escaping
the clutches of the Garda Síochána a year later after taking part in
the Feakle talks with the cross-community clergymen. In follow-up
searches, a secret document was found, tucked away in a pencil case
in a flat in Royal Terrace, Dun Laoghaire, a seaside resort just south
of Dublin, where Twomey had been hiding. It gave a rare insight into
the state of the Provisional IRA now being hit hard by 'criminalisation'
and extended interrogation periods. The document was headed 'Staff
Report'. The main points included:

- The three-* and seven-day detention orders are breaking volunteers,
  and it is the Republican Army's fault for not indoctrinating
  volunteers with the psychological strength to resist interrogation.
- Coupled with this factor, which is contributing to our defeat,
  we are burdened with an inefficient infrastructure of commands,
  brigades, battalions and companies. The old system with which
  Brits and [Special] Branch are familiar has to be changed. We
  recommend re-organisation and re-motivation, the building of a
  new Irish Republican Army.
- We emphasise a return to secrecy and strict discipline. Army men
  must be in total control of all sections of the movement.

---

*The three-day detention orders were introduced under the Emergency Provisions Act (1973).
Detention of up to seven days was the result of the Prevention of Terrorism Act (1974).

- We must gear ourselves towards long-term armed struggle ... based on a cell system.
- Sinn Féin should come under Army organisers at all levels [and] should be radicalised (under Army direction). It gains the respect of the people which in turn leads to increased support for the cell.[10]

The IRA, under its new Northern leadership, was now making its direction clear, mirrored in much greater detail in the output of an anonymous prisoner in Long Kesh writing under the pseudonym 'Brownie'. The author was alleged to be Gerry Adams, although Adams has always denied it as he has always denied membership of the IRA. When I was once about to identify Adams as 'Brownie' in a BBC *Panorama* investigation, 'The Long War' (on 29 February 1988), his office threatened me with a solicitor's letter.

The 'Brownie' articles were regularly published in the republican movement's newspaper, *Republican News*, edited by Adams's close friend and comrade Danny Morrison. Morrison knew who 'Brownie' was. As the anonymous writings evolved in the paper's columns from late 1975 to 1977 they provided a blueprint for the Provisionals' direction over the next twenty years. They outlined the strategy of the 'Long War' with the IRA's 'armed struggle' at its centre but with Sinn Féin building a broad political base. The duration of the 'Long War' was indefinite, to be waged, so its supporters believed, until victory was finally achieved in a united Ireland.

On 8 May 1976 on the sixtieth anniversary of the Easter Rising, 'Brownie' took the opportunity to criticise the recent IRA leadership which he claimed had led the IRA into the ceasefire trap set by the British: 'There is only one time to talk of peace and that is when the war has been won not while it is raging. The time to talk of peace is when the British have left Ireland.'[11]

Ceasefires and talks with the British were now firmly off the agenda. Inside the H Blocks of the Maze prison, the IRA's 'Long War' against the British was developing a second front. The prison protest against 'criminalisation' was to have monumental repercussions, ultimately leading to the hunger strike and the return of Michael Oatley and Brendan Duddy to this new arena of conflict.

14

The Second Front

At the outset, the IRA leadership could never have foreseen the game-changing, long-term repercussions of the prison protests. They were never planned but evolved as one thing inexorably led to another: the hunger strike and the dramatic rise of Sinn Féin on what was to become a historic political journey.

The prison protest began on 14 September 1976, four days after Roy Mason succeeded Merlyn Rees as Northern Ireland Secretary. Special Category Status had ended on 1 March that year and all prisoners convicted of crimes committed after that date had to wear prison uniform and not their own clothes. The IRA leadership saw the confrontation coming and was ready to respond. It was decided that the first IRA volunteer to be ordered to put on prison uniform would refuse. A nineteen-year-old IRA volunteer from West Belfast, Kieran Nugent, was the first in line. He had just been sentenced to three years for an armed hijacking. The offence was committed in May, two months after the 1 March cut-off point for the ending of Special Category Status. On entering the newly constructed H Blocks of what was now the Maze prison, Nugent was ordered to put on prison uniform as he was now categorised as a criminal. He refused, saying he was a political prisoner, and demanded political status and the right to wear his own clothes. He said the prison officers would have to nail the uniform on his back. His protestation cut no ice and he was escorted to his cell naked. The cell was empty except for basic furniture, a chamber pot, a Bible and a blanket on the bed. Nugent wrapped himself in the prison blanket to hide his nakedness. It was a symbolic gesture, a protest against 'criminalisation'.

Kieran Nugent wasn't alone in the H Blocks for long. Gerard Hodgins and others soon joined him. Hodgins was sentenced to fourteen years in December 1976 for a firearm and bombing offence and IRA membership.

> I didn't identify myself as being a criminal. The prison officer was
> there saying, 'Right, you're here to do your time. You can do it the
> hard way or the easy way. If you take my advice, you'd get them
> uniforms on you now. If not, strip.' So you stripped there and
> then, whilst you were being ridiculed and jeered at by the screws.
> We wouldn't wear the uniform. There wasn't a physical beating or
> anything at this stage.[1]

By Christmas 1976, forty more sentenced prisoners had wrapped themselves in prison blankets. By the end of the decade there were nearly 300 non-conforming inmates in the province's jails, including blanket women as the protest escalated to the women's prison in Armagh.[2] The only human contact the blanket men had was with prison officers whom they encountered when their cells were unlocked to slop out their chamber pots. Hodgins felt very isolated, standing there alone naked except for a blanket: 'Believe it or not, you were hoping against hope that we'd get political status. Being honest about it, within a few months we really believed we'd get it.'[3]

In 1977 the blanket men's morale was lifted when Brendan Hughes – known to his comrades as 'Dark' or 'Darkie' because of his swarthy complexion and jet-black hair – joined their number in the H Blocks. He had been the IRA's OC in the compounds and had been sentenced to five years after a fracas with prison officers. As the fracas happened after the ending of Special Category Status on 1 March 1976, he was locked up in the H Blocks. He immediately recognised the dramatic difference between being regarded as a Special Category Prisoner in the compounds and a common criminal in the H Blocks.[4]

> Every morning [as OC], I would go out from the 'cage' and
> negotiate with the Governor. He would call me 'Brendan' or 'Mr
> Hughes'. It was a military situation where I was a representative of
> the prisoners and I got all the respect I was entitled to. Then one

morning I was taken to court and sent back, only this time to the H Blocks. I was told to strip and given a prison uniform. I was called 'Hughes 704'. Earlier that morning I was called 'Mr Hughes'. Obviously I refused to wear the prison uniform. It didn't matter whether it had arrows on it or Mickey Mouse, it was still the prison uniform.

Hughes was locked up in H Block 5, where he soon became the OC of all the IRA prisoners in the Maze.

As the months passed, there was no sign of the Government being prepared to make even the slightest move. Hell would freeze over before Roy Mason would consider reintroducing Special Category Status. The Government believed that the protest had singularly failed to get traction outside the IRA's heartlands, where it was mirrored in parades of supporters wearing blankets. Media interest soon waned. The Government believed that to win it needed to do nothing, calculating that in the end the protest would die and the blanket men would give up, put the blankets back on the bed where they belonged and accept the comfort and warmth of a prison uniform, using the blankets for the purpose they had been intended. Not for the first time, ministers and officials underestimated republicans' commitment. To the prisoners, political status was the core of their being.

Outside the jail, the IRA increased pressure on the prison authorities by murdering prison officers. By the end of 1978, seven had been shot dead, four of them at home.[5] One of their victims was Desmond Irvine, the Secretary of the Prison Officers' Association (POA), whom I'd interviewed in 1977 for an ITV *This Week* documentary on the Maze prison, 'Life Behind the Wire'.[6] What he told me was remarkable for a Protestant/unionist prison officer as he seemed to acknowledge the legitimacy of the IRA's protest.

If one studies the history of republican prisoners, you will find that this was always a very strong point with them, that they would not wear prison clothes. So I don't think they do it mainly for publicity but they do it because it is their belief. I suppose one could say that a person who believes sincerely in what he is doing and is prepared to suffer for it, that there must be a measure of respect for him.[7]

When I heard he'd been gunned down by the IRA when leaving a Prison Officers' Association meeting, I felt sick. It was just over a fortnight after the programme had been transmitted. I couldn't understand why he had been targeted after his words, coming from a totally unexpected source, had helped explain the protesters' position to a national television audience. I then received word from the IRA that he had been killed, not because of his television interview, but because he was Secretary of the POA. I went to his funeral and watched his coffin being lowered into the grave on a windy hillside on the outskirts of Belfast.[8]

The next stage in the protest wasn't planned but grew out of circumstances. Prisoners said that as they left their cells and walked down the wings to wash and shave or slop out their chamber pots, they were humiliated, abused and beaten by prison officers. As a result, protesting prisoners refused to wash, shave or slop out and remained in their cells. The problem then arose of what to do with the contents of the pots. They tried to pour urine under the cell door and then built bread dams to stop the prison officers brushing it back again but the main problem remained: how to dispose of the faeces. Hughes as OC gave the prisoners the answer: daub them on the wall.

> It was me who gave the order to do that. Anyone who felt they could not do it, was not ordered to do it. Other people were suggesting we smear excreta on ourselves. If the first step hadn't come about, that was the alternative. It was a step I wasn't prepared to take.[9]

The 'dirty protest', or, as the IRA preferred to euphemise, the 'no-wash protest', began in March 1978. Nineteen-year-old Gerard Hodgins, who had lied about his age to join the IRA during the ceasefire, never imagined that signing up would lead to this.

> I just smeared [the excreta] on the wall. I ripped off a lump of the mattress to do it with. You were going against everything you'd ever learned about basic hygiene and manners. I lived like this for three years from 1978 to 1981. After a time you became used to it.
> The maggots. Nobody likes maggots. I don't think I could touch a maggot now. You were literally waking up in the morning and

there were maggots in the bed with you. It just gets to the stage where you brush them off. I think the human spirit can become accustomed to any environment. You'd wonder, is this ever going to end? I just couldn't bring myself to wear the uniform. I don't think I could have lived with myself.[10]

Cathal Crumley, like Gerard Hodgins, was jailed in 1976 and sentenced to four years for IRA membership. He joined Hodgins on the 'dirty protest' and told me how he improvised ways of sweeping urine and other 'stuff' under the cell door, only to find prison officers retaliating.

We had this process of putting the stuff out through gaps in the door and virtually every night in the week they'd come round and sweep it all back in again. I remember for years sleeping on a piece of sponge [the mattress] that had been soaked that many times by urine that was pushed back under the doors.[11]

On his release, Crumley was one of the first IRA prisoners to be elected as a Sinn Féin councillor and went on to become Mayor of Derry. I remember he always wore a collar and tie, one of a new breed of Sinn Féin politicians, hardened by the IRA's 'armed struggle' and the H Block protests.

By the summer of 1978 the 'dirty protest' showed no sign of ending, despite interventions by outside bodies including, most prominently, the Catholic Primate of All Ireland, Cardinal Tomás Ó Fiaich, an avowed nationalist coming from the republican stronghold of Crossmaglen in South Armagh. He was taken aback by what he saw on a Sunday-afternoon visit to the Maze.

I was shocked at the inhuman conditions in the H Blocks where over 300 prisoners were incarcerated. One would hardly allow an animal to remain in such conditions, let alone a human being. The stench and filth in some cells, with the remains of rotten food and human excreta scattered around the walls, was absolutely unbelievable.[12]

Roy Mason was furious and, typically, didn't mince his words.

He [Cardinal Ó Fiaich] seemed to be undermining the legitimacy
of our entire struggle against terrorism. In fact his words could have
been written by any propagandist from Sinn Féin. I was appalled
that such a prominent churchman could appear so indulgent
towards gangsters who had caused such pain to so many innocent
people over the years, including members of his own flock.[13]

Mason knew that the protest was entering a new and potentially
dangerous stage politically. If the media had come to develop a distinct
lack of interest in prisoners wearing blankets, the images of Christlike
figures with long hair and even longer beards in cells covered in shit
were a different matter. Mason was determined to stand firm.

Despite the adverse publicity, I couldn't give way. To do so would
give the IRA its biggest victory in years. It would appal the law-
abiding majority. It would dismay the security forces. It would
mean the abandonment of police primacy and the rule of law. It
would in the end lead to more death and misery.[14]

Of course, as the Government repeatedly pointed out, the conditions
were self-inflicted. Mason told the House of Commons:

If the conditions in which they now live are obnoxious, they are entirely
of their own making. The form of protest that they have chosen is
revolting to any civilised society, and I must pay a sincere tribute to the
prison officers whose dedication to duty ensures the regular cleaning
and disinfecting of the filth for which these prisoners are responsible.[15]

Mason's analysis that the conditions were self-inflicted was vehemently
rejected by the protesters.

British ministers and civil servants may have underestimated the protesters in the stinking cells of the H Blocks and the men and women of
the IRA outside, but elements in the senior ranks of the British army
did not. In 1978 Brigadier James Glover, the head of army intelligence
in Northern Ireland, wrote a report called 'Future Terrorist Trends'.
It was marked Secret but was leaked, perhaps deliberately given the
explosive nature of its analysis, which flew in the face of all that the

Government, the Northern Ireland Secretary Roy Mason and the RUC Chief Constable Sir Kenneth Newman had been saying. Mason dismissed the IRA as 'gangsters and gunmen'.[16] Roy Mason's deputy, Don Concannon, dismissed the IRA as 'criminal thugs' whom we should never recognise as political prisoners.[17] This was not the conclusion that Brigadier Glover reached in his report.

> Our evidence of the calibre of rank and file terrorists does not
> support the view that they are merely mindless hooligans drawn
> from the unemployed and unemployable. PIRA [Provisional IRA]
> now trains and uses its members with some care. The Active Service
> Units are for the most part manned by terrorists tempered by up to
> ten years operational experience ... We can therefore expect to see
> increased professionalism and the greater exploitation of modern
> technology for terrorist purposes.[18]

I later interviewed General Sir James Glover, by then promoted and knighted, for my *Panorama* programme, 'The Long War', which was broadcast in February 1988.[19] He was equally forthright in his comments. His report did not receive universal applause from his senior colleagues.

> It didn't find all that much favour [and] I was accused of
> encouraging the enemy. I think it revealed for the first time the
> strength of the IRA's commitment to the 'Long War' and their
> own confidence in their ability to sustain it politically and their
> confidence that they had the wherewithal to sustain it with the
> people, the weapons and public support.
>   One of the messages in the Report was that we believed that
> the IRA could not be defeated militarily. That again was a slightly
> unpopular message at the time because there was a school of
> thought that they could be brought to their knees by military means
> alone, which of course they can't. Peace can only reign when there
> is a political solution and the military situation has been contained.
> The IRA will never be totally defeated. The cause of republicanism
> will remain as long as the island of Ireland is divided.[20]

Glover was a prophet ahead of his time. Waiting in the shadows, Michael Oatley and Brendan Duddy were about to reappear on the scene to try and find a solution to the conflict in the H Blocks and would no doubt have agreed with much of Glover's analysis.

The warning that Brigadier Glover had given in his report nine months earlier about the IRA's 'increased professionalism' and 'greater exploitation of modern technology for terrorist purposes' was spectacularly and tragically borne out on 27 August 1979. Glover was flying back from Derry to army headquarters, Thiepval Barracks in Lisburn, when a distorted message came over the helicopter's radio – something or other about 'a lord' – the name was indistinct – being murdered in the South. It was only when the flight touched down on the helipad that Sir James was told that the victim was seventy-nine-year-old Lord Mountbatten, Prince Philip's uncle and a distant cousin of the Queen. He was also the last British Viceroy of India, who had overseen Britain's withdrawal from that part of Empire, after 300 years, and its partition into two independent nation states, Hindu-majority India and Muslim-majority Pakistan. The birth of each had been violent and bloody.

Sir James later learned the grim details of the assassination. He was deeply shocked. The IRA had placed Mountbatten under surveillance at his holiday home in the coastal village at Mullaghmore in County Sligo, and had planted a remote-controlled 50lb bomb under the floorboards of his small fishing boat, *Shadow V*. It was triggered from the shore once the IRA had seen that Mountbatten had embarked for a morning fishing trip with three others: his fourteen-year-old grandson, Nicholas Knatchbull, the elderly dowager Doreen, Lady Brabourne and fifteen-year-old Paul Maxwell, a young boatman from Enniskillen. All four were killed in the blast. Three people who were on board when the bomb exploded survived: Nicholas Knatchbull's twin, Timothy, their mother, Lady Patricia Brabourne and her husband Lord John Brabourne. Lord Mountbatten had shunned close Garda Síochána security, which irritated him. Irish police, stationed on a clifftop, saw the explosion from a distance, but could do nothing. They had failed to see the bomb being planted, presumably at night when the boat was moored in harbour. Former Garda Síochána Chief Superintendent John Courtney, head of the Murder Squad, described what his colleagues saw.

Suddenly, to their horror, a massive explosion ripped through the boat, which disintegrated before their eyes. Bodies were flung into the sea and debris showered from the sky. The noise of the blast was heard miles away. The shocked Garda Síochána rushed to the shore, the air now full of agonised screams of survivors as they struggled in the water.[21]

The IRA issued a statement to *Republican News* describing the operation as 'one of the discriminate ways we can bring to the attention of the English people the continuing occupation of our country'.[22]

Although the planning of the operation would have involved several IRA volunteers, only one was ever convicted of the murder of Lord Mountbatten. He was Thomas McMahon, one of the most experienced operatives of the IRA's South Armagh Brigade and one of the first IRA members to be sent to Libya to study detonators, timing devices and explosives. On the basis of forensic evidence he was sentenced to life for preparing and planting the bomb. Green and white paint flakes from *Shadow V* were found on his clothing, which also bore traces of nitroglycerine and ammonium nitrate.[23] McMahon was later released under the 1998 Good Friday Agreement, having served less than twenty years.[24]

But more tragedy was to follow that same day, just across the border in the North near Warrenpoint where Carlingford Lough flows into the Irish Sea, marking the border between Northern Ireland and the Irish Republic. Just after 4.30 on a gloriously sunny afternoon, only a matter of hours after the IRA had assassinated Lord Mountbatten, a convoy of paratroopers from the Regiment's 2nd Battalion was driving from their base at Ballykinler in County Down to relieve the Queen's Own Scottish Highlanders in Newry, who were about to return home, their tour of duty over. The convoy consisted of two four-ton trucks preceded by a Land Rover. At 4.40 p.m., as the second truck at the rear of the convoy passed a trailer piled high with hay bales parked at the side of the dual carriageway, there was a huge explosion, detonated by remote control from a firing point across the Lough on the Irish side of the border. The IRA had packed 800lb of explosives inside milk churns surrounded by petrol cans, all hidden by the hay bales. The second truck was thrown 100 feet into the air and landed on the central reservation. Six Paras were killed. One of the passengers in the Land Rover leading the convoy was Stuart (surname withheld). He'd driven past the hay lorry and hadn't given it a second thought as hay lorries were a common sight in late summer in South Down and neighbouring South Armagh. He was devastated by the loss of his mates and told me what he remembered about the ball of fire.

> The hay lorry and the second truck just disappeared together. There was smoke, debris and straw all over the place. We immediately turned our Land Rover and went back to the seat of the explosion to render what assistance we could. There were bodies and bits of bodies everywhere and there was ammunition exploding in some people's pouches. We were putting some people out who were on fire and we were just checking to see if anybody was alive. I never felt an anger like it. It just didn't seem fair that a bunch of really good mates, each one a thoroughly professional soldier, should die in such a way in such a cowardly attack. They were just helpless. They were just sat in a truck.[25]

The rest of the convoy ran for cover near the ruined gatehouse of an old castle. The IRA had anticipated this was what the survivors of the explosion were likely to do and had hidden a second 800lb bomb close by. After the first explosion the Paras had telephoned the Scottish Highlanders in Newry for help. The IRA bombers, still hidden on the other side of the border, bided their time until reinforcements in the form of a Quick Reaction Force (QRF) and a helicopter to evacuate the wounded from the first explosion arrived. When they reached the scene of the carnage, at 5.12 p.m., the bombers triggered the second bomb. The explosives had been hidden in milk churns concealed behind a wall.[26] Twelve more soldiers were killed – bringing the total to eighteen in the space of half an hour. The IRA was jubilant, seeing the attack on the Parachute Regiment as revenge for 'Bloody Sunday'. Triumphant graffiti appeared in republican areas, 'We got 18 and Mountbatten'. It was the meticulously planned IRA spectacular that Sir James Glover had warned about, now come doubly true.

> It was arguably, I think, the most successful and certainly one of the best-planned IRA attacks of the whole campaign. It was almost inevitable that at some stage they were going to succeed because we'd failed to interdict them. The event was not a surprise but the nature of it was. It was ghastly.[27]

In the fetid H Block cells, there was jubilation at the IRA's 'double whammy'. Morale, sinking ever lower as the 'dirty protest' was still failing to move an obdurate Government, rocketed sky high, boosted by the dual slaughter on a single day. It was, as the prisoners' OC Brendan Hughes described it to me, 'us hitting back at what they were doing to us. Certainly nobody was going to cry over Mountbatten or the soldiers getting killed.'

The assassination of Lord Mountbatten and the killing of eighteen British soldiers only served to strengthen the protesters' resolve. Cathal Crumley, now into the fourth year of the blanket and 'dirty protest', knew he and his comrades faced a stark choice. 'It was uncomfortable, it was stomach churning. It was very, very difficult to live in those conditions for all those years but that was the battleground that had been created for us and we either survived or gave up.'[28]

The prisoners were not in the mood to give up nor was the Government in the mood to give in, especially as it was now a new administration led by a new Prime Minister, Margaret Thatcher, elected on 4 May 1979, three months before Mountbatten and Warrenpoint. As events were to prove, Mrs Thatcher did not earn the sobriquet the 'Iron Lady' for nothing. Six weeks before the General Election that brought her Conservative Government to power, the republican Irish National Liberation Army (INLA)[29] assassinated the shadow Northern Ireland Secretary, Airey Neave, one of Mrs Thatcher's closest friends and confidants. He had been steeled in the Second World War as a prisoner of war incarcerated in Colditz Castle, from which he escaped in 1942. Neave's attitude to dealing with terrorism made Roy Mason look soft. Mrs Thatcher developed a visceral hatred for the IRA, intensified by escalating events in the H Blocks that were now coming to a head. The 'Iron Lady' had no time for 'political status' and, to her, Sinn Féin was simply the IRA in jackets and ties.

By the beginning of 1980 the protesters were becoming increasingly anxious about the lack of progress in meeting their demands for political status. They then set about devising a set of Five Demands which, if granted, would, in the prisoners' eyes, amount to what they were fighting for. In fact they were a refinement of the demands that Billy McKee's hunger strike had extracted from Willie Whitelaw in the lead-up to the Cheyne Walk talks in 1972. They were:

1. The right not to wear prison uniform.
2. The right not to do prison work.
3. The right to associate freely with other prisoners.
4. The right to a weekly visit, letter and parcel and the freedom to organise educational and recreational pursuits.
5. Full restoration of remission lost through the protest.

It was a subtle repackaging to make it appear to the world outside that all the prisoners were asking for was to be allowed to serve their sentences in civilised and humane conditions, the antithesis of the bloody events that led to their incarceration. The hope was to broaden the appeal to a wider liberal constituency that would never contemplate supporting the IRA's violent campaign but might consider supporting the call for a more humane treatment of prisoners on human rights grounds. It was noticeable that the toxic words 'political status' were absent from the Five Demands.[30] The fact that Mrs Thatcher was trumpeting the mantra that conditions in the Maze prison were among the best in prisons anywhere cut no ice. But that was to miss the point, perhaps deliberately. The real issue at stake wasn't about prison conditions. It was fundamentally about the nature of the war and the motivation of the combatants fighting it. The Prime Minister remained unmoved.

> The IRA and prisoners were determined to gain control of the prison and had a well-thought-out strategy for doing this by whittling away at the prison regime. The purpose of the privileges they claimed was not to improve prisoners' conditions but to take power away from the prison authorities. They were also keen to establish that their crimes were 'political', thus giving the perpetrators a kind of respectability, even nobility. This we could not allow... The IRA were pursuing with calculated ruthlessness a psychological war alongside their campaign of violence: they had to be resisted at both levels.[31]

By the autumn of 1980 the protest had reached a critical point. All attempts at negotiating a settlement had failed. Tommy McKearney summed up the feeling in the republican wings of the H Blocks: 'Something had to be done to bring the cycle of protest to an end. We had no option but to use the last available weapon that a prisoner has, in our eyes, the weapon of the hunger strike.'[32]

The Provisionals' Army Council was initially against the hunger strike, fearing it would divert attention and energy from its priority, its military campaign. The prisoners could not use the 'last available weapon' without the PAC's blessing. In the end, faced with the prisoners' implacable determination to go ahead, the Army Council reluctantly agreed, not wishing to cause a damaging rift with the prisoners that would have risked undermining what they were trying to achieve.

By now there were about 500 protesting prisoners. In his capacity as OC, Brendan Hughes asked for volunteers. One hundred and seventy came forward. Seven prisoners were chosen to reflect the broad geography of the province. Hughes was to lead the strike. The fast to the death began on 27 October 1980 when the seven volunteers refused breakfast. All started the hunger strike together, which meant that it was only as strong as the weakest link. The British calculated that the protesters would never go through with it but, as the days and weeks rolled by, the anticipation of capitulation seemed less certain. The prisoners did not want their comrades to die and the Government did not wish to have martyrs on its hands, turbocharging the campaign for political status. All attempts at compromise failed. One involved the Northern Ireland Office's offer to provide all protesters with 'civilian-type' clothes from Marks and Spencer. I remember discussing the offer at Stormont with a Northern Ireland press officer who produced from his desk drawer an M&S shirt wrapped in cellophane. He told me it seemed a sensible compromise. I said I thought the prisoners would, literally and metaphorically, never wear it. The compromise was rejected. The protesters wanted their own clothes, not M&S substitutes provided by HMG and the prison authorities.

15

'The Mountain Climber' Returns

Michael Oatley had left Northern Ireland in the early months of 1975 once the ceasefire was in place and was now abroad, which meant that throughout the escalating prison protest he was out of the loop. Nevertheless, he had kept in touch with Brendan, in direct contravention of Roy Mason's order that there was to be no further communication of any kind with the IRA or its intermediaries. Oatley made no apology for turning a semi-deaf ear to the new Northern Ireland Secretary's instruction.

> This was a personal decision. I didn't report it to anybody and
> I didn't seek anybody's permission for doing it. I merely allowed
> the situation to develop where some members of the Provisional
> IRA leadership were aware that the [bamboo] pipe was still there
> and that I was at the other end of it. From my own point of view,
> I think that people on the IRA side thought I had come out of it as
> a reasonably reliable person with whom to deal. And I, for my part,
> had been quite clearly convinced that people on the other side were
> able to keep secrets. So I didn't think I was running any serious risk,
> politically, for the Government, in letting the IRA know that there
> was still a point of contact if they should ever need it and it would
> operate wherever I happened to be in the world, and that remained
> the situation for a considerable time thereafter.
>   I did tell a friend who was a senior official in the NIO so he
> could brief the Permanent Under Secretary on my behalf should

it become necessary to do so. People would know that there was a
means of communicating should it ever be required.[1]

Oatley was aware that if Mason (or his successor) and the Northern
Ireland Office ever found out that Michael's pipe was still operational,
he would have been 'very severely reprimanded'. Nevertheless a
considerable rap over the knuckles – or the sack – was a risk he was
prepared to take.

Meanwhile in the H Blocks, the hunger strike was reaching a critical
stage as the fiftieth day without food approached. Tommy McKearney
realised that, without a last-minute settlement, death was close. He was
slowly going blind. 'I was drifting between delirium and consciousness
and then back to lucidity. I was in extreme pain. I was vomiting, running
a temperature and having severe headaches. I was prepared to die.'[2]

As the months went by and Christmas 1980 approached, Brendan,
at home in Derry, was becoming increasingly concerned that one or
more hunger strikers might soon be about to die. He knew that the
consequences would be disastrous. It was brought home to him when
Billy McKee rang and then paid him a visit in the 'wee room' as he had
done during negotiations for the 1975 ceasefire. 'He was really upset about
the hunger strike due to his own experience in jail. He was completely
opposed to hunger strikes having gone through the experience himself.
He said he preferred a man to die on the front line rather than in prison.'
Brendan had become increasingly depressed about the collapse of the
ceasefire and with it the end of dialogue with the IRA:

> We had the two sides getting further and further apart. The IRA
> didn't want to know and didn't want to be involved in anything,
> discussions or dialogue. I saw this as a possibility of reopening
> negotiations. That's how I read it.[3]

On 18 December 1980, Duddy picked up the telephone in the
small hours of the morning and called Michael Oatley, who was now
back in London. Time was of the essence. One of the hunger strikers,
Sean McKenna, was thought to be facing death in only a day or two.
Duddy told Oatley the IRA was ready for compromise, the message
Billy McKee had relayed. Oatley too recognised a narrow window for
dialogue. He remembers it all happening very quickly.

The IRA leadership was, I think, very concerned about community reaction to the hunger strike as it would make them rather unpopular. Of course, the British Government was very concerned about it too. It seemed that one might be able to develop a formula with, no doubt, some ambiguities, which would be a gesture by the British Government to the demands of the hunger strikers.[4]

Oatley and Duddy spoke on the phone for an hour or so. Duddy outlined the kind of compromise the IRA might be prepared to accept, while Oatley mulled over the kind of compromise the British Government might be prepared to go along with. It was all based around possible changes to the prison regime and crucially the sequencing of prisoners being allowed to wear their own clothes. At the end of the conversation a rough form of words had been agreed, based on Duddy's understanding of the IRA leadership's position.

Oatley didn't get much sleep that night. As dawn broke, he made his way to MI6 headquarters, Century House in Waterloo, where he had a secretary type up his notes of the agreed draft formula so it looked like a semi-official working paper.[5] By 9 a.m. he had crossed central London to the Northern Ireland Office in Westminster to discuss the document and the potential compromise formula with Sir Kenneth Stowe, the Permanent Under Secretary, the NIO's senior official. Sir Kenneth told me he was fully aware of the dilemma the Government faced.

One knew that force-feeding was out, therefore if the hunger strike continued, these people would die. Then we would have more martyrs, and Northern Ireland is not a place to grow martyrs if you can avoid it. Therefore we were very anxious to try to get some way of enabling the hunger strikers to get off the hook. The stakes were very high. We needed to explore whether the rules regarding prison could in any way be adapted in a UK context so that some of the steam could be taken out of the issue ... We knew we had to act speedily if we were to resolve this situation before we had a martyr.[6]

Stowe agreed to take up Oatley's draft and ran it past Mrs Thatcher's new Northern Ireland Secretary, Humphrey Atkins, who made no changes. Stowe then phoned the Prime Minister 'in a few crowded hours' who signed it off. Stowe had been her Principal Private Secretary and had a close relationship with her. The Prime Minister was equally keen to avoid a martyr. Stowe described the compromise as 'a face-saving formula' and 'a façade of concessions about the treatment of prisoners which gave them a ladder to climb down'.[7] Essentially the final draft which Oatley was to take to Belfast contained concessions designed to be interpreted as humanitarian gestures to be applied to all prisoners in Northern Ireland: clothing from prisoners' families to be worn during visits and recreation; civilian-type clothing (as purchased from M&S) to be worn during the working day; free association at weekends; and the prospect of restored remission. The Government's main concern was to ensure that the Governor remained in control of the prison and its wings.[8] In essence, the statement was aspirational and workable, given goodwill on both sides.

With Sean McKenna ever nearer to death, there was little time left. Stowe told Oatley to take his official car and get to Heathrow as quickly as possible to hand over the now agreed compromise document. Oatley was driven at top speed along the then hard shoulder of the M4. Brendan, who was kept in the loop, was also on his way to Aldergrove airport, sixty miles from Derry, to collect the document from Oatley and hand it over to the intermediary, Father Brendan Meagher, an Irish Redemptorist priest, codenamed 'The Angel', who would be waiting there. Father Meagher was a chaplain in the Maze prison and was trusted by the prisoners. Given the sensitivity of the operation and the (unlikely) risk of Oatley being assassinated or kidnapped, RUC Special Branch officers were dispatched to Aldergrove to make sure nothing untoward happened and that the handover was accomplished.

By the time Oatley landed at Aldergrove, the last flight had gone and the terminal was eerily empty. The timing was determined by security considerations. Brendan says he told Michael it would have been easier to have met him in the centre of Belfast on top of a Christmas tree. Oatley remembers the bizarre scene.

> There were various people there who were concerned, I think quite
> unnecessarily, for my personal safety. I was required to have my
> meeting in Aldergrove airport, fairly late in the evening, in a rather
> curious circumstance because there was nobody in Aldergrove
> airport at that time of night. So we had this situation where our
> meeting took place in an entirely empty airport with burly [Special

Branch] figures standing behind every pillar – which was quite grotesque and not entirely designed to keep the thing entirely discreet.[9]

Oatley handed the envelope containing the document to Father Meagher, who then conveyed it to the republican movement's leadership meeting in West Belfast. This all took time and it was already late in the evening. But time had run out. It was 11 p.m. before Father Meagher finally got to the H Blocks with the document.[10] As the leadership was poring over it, word came that the hunger strike had been called off. Events in the hospital wing of the Maze had raced ahead of Father Meagher and Oatley's document.

In what appeared to be McKenna's final hours, prison doctors made the decision to transfer him to Musgrave Park Hospital where he was expected to die. In a dramatic and controversial move, without consulting Bobby Sands, who had taken over from Hughes as OC, Hughes, himself perhaps only days from death, called the strike off without anything having been achieved – although there was encouraging news that the document from London was on its way. Hughes later confirmed that McKenna had initially told him that he, McKenna, was prepared to go on hunger strike but was not prepared to die. Hughes assured him that he would stand by his wish. 'I gave him a guarantee that I would not let him die.'[11] Hughes was true to his word. A confidential Government document later summed up what happened and why. Its analysis was painful and blunt.

> Probably the single most important factor was that the seven hunger strikers just did not have the will to die. They may have been misled into thinking that their protest would succeed easily, and as it became increasingly clear that their deaths were going to be in vain, the fear of death probably became an increasingly significant factor.
>
> This effect was undoubtedly enhanced by the different rates of deterioration of health (in particular McKenna's distressing and rapid decline towards the end of the fast). The other six were given a preview of the fate which awaited them. Their death was clearly going to be painful and degrading and the leader Hughes was burdened with the responsibility of standing by and watching one

of his subordinates die, probably in vain, while he still lived. Then
when the decision was made to remove McKenna to the Musgrave
Park Hospital, the doctors made it very clear to Hughes and the
others that he [McKenna] was about to die and that the other
hunger strikers would follow soon. This was the critical point for
the strikers. It is evident that Hughes' determination had given way
at this point under the double stress of responsibility for McKenna's
death and the imminence of his own death. Once the group's leader
had succumbed, it was almost inevitable that the others would
eventually follow suit ... Because the hunger strikers had achieved
nothing and the Government's firmness of purpose was apparent,
the futility of their action was manifest.[12]

The analysis was hard but realistic given Brendan Hughes' promise to
Sean McKenna. Mrs Thatcher believed she had won. She later wrote, 'I
had hoped this would be the end of the hunger strike tactic, and indeed
of all the prison protests. But it was not to be so.'[13] It was a Pyrrhic
victory. Worse was to come.

16

The Final Showdown

The republican movement leadership outside the Maze presented the end of the first hunger strike as a victory. They could hardly do anything else given all that had been invested in it. Perhaps many of their supporters were doubtful too. A 'victory' parade in the republican stronghold of West Belfast did not attract the hoped-for numbers on to the streets. Brendan Hughes, now embroiled in mutual recriminations with Bobby Sands, his successor as OC, harboured no illusions.

> The first hunger strike was a failure. We did not win our demands and the lie was perpetrated. People on the outside and Bobby [Sands] were dictating the line. I was totally and utterly demoralised, full of feelings of guilt, and thinking, 'Should I have let Sean die?' I was suicidal. I had a constant clear image of having a gun and just blowing my head off. It was the worst period of my life. It took me years and years to get over it.[1]

Some years later, after his release from jail, Hughes bumped into Sean McKenna across the border, in Dundalk. 'Fuck you, Dark,' Sean said. 'You should have let me die.'[2]

But what happened to the compromises listed in the document that Michael Oatley had brought over from London? It finally reached the Maze, albeit too late, but according to Oatley what was on offer was all rather vague and imprecise.

I think the Government was very keen to do what it could to
calm the situation down and stop the hunger strike, if it could
do so in a way which was consistent with not making politically
damaging concessions. It had a formula which was basically the
formula which had been devised during the long night's [telephone]
conversation [with Brendan] which was accepted as being within
what was politically acceptable to Government. There was a lot
of consideration being given, at that stage, to the regime in the
prison and whether anything could be adjusted which would make
a gesture to the hunger strikers' demands which were to do with
things like parcels and clothing and visits and so forth. What we did
was to produce a formula which was fairly open-ended, and in some
ways ambiguous, which we felt would enable the hunger strike to
be called off. It had to be their decision, it was not something which
the Provisional leadership could impose upon them.

Peter Taylor: *Did the formula allow for prisoners to wear their own
clothes?*

No, it didn't. I think it left that sort of question rather open.
It did suggest some concessions. The regime was not altered
sufficiently to meet the expectations of the prisoners.[3]

Although the hunger strike had fallen apart, the document was still
in play. The problem was the interpretation of it. The prisoners took
it, over-optimistically, to mean that they could now wear their own
clothes, the result of which was that families brought them into the
prison expecting them to be handed over to the recipients, but that was
not to be. The prison authorities saw it differently, insisting it was a
matter of sequencing. The Government's intention was that prisoners
should put on civilian-type clothing first – as a gesture to putting on
prison uniform – end the 'dirty/no-wash protest' and not foul their cells
again, and basically show their intention to abide by prison rules. After
the blanket protest, the 'dirty protest' and the collapse of the first hunger
strike, goodwill was in short supply. Prisoners' clothes were brought into
the Maze by families on 23 January 1981, but they were withheld by
the prison authorities until the prisoners had shown their willingness to
comply with the enforced sequencing and the prison rules. To Bobby
Sands this was unacceptable. He decided that if the authorities were
prepared to play hardball, he, as OC, was ready to play hardball too.

Sands had made it clear that if his interpretation of the compromise on offer wasn't adopted, then a second hunger strike would follow which he would lead. He also made it clear that he was prepared to die. From the outset the British had little doubt that Sands, who they knew was a formidable adversary, meant it. There would be no surrender as in the first hunger strike. Both sides now had their heels firmly dug in. Mrs Thatcher wasn't going to capitulate, nor were the hunger strikers. I sensed what the outcome would be. It was not a question of whether Sands would die but how many others would follow him to the grave. Should this happen, the political repercussions were likely to be enormous.

But what about the back channel at this critical time? Could it break the impasse? Could Michael Oatley and Brendan Duddy have come to the rescue as they had before in the lead-up to the 1975 ceasefire and 1980 hunger strike? It was now more difficult because the situation and the personnel involved in the back channel had changed. Oatley was now abroad once again, although he maintained contact with Brendan in Derry, who was still plugged into the IRA channel. When Brendan heard of Sands's intention to lead a second hunger strike, his reaction was entirely predictable.

> Despair because of the mood at that time. The British Government had moved away from thinking of any form of agreement in Northern Ireland. Mrs Thatcher was not terribly interested. [The 'Brits'] were on the winning trail. They felt the IRA is beaten and we're going to hammer them.[4]

Michael Oatley, although abroad and no longer directly involved, shared that view and threw another consideration into the mix that made compromise more difficult.

> The Governor of the Maze had a totally different set of problems from those that he might have had five or six years earlier [before Special Category Status was abolished and the blanket protest began]. He had to accommodate a long-term situation and had to secure and maintain the cooperation of the Prison Officers' Association, and the prison officers in the Maze. He couldn't afford to make the sort of concessions perhaps that we might have urged

on him some years previously. And I think the Government's attitude and the Prime Minister's attitude to the situation was probably that she wasn't in a mood to do any deals or to make life easier for people [that is, the protesters].[5]

During the first few weeks of 1981, as negotiations on the compromise formula proved inconclusive, a second hunger strike looked increasingly likely, despite the fact that initially the Provisional Army Council opposed it on the same grounds on which it had initially opposed the first hunger strike: that it would distract attention and drain energy from the war. However, Sands's determination to lead it to the death, supported by the majority of the protesters incensed by what they saw as British duplicity, made it difficult for the Army Council to do anything other than, in the end, agree. When I put the IRA's conundrum to Gerry Adams, talking to me in a retrospective interview broadcast over forty years later, he insisted that the final decision was made by the prisoners and not by the IRA leadership outside.

> The IRA tried to prevent the hunger strike. In the process, where
> it failed to do this, it supported the hunger strike. We are morally,
> strategically and tactically opposed to the hunger strike. The
> situation was created out of the intensity over which nobody on the
> outside could have control.[6]

Any hopes that the IRA might have dialled down its campaign outside the jail to gain wider nationalist support for a second hunger strike were dashed by a series of killings in January 1981. The most shocking was the murder of the eighty-six-year-old Sir Norman Stronge and his son, James (forty-eight), on 21 January – two days before the families took protesters' clothes into the Maze. Sir Norman was the epitome of the unionist establishment, a former Stormont MP, Speaker of the parliament and one of the oldest people to have been targeted by the IRA during its current campaign. His son James was a merchant banker, educated at Eton and Oxford, a former captain in the Grenadier Guards and an RUC reservist who had gone on to inherit his father's Stormont seat. The family home was Tynan Abbey, a neo-gothic eighteenth-century pile in County Armagh, close to the border with the Irish Republic, which afforded the IRA a quick and convenient escape route.

The murders were particularly shocking. An armed ten-man IRA unit in combat gear crossed the border, hijacked two vehicles and forced their way into the family seat. They searched out father and son, and shot both of them dead. The gunmen then planted incendiary bombs and set fire to the Abbey, leaving a burned-out shell which still stands today. The IRA said the Stronge family had been targeted as 'the symbols of hated unionism', and the attack was 'a direct reprisal for a whole series of loyalist assassinations and murder attacks on nationalist people and nationalist activists'. Five days earlier, the UDA/UFF had tried to assassinate 'the nationalist activist' Bernadette Devlin McAliskey, the former Westminster MP and H Block and hunger-strike campaigner.[7] On 1 March 1981, Bobby Sands refused food. The date was symbolic, the fifth anniversary of the abolition of Special Category Status. The scene was set for the final showdown.

Bobby Sands and the protesters had learned the grim lessons from the collapse of the first hunger strike. Its Achilles heel had been that all the hunger strikers had embarked on the strike together so that the strike was only as strong as its weakest link, which turned out to be Brendan Hughes. The same mistake was not to be made again. In consultation with his colleagues, Sands, as OC at the time, decided that the second hunger strike was to be staggered, with volunteers joining at intervals and others joining in the event of one striker dying. Not only would the deaths be lingering but the protest would be lingering too, putting maximum pressure on Mrs Thatcher, the Government and the prison authorities. Sands may also have calculated that, once he had died, others would follow suit as they could not afford to let their dead colleague's sacrifice be in vain. It was a gruesome and high-risk strategy. A senior Northern Ireland Office official described it as 'another desperate, doomed throw'.[8]

Sunday 1 March 1981 dawned a cold, rainy day in Belfast. Sinn Féin marked it with a march through its heartland of West Belfast. Four months before, on 27 October 1980, Bernadette McAliskey had taken part in a march to mark the beginning of the first hunger strike, perhaps thinking back to the great civil rights marches of the late 1960s and hoping that the first hunger strike would lead to a similar mass movement. Ten thousand had joined the march in October 1968. Only about a third of that number turned out on that grim, wet day in 1981.[9] It was hardly an auspicious beginning for a potential mass movement. People were understandably weary after the drama and anticlimax of the first hunger strike. Getting supporters enthused and revved up again wasn't going to be easy. A statement was read out at the rally, hoping to rekindle the enthusiasm and determination that had been evident at the beginning of the first hunger strike.

> We have asserted that we are political prisoners ... our interrogation, trials and prison conditions show that we are politically motivated and not motivated by selfish reasons for selfish ends. As further demonstration of our selflessness and the justice of our cause, a number of our colleagues, beginning today with Bobby Sands, will hunger-strike to the death unless the British Government abandons its criminalisation policy and meets our demands.[10]

Three days before the beginning of the second hunger strike, Margaret Thatcher had made her position clear in a personal message to the Irish Taoiseach, Charles Haughey, in the hope of enlisting his support for the British Government's steadfast position.

> We are not prepared to concede these demands and we believe the prisoners know it. We think their object now is to bring about one or more deaths of hunger strikers to inflame community passions. All the evidence is that community support for the protesters is at its lowest ebb ... If there is anything you feel you can do to reinforce the actions we shall be taking ... [this] would be very helpful.[11]

Sands planned to keep a diary of his hunger strike. The entry for 1 March sets out his political credo, the end reflecting the republican movement's past and future negotiations with the British.

> I am a political prisoner because I am a casualty of a perennial war that is being fought between the oppressed Irish people and an alien, oppressive, unwanted regime that refuses to withdraw from our land. I stand by the right of any Irishman or woman to

assert this right in armed revolution. That is why I am incarcerated, naked and tortured ... There can never be peace in Ireland until the British presence is removed, leaving all the Irish people as a unit to control their own affairs and determine their own destinies as a sovereign people ...[12]

The following day, two significant events happened. Republican prisoners ended their 'no wash' protest and the Bishop of Derry, Edward Daly, urged young people not to support the hunger strike as it was not 'morally justified'. Sands took issue with the Bishop's analysis. 'If I die, God will understand,' he reflected.[13] At the end of his first week on hunger strike, Mrs Thatcher visited Northern Ireland, which she described as 'a most important part of the United Kingdom'. On 6 March, she gave a typically forthright interview to ITN, the 'Iron Lady' at her most adamantine.

Once again we have a hunger strike at the Maze prison in the quest for what they call 'political status'. There is no such thing as political murder, political bombing or political violence. There is only criminal murder, criminal bombing and criminal violence. We will not compromise on this. There will be no political status. That hunger strike will achieve nothing.[14]

On 15 March 1981, two weeks into Sands's fast, he was joined by Francis Hughes, an IRA icon detained after a gun battle in 1978, believed to be with the SAS, in which Hughes shot one British soldier, Corporal David Jones, a paratrooper, dead. Hughes was wounded in the shootout, arrested at the scene, prosecuted and sentenced to life imprisonment to be served in the H Blocks. A week later he was joined by two more hunger-strike volunteers: the Provisionals' Raymond McCreesh from South Armagh and Patsy O'Hara, the prison OC of the Irish National Liberation Army (INLA).

By this time, attention had been diverted from the hunger strike to an event that caused barely a ripple at the time outside the republican movement: the death of the Independent Nationalist MP for Fermanagh and South Tyrone at Westminster, Frank Maguire, hardly a household name beyond the borders of his constituency. But his death was to have conflict-changing consequences and become a turning point in the history of the Troubles by accelerating the phenomenal rise of Sinn Féin. Few would have guessed it at the time.

Following Maguire's death there was an intense and sometimes acrimonious debate within the ranks of Sinn Féin and the IRA over whether the republican movement should field a candidate to stand in the by-election. And if so, who? Opinion was divided between the republican traditionalists who opposed any involvement in conventional politics and Sinn Féin's young Turks in the new leadership who saw the opportunity to transform the profile of the party and the hunger strike their candidate would be supporting. The hunger-strike campaign had still to catch fire outside of the prison walls. The media and the public had been there before. There was a certain weariness. Why go through it all again?

Sinn Féin's Jim Gibney is credited with being the person who first suggested to Gerry Adams that Bobby Sands should be the candidate to fight the vacant Westminster seat. Adams agreed with Gibney, seeing the potential for radicalising and extending Sinn Féin's base, although Sands was standing not for Sinn Féin but as an 'H Block/Armagh' candidate (Armagh city is where the women's jail is situated). Gibney's judgement was fully vindicated.

> We had extreme difficulty in getting publicity for Bobby during his
> hunger strike. The idea that he would stand, the idea that he would
> be in a contest that would last for a month or so, in terms of his
> cause and the prisoners' cause was excellent.[15]

Opposition within the republican movement was based on the fear that running Sands as a candidate in a field that contained a moderate nationalist, the SDLP's Austin Currie, and the republican firebrand Bernadette McAliskey, as well as a strong unionist candidate, Harry West, a dour but affable local farmer, was risky. The anxiety was that the nationalist/republican vote would be split, thereby letting the unionist Harry West in. That would be damaging to Bobby Sands, the republican movement and the hunger strikers' cause. To avoid that eventuality, pressure was brought to bear, gentle or otherwise, to get the other nationalist candidates to withdraw and so give Bobby Sands a free run against Harry West. Mrs Thatcher remained unmoved.

The IRA were on the advance politically. There was some
suggestion, to which even some of my advisers gave credence, that
the IRA were contemplating ending their terrorist campaign and
seeking power through the ballot box. I never believed this. But it
indicated how successful their propaganda could be.[16]

Mrs Thatcher miscalculated. The high-stakes by-election gamble
paid off. On 9 April 1981, on the fortieth day of his hunger strike and
having lost 28lb in weight, Bobby Sands beat Harry West by 1,500 votes
on a massive turnout of 86.9 per cent. Sands received 30,492 votes
to West's 29,046. I remember being at the count in Enniskillen and
sensing the excitement of republicans in the huge crowd and the shock
and disappointment of unionists, who saw their candidate narrowly
defeated by a convicted 'terrorist'. I didn't need convincing that this
was a profound moment of change in the conflict and a historic turning
point for Sinn Féin. A convicted IRA 'terrorist' had been elected to
the British House of Commons, although, in keeping with republican
policy and tradition, he would never take his seat at Westminster. To do
so would mean recognising the sovereignty of the British parliament,
which would have been anathema to the IRA.

As the IRA prisoners in the H Blocks waited for the result, the
tension was almost unbearable. Their only source of information
from the outside world was a crystal set, affectionately known
as 'Mrs Dale', that had been smuggled into the H Blocks.[17]
Incongruously the wireless was named after a popular radio soap
opera broadcast throughout the 1950s and 1960s called *Mrs Dale's
Diary*. Communication from the pivotal cell that looked after 'Mrs
Dale' was conveyed by tapping a form of code on the heating pipes
that ran in a chain from cell to cell. Any noise indicating jubilation
would have alerted prison officers that there was a contraband source
of information abroad in one of the cells. And that would have been
curtains for 'Mrs Dale'. Laurence McKeown, who later joined the
hunger strike, has never forgotten the moment he heard of Bobby
Sands's victory.

I remember in our particular wing when we heard the news, there
was like a suppressed cry, like someone was yelping. The next
minute someone banged the pipes and then I heard someone

saying, 'He's won!' Then the place just went mad. Doors were
banged, pipes were banged, everything was banged. People danced
around their cells. It was the highest point of my existence and I've
no doubt every other prisoner's existence during that period.[18]

Sinn Féin spun Sands's historic victory as a humanitarian vote for better
prison conditions and not a vote for the IRA. Brendan 'Bik' McFarlane,
who replaced Sands as OC, knew the opposite was true. 'What a day!'
he wrote in a 'com'.* 'I wonder if the opposition [Austin Currie, the
SDLP's candidate, withdrew so as not to split the nationalist vote] will
be just as quick to declare that the IRA have that popular support they
were claiming would be seen if they won this seat ... Up the good old
"RA" [IRA], onward to victory.'[19]

A month later, Bobby Sands carried out his promise. He died on 5
May 1981 on the sixty-sixth day of his hunger strike. Jim Gibney was
with him and Sands's family during his final hours.

It was one of the saddest scenes that I can recall in my time in the
struggle. His mum and his sister were standing by his bedside. He
had a pair of rosary beads around his neck that had been sent to
him by the Pope through his envoy. At that stage he was blind but
he said, 'Is that you, Jim?' And I said, 'Yes, it is, Bobby.' I took his
hand and he said, 'Tell the lads I'm hanging in there.' And I wished
him goodbye. He died shortly afterwards.[20]

On the day he died, Mrs Thatcher lost no time in telling the House of
Commons how she saw his death: 'Mr Sands was a convicted criminal.
He chose to take his own life. It was a choice that his organisation did
not allow to many of its victims.'[21]

Almost 100,000 people turned out for Bobby Sands's funeral in
Belfast's Milltown cemetery, conducted with full IRA military honours,

---

*A 'com' was a communication written on toilet paper in tiny handwriting, wrapped in cling
film and smuggled out of the jail, usually in the mouth and then passed on orally during a
family visit. The 'coms' provide a detailed record of the H Block experience from the blanket
and no-wash protests to the hunger strikes and beyond. David Beresford's seminal book,
Ten Men Dead, is based around them (Grafton Books, London, 1987).

including masked men in combat gear firing shots over his coffin. It was a transformational moment, the riposte to the Government's repeated claim that the IRA and the hunger strikers had dwindling support. To his supporters, Sands was a martyr and Mrs Thatcher a murderer. She later noted that it was a date 'of some significance for me personally. From this time forward I became the IRA's top target for assassination.' Three years later, the IRA almost succeeded.[22]

17

The Rise of Sinn Féin

In the two weeks after Sands's death three other hunger strikers followed him to their deaths. Francis Hughes, from Bellaghy, County Derry, died on 12 May 1981 after fifty-nine days without food. Raymond McCreesh, from Camlough, South Armagh, and Patsy O'Hara, from Derry City, both died on 21 May after sixty-one days without food. At the end of May, the month that had seen the deaths of four hunger strikers, Mrs Thatcher visited Belfast and dismissed the hunger strikers and their cause.

> Faced with the failure of their discredited cause, the men of violence
> have chosen in recent months to play what may well be their last
> card. They have turned their violence against themselves through
> the hunger strike to death. They seek to work on the most basic
> of human emotions – pity – as a means of creating tension and
> stoking the fires of bitterness and hatred.[1]

By now there were increasing divisions between the IRA leadership in the prison and the IRA leadership outside, which had never been enthusiastic about the hunger strikes in the first place. As Sands was approaching death, a 'com', presumably from the Army Council, had ordered that should Sands or any other hunger striker die, they were not to be replaced. The instruction was ignored, again a sign that the prisoners were making the decisions, not the IRA's external leadership. The prisoners' OC, 'Bik' McFarlane, grew increasingly depressed and frustrated by the lack of movement from the Government – even after the death of Bobby Sands: 'Everything seemed to freeze. Nothing moved – not even a hint of an opening for dialogue – no offers from the British that would go some way to negotiating a settlement. It was like living in a vacuum.'[2]

Outside the prison, Brendan Duddy desperately tried to broker a compromise based on the December document Michael Oatley had brought from London and handed over to Father Meagher at Aldergrove airport. Brendan shared McFarlane's intense frustration at the lack of progress.

> It was easily the most traumatic time of my whole work in this field.
> It was awful, absolutely awful. I fought for every one of the hunger
> strikers' lives. Every one. It was a political strike. Bobby Sands knew
> what he was doing and he went on that hunger strike to die. He set
> the agenda. It was a strike to politicise the people of Ireland. That's
> what he set out to do and that's what happened. He was determined
> to die and at that point the British Government was saying, 'If he
> wants to die, let him die.' I was saying to the British, every hour of
> every day, 'This is completely crazy. We don't need it.'[3]

Years later when I talked to Brendan Duddy about his attempts to resolve the second hunger strike in 1981 and prevent more men dying, he produced a 'com' that Bobby Sands had sent him from inside the jail. He read it aloud to me, periodically breaking down, with tears running down his cheeks. He said it was a 'precious' memento. I had no doubt how much it meant to him and how reading it brought all the painful memories flooding back.

> It says, 'To you and yours, may I be permitted to say a last goodbye.
> If my passion is to mean anything, may it mean peace and freedom
> for you and all of yours. May I be permitted to say ... [at this point
> Brendan broke down completely] ... I much appreciate all the
> efforts you've done on our behalf.' Signed 'Marcella'.

'Marcella' was Bobby Sands's sister and the pseudonym he used for his writings from the H Blocks.

The prisoners were determined to keep up the pressure in defiance of the Army Council's order that once one hunger striker died, no more were to follow. The day after Sands's funeral, Joe McDonnell from Belfast took Sands's place. He had been arrested with Sands and others following a gun battle with the RUC after the bombing of the Balmoral Furnishing Showrooms in Dunmurry in October 1976 which, because of the date of the incident, was why both ended up in the H Blocks.[4] Sands and McDonnell were both sentenced to fourteen years for possession of a firearm.

Seventeen days after Sands's death, Kieran Doherty from Belfast joined the hunger strike. He was followed the next day by Kevin Lynch, an INLA prisoner from County Derry. 'Bik' McFarlane had the lonely task of selecting the volunteers from those who had indicated their willingness to join. The strategy was for prisoners to join at regular intervals so there would be no long breaks to ease the pressure on the Government in the event of no settlement. Instead it would be faced with a steady stream of coffins. The others who went on to join were Martin Hurson, from Cappagh, County Tyrone; Thomas McElwee from Bellaghy, County Derry; Paddy Quinn from Camlough, South Armagh; Michael Devine (INLA) from Derry City; and Laurence McKeown from Randalstown, County Antrim. Just before refusing food for the first time, McKeown got a 'com' from the Army Council. It warned, 'Comrade, you have put your name forward to embark upon the hunger strike. Do you realise the full implications? What it means, comrade, is that in a short time, you will be dead. Rethink your decision.' McKeown ignored the entreaty and refused food.

On 11 June 1981 the hunger strikers received a boost to morale when Kieran Doherty, one of the nine H Block prisoners who were put up as candidates in the Irish General Election, was elected and became an *in absentia* member of the Irish parliament, Dáil Éireann. In total the prisoners in the Maze won 40,000 votes, underlining the message that Bobby Sands's victory had sent to the British Government and that had now percolated across the border and reached the new Irish Taoiseach, Fine Gael's Dr Garret FitzGerald, who took over from the defeated Fianna Fáil's Charles Haughey. Sinn Féin's growing political base was now extending into the Irish Republic.

By the end of June, there appeared to be a slight softening in the British position after the intervention of the Dublin-based Irish Commission for Justice and Peace (ICJP), which entered a dialogue with the British Government and the prisoners. The Government stressed that the meetings were for 'clarification' not 'negotiation'.[5] The ICJP was working on a formula in which all prisoners could wear their own clothes, there would be greater freedom of association and the definition of prison work could be broadened to include cultural and educational pursuits. But the initiative failed, rejected by 'Bik' McFarlane, who saw it as an attempt to split the prisoners by dealing with only three of their Five Demands. He also saw it as collusion with the Dublin Government.

At about the same time, Brendan Duddy's re-emergence appeared to be producing results. The back channel he and Michael Oatley had used to resolve the first hunger strike came to life again. As far as the IRA was concerned, the connection at the British end was still 'The Mountain Climber'; they were unaware that Michael Oatley was now thousands of miles away in a new posting. It has not been possible to establish the identity of Oatley's successor with certainty.

Whoever the contact was, he informed Brendan via the back channel that the Government was prepared to issue a public statement outlining agreed concessions, on the understanding that they would bring an immediate end to the hunger strike. Brendan then informed his IRA contact, who then passed the message to Gerry Adams, who took charge of events on the ground. The concessions on offer were that all prisoners in Northern Ireland, not just in the Maze, would be allowed to wear their own clothes; visits and other privileges would be agreed; prison work would be open to wider interpretation; and there was a vague offer to restore some percentage of lost remission. Crucially the British informed Adams via the back channel that, if any word leaked out, the deal was off. To clear the decks, Adams told the ICJP about the back-channel initiative and asked them to withdraw their formula to avoid any confusion. The contact probably reflected the anger felt in London at this unauthorised revelation but agreed to carry on. Word then came to Brendan, again via the back channel, that a Northern Ireland Office official would come into the prison that evening, by now 7 July 1981, to confirm directly what was on offer. As fate would have it, the official wasn't able to make the date but said he would come into the jail the following morning. But by then it was too late.

Joe McDonnell died at 4.50 on the morning of 8 July after sixty-one days on hunger strike. If the official had been able to keep to the original date, it's possible that Joe McDonnell's life might have been saved as well as the lives of others bent on starving themselves to death. By now, as the crisis escalated, some of the back-channel communications were being conducted in coded language as if it were an industrial dispute. The 'management' was the British Government; the 'shop stewards' were the Provisionals; and the 'workers' were the prisoners and the hunger strikers.

On 11 July, three days after the death of Joe McDonnell, the back channel became operative again. At 4.00 in the morning of 11 July, Brendan was contacted with a message from the 'management'. He kept a handwritten note of the somewhat convoluted communication: 'The management [the Government] is reassessing its position with a view to offering a settlement through their best possible option i.e. the Church [the ICJP] or Garret FitzGerald [the Irish Taoiseach], or both.' The message also pointed out a potentially dangerous split developing in the 'management', reflecting how sensitive the issue was in 10 Downing Street with its own 'hawks' and 'doves'.

> A section of the management still believes that the shop stewards [the Provisionals] are the best long-term hope but this section of management has lost ground. If face is to be saved for this section of management, they would need assistance. Only the shop stewards can do this.[6]

After spending most of the day digesting the late-night message from the management (the British Government), the 'shop stewards' (the Provisionals) gave Brendan their reply at the end of the day, at 10.15, as Brendan noted.

> The shop stewards, being aware of present management moves and intentions for ending the conflict on the factory floor to the management's satisfaction, wish to state that it is impossible for the present conflict to end unless the management grant *in full* [author's emphasis] the shop stewards' and trade union terms for settlement in clear, unambiguous terms. If a settlement cannot be reached to the shop stewards' satisfaction, then escalation will surely follow.[7]

'Escalation' was an ominous warning. The key words were 'in full'. The 'shop stewards', the Provisionals, were not prepared to compromise

and give the 'management', the Government, the assistance it required
(that is, further compromise on the part of the prisoners). Not only
was that not forthcoming but, to pile on the pressure even more,
at lunchtime the following day, 12 July, Martin Hurson became
unconscious and died in the early hours of the following morning
after a series of violent convulsions. It had been the forty-sixth day of
his hunger strike.

On 19 July there were signs that the 'management' was showing
flexibility, although it firmly ruled out any direct talks with the prisoners
or their OC, having insisted that there are no OCs in prisons, flying
in the face of the reality on the H Block wings. It sent its message
down the back channel, crucially on the central issue of prisoners being
allowed to wear their own clothes.

> In the conviction that the prisoners themselves will see no further
> point in their action, the Government reiterates its firm intention
> to continuing to improve the regime. When the hunger strike in
> support of the prison protest is brought to an end, it will extend
> to all male prisoners in Northern Ireland the clothing regime at
> present available to female prisoners* in Armagh prison.[8]

The 'management' also displayed a degree of movement on some of the
other Five Demands, although not on 'free association', the freedom
to mix on the wings at any time of the day, except during 'lock-up'
when prison officers went off for their lunch. The message concluded
by saying this was not a negotiating position but 'further evidence
of the Government's desire to maintain and improve an enlightened
and humane prison regime'. But the two sides were still too far apart.
Brendan was exhausted. 'The position has gone dead,' he wrote in the
small hours of 20 July 1981.

> Neither side can nor will move. Everyone is tired. Time is running
> out. I am almost defeated. I can't move forward. The British are

---

*Women prisoners in Armagh had always been allowed to wear their own clothes. For that
reason they did not join the blanket protest but expressed solidarity with the 'no wash' protest
by smearing menstrual blood on the walls.

asking for their plan to be accepted. I am so tired. It is so tragic. It is regrettable that a solution does not seem to be possible.[9]

With six prisoners now dead, the final phase of the showdown in the H Blocks began as the first cracks in the hunger strikers' resolution began to appear. The cracks were destined to spread. The instigator was Father Denis Faul, the Dungannon Roman Catholic priest who had been against the hunger strike from the very beginning. He was the IRA's bête noire. To the prisoners he was known as 'Denis the Menace' as he had no time for the Provisionals' revolutionary ideology or their use of violence, but, as an authorised visiting priest to the Maze, he cared passionately about prison conditions and the prisoners' welfare. He was also opposed to the hunger strike on theological grounds and had originally tried to persuade Bobby Sands not to go ahead. Sands refused, telling him, 'Greater love than this no man has than that he lay down his life for his friends'. Father Faul felt he had no option but to accept Sands's decision. 'I had to let him go ahead. He was in good conscience. He felt he was doing the right thing for the right motives.'[10] With others on the brink of dying, Father Faul met the families, some of whom had become increasingly frustrated and angry at the lack of progress in reaching a settlement while the macabre conveyor belt of death continued. He told them how bleak the situation was and how he didn't think that Mrs Thatcher was going to capitulate to the hunger strikers' demands. The message hit home.

On 31 July, Paddy Quinn's mother intervened and asked for medical intervention to save her son, now on his forty-seventh day without food. Families were entitled to request direct medical intervention. Quinn's mother said she was not prepared to let her son die.[11] But it was too late to save others still determined to end their lives.

On 1 August, INLA'S Kevin Lynch died after seventy-one days on hunger strike. The next day, Kieran Doherty passed away after refusing food for seventy-three days. He had recently been elected to the Irish parliament in Dublin. The following week, on 8 August, Thomas McElwee, from County Derry, died after sixty-two days on hunger strike. With no sign of any breakthrough concession from the Government, especially on work and free association, that was likely to end the hunger strike, others continued to replace their dead comrades.

On 20 August, Michael Devine, an INLA hunger striker from Derry, died, having refused food for sixty days. The same day the McGeown family requested medical intervention for their son Patrick, who had joined the hunger strike on 9 July and refused food for forty-two days. I remember it was McGeown who had planted a bomb outside Belfast's Europa Hotel when I was having a bite to eat inside. The abandonment of his protest changed the dynamic of the protest as more families went on to request medical intervention for their sons. The dam was breaking.

Michael Devine was the tenth and last hunger striker to die. I went to film his funeral in Derry and noted the long line of mourners who came to pay their respects to the dead INLA volunteer lying in an open coffin, surrounded by memory cards and guarded by masked men wearing white shirts and black berets. The numbers should have come as no surprise given that the same day, in the by-election in Fermanagh and South Tyrone following the death of its MP, Bobby Sands, his successor, Sinn Féin's Owen Carron, increased Sands's majority by 786 votes on an even bigger turnout of 88.6 per cent.

I knew the hunger strike would have to end at some stage and wondered how it would finally happen. The answer came a month later on 17 September 1981 when Mrs Thatcher moved James 'Jim' Prior sideways from Employment Secretary to Secretary of State for Northern Ireland. Prior, regarded as a Cabinet 'wet', and the Prime Minister were not close, as he later told me. He was a liberal, Conservative conciliator of the old school and did not see eye to eye with the 'Iron Lady', not least on the hunger strike:

> She wanted to get rid of me from London, I think, more than
> anything. Perhaps she thought I had some of the qualities that
> could be useful in Northern Ireland but I suspect that it was much
> more that she wanted me out of the way. I saw the hunger strike
> as an obstacle and I didn't think I could begin to make political
> progress with the hunger strike still in operation and therefore
> I wanted it ended. Mrs Thatcher never really understood what the
> problem was and she didn't like being told these things.[12]

Once Prior had arrived in Northern Ireland, everything began to change. He wanted to see the situation for himself. Within three days of his arrival, he went into the Maze prison where he had a three-hour meeting with the hunger strikers. He also met some of their families.

> I was influenced to a great extent by the lady who was the mother of one of the hunger strikers. She made it perfectly clear that she was not going to let her son die, and she would take him off hunger strike. And I always remember her words. 'My son has been a bad boy and he shouldn't have used that gun, but he's not a criminal, and I will take him off hunger strike, but just remember, he's not a criminal.' And that had quite a big influence on me.[13]

Three weeks later, on 3 October, the hunger strike ended with two more prisoners, Bernard Fox and Liam McCloskey, having called off their fast after thirty-two and fifty-five days respectively. The prisoners feared that the trickle of medical interventions was about to become a flood. The dam had broken. They knew the game was over and issued a statement:

> We have reluctantly decided to end our fast. We have been robbed of the hunger strike as an effective protest weapon principally because of the successful campaign waged against our distressed relatives by the Catholic hierarchy aided by the Irish establishment.[14]

Mrs Thatcher, abroad in Australia at the time, tersely remarked, 'I am delighted to hear that this waste of life is at an end.' The hunger strike now over, she authorised further concessions on clothing, free association and loss of remission. It marked, she said, 'a significant defeat for the IRA'.[15] Prior then included the concessions in a raft of measures that pretty much gave the protesters the essence of their Five Demands.

The 1981 hunger strike, along with internment and 'Bloody Sunday', was one of the great watersheds of the conflict. On the face of it, it was clear that Mrs Thatcher, through her steadfast defiance, had won the epic showdown and the prisoners, with ten of their comrades having starved themselves to horrific and lonely deaths, had lost. But that is looking through the wrong end of the telescope. Historically the bigger picture looks very different.

The hunger strike and the election of Bobby Sands and Owen Carron to Westminster, plus the election of hunger strikers to the Irish parliament, gave Sinn Féin a boost that Gerry Adams could scarcely have hoped for when he was incarcerated in the 'cages' of Long Kesh and the H Blocks of the Maze prison contemplating the future of the republican movement and the furtherance of its goal – the reunification of Ireland. These electoral victories laid the foundation for the political base that Adams knew had to be built if the 'struggle' was to progress and evolve. The hunger strike and the rise of Sinn Féin over the following decades, no longer the junior partner in the republican movement, were to change the course of Irish history. The end of the hunger strike also seemed to mark the end of the back channel that had resolved the first hunger strike in 1980 but not the second in 1981. It seemed to have served its purpose and would no longer be required. But Brendan Duddy, still in contact with Michael Oatley, thought differently:

> After the hunger strike, absolutely nothing happened. We went into a frozen period. Michael agreed. Mrs Thatcher was absolutely determined there would be no dialogue with terrorists. Michael would tell me, 'The lady is an iceberg.' The qualities and abilities that the earlier IRA delegations had shown in speaking to the British had gone. Billy McKee had gone, David O'Connell had gone, Ruairí Ó Brádaigh had gone. The new men, Gerry Adams and Martin McGuinness, hadn't got any experience [in these kind of dealings] but they handled them as honourably as they could. I knew the British would be back and the opportunity for dialogue would recur. I knew the conflict had to be solved and would be solved. It was simply a matter of waiting. So I waited ...[16]

18

The Armalite and the Ballot Box

Sinn Féin's electoral success during the 1981 hunger strike did not mean that the IRA was in the business of giving up its 'armed struggle'. On the contrary, throughout the decade that followed the gloves were off – on both sides. The obduracy of Mrs Thatcher who, in the eyes of IRA volunteers, 'murdered' ten of their comrades, only fuelled their determination to hit back at the 'Brits' and ultimately to target the Prime Minister herself. The British were equally determined to hit the IRA hard and use the full force of the security and intelligence services to eliminate the 'terrorists', in particular through the use of the SAS and its eyes and ears, the undercover men and women of 14 Intelligence Company, colloquially known as the 'Det', short for military 'Detachment'. The 'Det' and other agencies helped provide the intelligence on which the SAS could act. In this, they had the Prime Minister's full support. Intelligence was to be the British trump card, penetrating all levels of the IRA with a formidable array of human and technical resources.

During the hunger strike, Mrs Thatcher had dismissed any thought that the IRA might give up violence for politics. She was wrong.

On 31 October 1981, the end of the month in which the hunger strike ended, Sinn Féin held its annual conference, Ard Fheis, in the historic setting of the Mansion House in Dublin.*

---

*The Mansion House was a symbolic venue for the republican movement. After the 1918 General Election, in which Sinn Féin won a majority of seats on the pre-partitioned island of

It was in the slightly musty Georgian splendour of its Round Room, built in 1821 to receive King George IV, that Sinn Féin's wordsmith, Danny Morrison, rose to make a speech that few delegates imagined at the time would go down in history. Morrison was part of the Sinn Féin leadership who had played a prominent part in Bobby Sands's electoral campaign and in attempts to end the hunger strike by communicating with the prisoners in the H Blocks. He was selected by the leadership to deliver a morale-boosting speech to reassure the faithful that, despite the hunger strike not ending in any clear-cut victory, the republican movement remained strong, undefeated and ready to carry on the war on all fronts. It was in this context that he famously coined the phrase 'the Armalite and the Ballot Box'. In the years ahead, the words were to become synonymous with the republican movement's strategy of pursuing 'armed struggle' and electoral politics simultaneously. At the time, Morrison's actual words were rather more prosaic: 'Who here really believes we can win the war through the ballot box? But will anyone here object if with a ballot paper in one hand and an Armalite in the other, we take power in Ireland?'[1]

Any impression that these thoughts on the future of the 'struggle' had been carefully considered and scrutinised and approved by the leadership were wide of the mark. Indeed, nothing could have been further from the truth. Martin McGuinness, who was sitting next to Morrison on the platform, is said to have looked up and said in a whisper, designed only for Morrison, 'What the fuck is going on?' Morrison seemed to be articulating policy on the hoof. Approved or not, the policy became for ever known as the 'Armalite and Ballot Box' strategy.[2]

These two strands, violence and politics, are the twin threads that run through the decade after the hunger strike and culminate in Michael Oatley, aka 'The Mountain Climber', and Brendan Duddy, aka 'Soon', returning to the scene in one last back-channel endeavour to persuade the IRA to abandon the violence of the Armalite in favour

Ireland – taking 73 of the 105 seats – the newly elected Sinn Féin MPs refused to take their seats at Westminster, a British parliament they did not recognise, and adjourned to the Mansion House, where they established the first parliament of the Irish Republic, as declared by Patrick Pearse during the Easter Rising of 1916.

of constitutional politics, the Ballot Box. The reinvolvement of the back channel, with Michael Oatley and Brendan Duddy, can only be understood in the context of the escalating violence that happened in the decade after the hunger strike that in the end led to 'Operation Chiffon'.

In the year that followed Morrison's dropping of the Armalite and Ballot Box bombshell, the republican movement showed what the words meant. On a summer's day on 20 July 1982, the IRA killed eleven soldiers in London. The first bomb killed four Guardsmen of the Household Cavalry on their way to perform their ceremonial duties in the Changing of the Guard. Public outrage was further intensified by the deaths of seven horses that had to be put down and shot due to the seriousness of their injuries. The one horse that survived, Sefton, became a national hero and, to many of the public, a heroic symbol of defiance against the IRA.

The second bomb was detonated two hours later in Regent's Park where bandsmen from the Royal Green Jackets were performing a lunchtime concert in an open-air bandstand. The concert had been well advertised earlier in the year. The bomb had been hidden under the bandstand. One eyewitness described what he saw just after the band had started to play a selection from *Oliver*.[3]

> Suddenly there was this tremendous whoosh and I saw a leg fly past me. The bandstand seemed to lift off and I could see bandsmen flying through the air. I could not believe it. Everyone was stunned. Bandsmen were just staggering away from the bandstand. The whole centre was blown away. Only the railings were left.[4]

Sinn Féin's victories in the by-elections in Fermanagh and South Tyrone were shown to be no flash in the pan. Jim Prior, eager to capitalise on his resolution of the hunger strike by effectively giving the prisoners most of what they demanded, was anxious to get politics back on the agenda. On 20 October 1982, elections were held for the new Assembly that Prior had set up in the hope of a non-violent political future. Adams and McGuinness both stood and were elected. Sinn Féin won five of the seventy-eight seats with 10 per cent of the vote, just over half of the SDLP's 19 per cent. Prior was criticised in some parts of the establishment for giving Sinn Féin an opportunity to show its growing electoral credibility and presenting a threat to John Hume's previously unassailable SDLP as the dominant nationalist political party.

A week later, to show the IRA's rank and file that the Armalite was still in play and its leadership was not going soft on the 'armed struggle', a 1,000lb bomb was remotely detonated on the Kinnego Embankment in County Armagh, killing three RUC officers in a patrol car. But the most spectacular justification of the Ballot Box element of the new strategy came the following year in the General Election of 9 June 1983 when Gerry Adams was elected as an abstentionist MP to Westminster, with Sinn Féin winning 13 per cent of the nationalist vote, closing in on the SDLP's 18 per cent. In line with Sinn Féin policy, Adams never took his seat. Jim Prior was aware of the dangers of a Sinn Féin success.

> I think my reaction was almost one of despair, that they were going to elect someone whom we believed to be a terrorist and who was not going to play any part at Westminster. I had no doubts at all that he belonged to the Provisional IRA. I think he encapsulated the Armalite and Ballot Box completely.[5]

Adams's election also sealed the Northerners' takeover of the republican movement. At Sinn Féin's Ard Fheis, its annual conference, on 13 November 1983, Adams was elected President of Sinn Féin, displacing the outgoing President, Ruairí Ó Brádaigh, who had held the post since 1970. Ó Brádaigh, as a former IRA Chief of Staff, supported the Armalite but not the Ballot Box, because contesting elections north and south of the border was anathema given that participation recognised the authority of the Dublin and Westminster parliaments. Adams's election to Westminster and Ó Brádaigh's demise marked a profound ideological split in the republican movement. In his conference address, to tumultuous applause, Adams reassured the doubters in his audience that the IRA's military campaign remained central to the new strategy.

> I would like to elaborate on Sinn Féin's attitude to armed struggle. Armed struggle is a necessary and morally correct form of resistance against a government whose presence is rejected by the vast majority of the Irish people ... There are those who tell us that the British Government will not be moved by armed struggle. As has been said before, the history of Ireland and of British colonial involvement

throughout the world tells us they will not be moved by anything else. I am glad therefore to pay tribute to the freedom fighters – the men and women Volunteers of the IRA.[6]

The IRA leadership backed Adams in its defiant 1984 New Year message. 'The war is to the end,' it said. 'When we put away our guns, Britain will be out of Ireland and an Irish democracy will be established in the Thirty-Two Counties with a national Government.' To achieve this aim, the IRA would soon unleash its most devastating attack yet on the British Government.

19

The Brighton Bomber

Three years after the hunger strike and a year after Gerry Adams paid tribute to the 'freedom fighters of the IRA', the IRA planted a bomb in the Grand Hotel in Brighton where the Conservative Party was holding its annual conference. It came within an ace of assassinating Prime Minister Margaret Thatcher and wiping out her Cabinet. It was one of the most audacious attacks in the IRA's entire campaign. The bomber was Patrick Magee. It took me eighteen months to track him down and persuade him to do an interview.

Magee was born in Belfast, but the family moved to Norwich as the conflict was growing through the late 1960s and early 1970s. His mother tried to moderate his prominent Belfast accent, which stood out in the genteel English city in East Anglia. She tried getting him to say 'mum' instead of the ubiquitous Belfast 'mummy'. Mrs Magee didn't want her son to stand out, aware of the growing anti-Irish sentiment, a reaction to the IRA's killing of British soldiers and the Old Bailey bombings in London.[1] Magee returned to Belfast in 1970 when he was nineteen. 'It felt like a war zone,' he told me.

After 'Bloody Sunday' he joined the IRA. 'It just seemed a natural thing for me to get involved.' When he joined, was he prepared to kill? His answer was an unequivocal 'yes'. In 1973, he was interned in Long Kesh as a suspected member of the IRA. Released in 1975, he had no doubt what he wanted to do. 'Within an hour of getting off the bus in Belfast, I'd reported back to the IRA and from that moment I was active.' He soon appeared on the RUC's radar.

By the late 1970s Patrick Magee had become a recognised 'player' in Belfast, known to RUC Special Branch as a bomber with a brain which he used to exercise by doing *The Times* crossword. A Special Branch officer who interrogated him told me that he was in and out of the Castlereagh interrogation centre 'like a yo-yo'. But there was never any evidence that would stick and Magee would never make any admission. However, Castlereagh served another purpose in addition to getting confessions. Here, in the privacy and seclusion of Castlereagh's interview rooms, IRA detainees could be propositioned and recruited by British intelligence. In 1977 Magee claims to have been one of the many approached.

> I remember being offered £25,000. They didn't show me the money but they said, 'We can give you £25,000 if you'll agree to give us information.' I think I made some crack about 'What about £50,000?' but they never came back to me on that. Such was my value at that time to them.

One Special Branch officer who interrogated Magee assured me, 'The offer would have been made without doubt. He was a hard man and we knew what he was like. We would have loved to have had him on our side.' The temptation never entered Magee's mind.

He developed a particular skill: making bombs. 'A lot of people felt very nervous about explosives for absolutely correct reasons. But if you knew what you were doing, you had a certain confidence – and you did it.' And he had no doubt about the most effective way of putting pressure on the 'Brits', especially after the hunger strike.

> The campaign in the North was contained by the British strategies. In terms of the pressure needed to bring the British to the negotiating table and find a political way out of the conflict, we weren't going to achieve that by focusing on the war zone in the occupied Six Counties. The obvious recourse was to take the war to the enemy, to take it to England. I got out of internment with a very clear idea in my own head that that's what I wanted to do – to be part of the campaign to bomb England. I was very careful who I approached and it didn't happen overnight. But I got to the right people, said this is what I want to do and convinced them that I was up to the task.

Magee was given his target: the Grand Hotel, Brighton, the venue for the Conservatives' 1984 autumn conference, and the highlight of the party's year, starring the darling of the conference, Prime Minister Margaret Thatcher. Magee had no hesitation in targeting her. 'She was the leader of the British Government and she came into office determined to pursue a hard military line. You go up the chain of command and the buck stopped with her.'

On Saturday 15 September, Magee checked into Room 629 at the Grand Hotel, using the alias Roy Walsh, an IRA volunteer serving a life sentence for being part of the IRA team that bombed the Old Bailey in 1973. A risky choice of alias. No wonder Special Branch knew Magee as 'Chancer'. Once in his room, he put a 'Do Not Disturb' notice on the door and then barely appeared for the next three days.

Magee needed the privacy. He assembled the bomb behind the bath panel in room 629 and set the long-term timer to explode twenty-four days, six hours and thirty-six minutes later, the eve of the Prime Minister's eagerly awaited end-of-conference speech. Magee was matter of fact about how he felt at the time. 'You've got a job of work to do, you've been doing it for a long time and you just do it. You can be nervous after it but not while you're doing it.'

With the timer set, the thought of the bomb ticking away in the bathroom never left his mind. 'I'd have thought of little else. Quite honestly, you'd be concerned that the thing wouldn't go off.' That was the thought that was uppermost in his mind rather than the thought that it was about to kill any number of innocent people, in addition to the Prime Minister and members of her Cabinet. 'You don't dwell on things like that. You're putting a bomb in place to kill people. You've years afterwards to dwell on that.'

The police believe that Magee's bomb was made up of around 20lb of explosives. He insists it was five times that amount. Whatever its size, the impact was devastating. At 2.50 a.m. on Friday 12 October 1984, it exploded when most of the delegates were asleep. The explosion dislodged one of the Grand's great Victorian chimneys, which plunged downwards, collapsing the floors like a pack of cards. It was this that caused most of the deaths and injuries. Four people died, buried in the rubble: Mrs Joan Shattock, Mrs Roberta Wakeham, Eric Taylor and Sir Anthony Berry MP, Magee's only 'political' victim. Mrs Muriel Maclean, who'd been sleeping in room 629 next to the bomb, was

later to die from her injuries. Margaret Tebbit, the wife of the Trade
Secretary, Norman Tebbit, was paralysed for life until her death in
2020. Norman Tebbit himself, who had been trapped in the debris
for four hours, was saved by the resilience of an old-fashioned English
mattress. He survived with an injured spine, a punctured lung and a
dramatically curtailed political career, becoming carer for his severely
disabled wife. He never forgave the IRA. When I interviewed him
his words on his feelings about Magee and the IRA were unprintable.
Mrs Thatcher narrowly survived. Glass shards from the windows of
her sitting room were strewn across the carpet. At first she thought it
was a car bomb outside the hotel. Her bathroom was more severely
damaged. As she later wrote, 'Those who had sought to kill me had
placed the bomb in the wrong place.'[2] Her end-of-conference speech
was hastily rewritten.

> The bomb attack … was an attempt not only to disrupt and
> terminate our conference. It was an attempt to cripple Her
> Majesty's democratically elected government. That is the scale of
> the outrage in which we have all shared. And the fact that we are
> gathered here now, shocked but composed and determined, is a sign
> not only that this attack has failed, but that all attempts to destroy
> democracy by terrorism will fail.[3]

The Prime Minister received a rapturous standing ovation. The IRA
responded with a chilling reminder:

> Today we were unlucky, but remember we only have to be lucky
> once. You will have to be lucky always. Give Ireland peace and there
> will be no more war.[4]

Magee didn't go to ground, determined to return to the IRA's
campaign.

> I was a volunteer. I was committed to pursuing the war in England.
> For all the enormity of Brighton, it was one operation on its own
> and wouldn't have achieved the necessary leverage to change the
> British political establishment's mind. In order to do that, we had to
> sustain a campaign, so I returned to England with that in mind.

Eight months after the Brighton bomb, on 22 June 1985, Magee was finally caught red-handed in Glasgow as a member of an IRA cell plotting to plant bombs in seaside resorts and hotels across the south of England. At his trial the following year, he was given eight life sentences. The judge described him as 'a man of exceptional cruelty and inhumanity' and recommended that he serve at least thirty-five years. In the event, he served only thirteen and was one of the last IRA prisoners to be released under the Good Friday Agreement. He emerged from the H Blocks as Dr Patrick Magee, having studied for a PhD in the Maze prison.[5] He never believed he would serve thirty-five years. 'Quite honestly I was in no doubt about that. The whole prosecution of the war was linked to a political settlement. It was just a case of sustaining that war effort to achieve that end.'

Magee still had thirteen years in jail to mull over the enormity of Brighton, for which operationally he never had any regrets. 'I stand by my actions as a volunteer in the Irish Republican Army. I think our struggle was legitimate. There was no other way, but I still carry the burden of having killed people and hurt people and that doesn't rest easily with me.' He also had plenty of time to think about his victims and the alternative to violence. 'It's got to be dialogue,' he told me. 'Respect for the other person's position, preparedness to talk through issues.'

Following his release, he put his words into deeds. Back in Belfast he founded a charity called Causeway, a word with which both communities could readily associate because of the Giant's Causeway in County Antrim, one of Northern Ireland's most famous beauty spots and tourist attractions. The charity's purpose was to bring victims and perpetrators of violence together, the beginning of a process of reconciliation. He began a dialogue with Jo Berry, daughter of one of his Brighton victims, Sir Anthony Berry MP. I asked Magee if at his first meeting with Jo Berry he had said, 'I'm sorry I killed your father.' He said those were his exact words. What's more he said that during their first encounter 'we actually hugged'.

Patrick Magee, the Brighton Bomber, initially the embodiment of the IRA's Armalite, went on to become the personification of the Ballot Box and dialogue, rejecting the Armalite – as eventually did the IRA. But that was still to be many bloodstained, dramatic and painful years ahead.

20

Stalemate

Politically the second half of the 1980s was marked by Mrs Thatcher's determined attempt to stem the rise of Sinn Féin by signing the Anglo-Irish Agreement with the Irish Taoiseach, Dr Garret FitzGerald, at Hillsborough Castle on 15 December 1985. As far as the British Government was concerned, the Agreement was designed to boost the moderate Catholic/nationalist party, the SDLP, led by John Hume, and to encourage the Dublin Government to step up cross-border security in the hope of choking the IRA. In terms of stopping the rise of Sinn Féin, Dublin was at one with Downing Street, seeing Sinn Féin as a potential long-term threat to the duopoly of the traditional Irish parties, Fianna Fáil and Fine Gael, whose origins lie in the bloody Irish civil war of 1922–3.* Although the Agreement began by declaring that 'any change in the status of NI would only come about with the consent of the majority of the people of Northern Ireland', unionists were not convinced and screamed betrayal, seeing a closer relationship with the South, epitomised by Dublin being given a token symbolic advisory role in the administration of Northern Ireland as yet another step on the road to a united Ireland.[1] Dr FitzGerald, a moderate nationalist like John Hume, believed in a united Ireland to be agreed constitutionally, not by violence, and saw the Anglo-Irish Agreement as a step in that direction, but only with unionist involvement. That

---

*Fine Gael (Tribe of Ireland) supported the treaty negotiated by Michael Collins. Fianna Fáil (Soldiers of Destiny) opposed the treaty, as it fell short of a united Ireland, and fought on.

involvement was never forthcoming as loyalists took to the streets in violent demonstrations, the anomaly highlighted by the sight of a loyalist protester hitting a member of the Royal Ulster Constabulary over the head with a pole with the Union Jack at the end of it. For unionists, the Anglo-Irish Agreement was a step too far.

The republican movement was fully aware of the strategy of the British and Irish governments to marginalise Sinn Féin, but this was offset by the IRA's growing confidence in the long-term future of its military campaign, based on a secret operation likely to reflect the primacy of the Armalite over the Ballot Box for years to come. At the time, this confidence was shared by only a handful at the highest level of the Provisional Army Council to minimise the risk of any leak that might jeopardise the operation that could change the face of the war.

In the months just before and just after the signing of the Anglo-Irish Agreement, vast consignments of arms from Libya's ruler, Colonel Muammar Gaddafi, were on the way to Ireland. Gaddafi, who had supplied the IRA with arms before, saw the IRA as brothers in the revolutionary struggle and wanted to show solidarity, not least with the ten men who had died on hunger strike.[†] The result was that between August 1985 and October 1986 some 140 tons of arms, in four separate shipments, were offloaded in Zodiac inflatable dinghies at Clogga Strand, a wide and long sandy beach in County Wexford. Remarkably this happened under the noses of British and Irish intelligence. The fact that the agencies were blind is an indication of how tightly the secret was kept. The weapons were then stashed away in remote arms dumps across Ireland, again without the knowledge of the intelligence agencies, which is surprising as this involved a sophisticated logistical operation.

The four consignments of weapons consisted of hundreds of Czech-made AK-47 high-velocity rifles, heavy and light machine guns, rocket-propelled grenades (RPGs), Semtex plastic explosives and surface-to-air missiles (SAMs). Semtex was to play a devastating role in the intensified

---

[†]On 28 March 1973 a consignment of arms from Libya was seized by the Irish navy on board a Cyprus-registered boat, the *Claudia*. The haul included 250 rifles, 240 small arms, anti-tank mines and explosives. On board overseeing the operation was the veteran IRA leader Joe Cahill, who was arrested.

campaign. The IRA leadership believed that President Gaddafi's generosity could change the face of the 'Long War' first outlined by Gerry Adams and his comrades in Long Kesh – and, if necessary, make it even longer. It was only on 1 November 1987 when the French navy intercepted the fifth and largest consignment of arms off the coast of Brittany that the British and Irish governments – and the world – realised what had got under the wire. The huge shipment, concealed in the bowels of a Panamanian-registered ship, the *Eksund*, was believed to have contained a thousand AK-47s, a million rounds of ammunition, more than fifty SAMs and two tons of Semtex explosive.[2]

While the importation of these vast quantities of arms was secretly underway at sea, at home the Ballot Box strategy was being refined in one crucial area. If Sinn Féin was to make credible electoral advances north and south of the border, it could not do so as long as the party refused to take any seats in the Irish parliament, Dáil Éireann, which Sinn Féin had not recognised for almost a hundred years.[§] Seeing that Sinn Féin's policy of 'abstentionism' would have to change, the leadership of Gerry Adams and Martin McGuinness and their 'kitchen cabinet' of Danny Morrison, Richard McCauley, Jim Gibney, Tom Hartley and selected others, planned a coup against Ruairí Ó Brádaigh and the 'old' leadership for whom the principle of abstentionism was inalienable.

Adams knew that a further split on the issue was inevitable but wished the parting of the ways to be bloodless. The IRA leadership, with minority opposition, had already been squared off on the coup. It was in fact the second coup against the old IRA leadership of Ruairí Ó Brádaigh following the first coup in 1976 at the end of the 1975 ceasefire. This second coup was to mark the complete takeover of the republican movement by the Adams/McGuinness faction. It was carefully planned. Much backstage lobbying of delegates was done before a vote was taken at the party's Ard Fheis at the Mansion House on 2 November 1986. Brendan Hughes did his utmost to prevent blood being spilt in what might have been a ruinous and violent internecine feud.

[§]This had been an ideological tenet since the British General Election of 1918, after which Sinn Féin established its own parliament, claiming it to be the only true legislative body of the Irish Republic.

I went round asking Ruairí and his followers not to walk out. A lot
of them were friends and comrades of mine and I had a lot of
respect for them. Everything was done to try and avoid a split but at
least, for the first time in Irish history, they didn't split by shooting
each other. It didn't mean the end of the involvement of people
from the South in the leadership but it certainly meant the end of
their domination of the republican movement.[3]

The vote to end abstentionism was carried by 429 votes to 161. Ruairí
Ó Brádaigh and around twenty of his close allies walked out of the Ard
Fheis. McGuinness was heard to say from the platform, 'You're going
nowhere.' Ó Brádaigh went on to form Republican Sinn Féin, which in
turn gave birth to an armed dissident wing, the Continuity IRA.

Meanwhile through 1985 and 1986, the IRA was targeting RUC
stations in the south of the province, the strategy being to deny the
police and army the territory they held, particularly in areas close to
the border. On 28 February 1985 a devastating mortar attack on Newry
police station left nine RUC police officers dead and thirty injured. It
was teatime on a wet Monday evening. An officer who survived told me
what he saw:

> Nothing that I had ever been trained for or experienced prepared
> me for this. It was like a war-time bombing. There were dead people
> and people in the process of dying. The darkness and the bleakness
> and the gore will be with me for the rest of my days. They died a
> terrible death in a lonely place. They were my comrades and they
> were just snuffed out on a bleak Monday's night.[4]

Ten months later, on 7 December 1985, the IRA launched a full-frontal
attack on a police station in the village of Ballygawley, County Tyrone,
a few miles from the border. It came during an evening shift change.
The IRA shot two officers dead, raked the front of the station with
automatic rifles and left a 100lb beer-keg bomb that destroyed the
building.[5]

The following summer, on 11 August 1986, most of the police station
in the County Tyrone village of The Birches was destroyed by a 200lb
bomb that the IRA had loaded into the bucket of a mechanical digger

which then smashed through the perimeter fence. The station was unmanned at the time.[6] But the IRA's luck ran out. The next attack was seen coming as RUC Special Branch had by this time recruited an informer in the IRA Active Service Unit planning the operation. I was told this by one of the counter-terrorist officers involved in heading off the attack.

The target was the police station in the quiet village of Loughgall. The attack was planned for Friday evening, 8 May 1987. Again the IRA planted a bomb in a mechanical digger taken from a farm five miles from the village. A Toyota HiAce van was hijacked in the nearby town of Dungannon that was to carry the seven heavily armed IRA attackers, the eighth being the driver of the digger. The attack was designed to be a repeat of the Birches attack. The difference this time was that the SAS was inside the station, waiting for the visitors. The digger smashed through the station's perimeter fence, the bomb exploded, the IRA opened fire (the precise sequence of events is not clear) and the SAS responded with 200 rounds of heavy ammunition, cutting down all eight members of the Active Service Unit, the elite of the IRA's East Tyrone Brigade. One of those killed was the informant, who could not be credibly exfiltrated in time. An innocent civilian was also killed in the crossfire. It was the biggest loss suffered by the IRA since the so-called 'War of Independence' of 1920–1.[7] Gerry Adams warned that Loughgall would become 'a tombstone for British policy in Ireland and a bloody milestone in the struggle for freedom, justice and peace'.[8]

Nineteen-eighty-seven was to become the IRA's *annus horribilis*. On 8 November, six months after Loughgall, the IRA bombed the Remembrance Day parade in Enniskillen. The intention was to target soldiers and security-force personnel, but the operation did not go according to plan. The bomb had been placed against the gable wall of a building overlooking the Cenotaph where the wreath-laying ceremony was due to take place at 11 a.m. It was to be triggered by an electronic timer set for 10.43 a.m. When the bomb exploded, it collapsed the gable wall on the crowd of spectators watching below, many of whom were trapped under the rubble. Ten innocent civilians and one RUC reservist, all of them Protestants, were killed. Sixty-three people were injured, many of them seriously. One of the injured, Gordon Wilson, poignantly described holding the hand of his daughter Marie, buried under the rubble, and hearing her last words, 'Daddy, I love you very much.'***

Not surprisingly, Protestants regarded the Enniskillen bomb as an attack on their community as it honoured the sacrifice of their war dead. The atrocity provoked universal outrage at home and abroad and did the IRA incalculable damage, even among its own supporters. The IRA issued an apology. 'In the present climate, nothing we can say ... will compensate the feelings of the bereaved and the injured.' Gerry Adams declared that the republican movement could not withstand another Enniskillen. Martin McGuinness later described the attack as 'absolutely terrible and atrocious' and said he was 'ashamed' of it.[9] Many years later I confronted McGuinness by saying that, as he was believed to be acting head of the IRA's Northern Command at the time of the bombing, he must have known about the operation and given the go-ahead for it. His eyes hardened and went cold. He denied the allegation and said he had neither sanctioned nor known about it. Enniskillen was to provide a powerful impetus for peace and marked the beginning of the process that eventually led to it.

But the Armalite still remained the principal driving force. Four months after Enniskillen, on 6 March 1988, the IRA planned to bomb the Royal Anglian Regimental Band during the Changing of the Guard ceremony on the British overseas territory of Gibraltar as part of the IRA's extension of its campaign to Europe. The three experienced members of the Active Service Unit (ASU) had been carefully selected, all of them from Belfast: Mairead Farrell, Danny McCann and Sean Savage, a nephew of Billy McKee. As with Loughgall, British intelligence knew of the planned attack and had monitored Farrell, McCann and Savage and their accomplices all the way from Belfast to Spain and Gibraltar. In anticipation of the attack, an SAS unit was flown to Gibraltar to deal with the threat on the ground. As Farrell, McCann and Savage crossed the Spanish border into Gibraltar, they were intercepted by the SAS, believing they were about to trigger the explosives by remote control as the parade was due to begin. All three were confronted by

***Gordon Wilson devoted the rest of his life to becoming a campaigner for peace. At one stage, in 1993, he met IRA leaders and entreated them, without success at that stage, to end the 'armed struggle'.

the SAS, wearing plain clothes, and shot dead in highly controversial circumstances. None of the three members of the ASU was armed and there was a fierce dispute over whether the SAS gave warnings. The car in which the bomb was thought to have been placed, parked close to the Changing of the Guard ceremony, was later found to be empty. Two days later, a car containing 140lb of Libyan Semtex was located in a car park in Marbella.[10] To the IRA and its supporters, Gibraltar proved their long-held contention that the British security forces, the SAS, the army and the RUC pursued a 'shoot to kill' policy – shoot first and ask questions later – that had always been denied by the Government.

In the IRA's eyes, Farrell, McCann and Savage immediately became martyrs. Their daylight killings were to trigger an astonishing series of events that, ironically, helped bring peace closer. Ten days later, as thousands gathered in Belfast's Milltown cemetery to pay tribute as the three coffins were about to be lowered into the grave in the republican plot, the area set aside for the IRA's dead, shots rang out. The mourners, prominently led by Gerry Adams and Martin McGuinness, came under attack by a lone member of the loyalist UFF, Michael Stone, who had infiltrated the funeral procession. Stone, armed with handgun and grenades in a potential suicide mission, planned to take the funeral by surprise in the hope of killing Adams and McGuinness.

The surprise is evident from the TV footage of Stone's attack. He killed one IRA volunteer, Kevin Brady, and two civilian mourners. More than fifty others were injured. Stone then made his escape, pursued by elements of the crowd, towards the motorway that runs along the bottom of Milltown cemetery. If they had caught up with him, his chances of survival would have been slim. His life was saved by a passing RUC patrol that happened to be driving along the motorway.

But that wasn't the end of the deadly sequence of events. Three days later, in the heart of republican West Belfast, as the funeral procession of Stone's single IRA victim, Kevin Brady, was beginning to make its way towards Milltown cemetery, a silver Volkswagen suddenly drove into the procession at considerable speed and then rapidly tried to reverse only to find its retreat blocked by an IRA black taxi. The mourners and IRA security detail thought they were coming under attack from another Michael Stone, their alarm confirmed when one of the two unknown occupants of the car leaned out of the window brandishing a Browning pistol and fired a shot in the air. What no one knew was that the intruders were two British army corporals, Derek Wood and David Howes, of the Signals Regiment, thought to be associated with 14 Intelligence Company, which was, as we have seen, the eyes and ears of the SAS. They were on their way back to army headquarters at Lisburn from an army base in Belfast in the course of which Corporal Wood is thought to have been showing Corporal Howes, a recent arrival in the province, some of the security hot spots in the city. They hadn't reckoned on running into an IRA funeral.[11]

The corporals were then dragged from the car, bundled into the back of a black taxi, driven to nearby waste ground, stripped naked, beaten and then shot dead by the IRA with one of the soldiers' own pistols. One of the most harrowing images of the Troubles is the photograph of Father Alec Reid, having tried mouth-to-mouth resuscitation, administering the last rites to the dying soldiers.[12] Father Reid would become another important figure in the peace process that was soon about to evolve.

In that one bloody fortnight in 1988, beginning with Gibraltar and ending with Kevin Brady's funeral, the SAS had killed three members of an IRA Active Service Unit, the loyalist Michael Stone had shot dead one IRA volunteer and two civilians and the IRA had murdered Corporals Wood and Howes. All three parties to the conflict – the British army, the IRA and the loyalist paramilitaries – had blood on their hands. People cried out for the killing to stop. The SDLP and Sinn Féin were listening.

Even before the Enniskillen bomb, the SDLP's leader, John Hume, had tried to get the IRA to end its campaign by secretly meeting with some of its leaders. On 23 February 1985 he was blindfolded and driven to a secret location where he met Brendan McFarlane and other members of the leadership, but the meeting never got beyond first base as McFarlane insisted on filming the proceedings. Hume flatly refused, knowing what the repercussions were likely to be, not just within his own party but throughout the nationalist community at the sight of him meeting and talking to the enemy. At the time, only a few months after the Brighton bombing, such a video, if released, was likely to have done incalculable damage to Hume's reputation and that of his party, the SDLP.

Two months after Enniskillen, Hume tried another route, engaging with Gerry Adams as both shared the abhorrence of the Remembrance Day attack. On 11 January 1988, Hume sent Adams a letter.

> Is it not time for the IRA and members of the Provisional
> Republican Movement to seriously reconsider the methods they
> have chosen to achieve their objectives or are they in danger
> of moving to a situation – or are they already in it – where the
> methods have become more sacred than the cause?[13]

Hume pointed out to Adams that, if there was to be a settlement to end the conflict, unionists would have to be persuaded to accept it and not forced to do so at the point of a gun. Adams was already moving in a similar direction. Having warned that 'there is no military solution', he outlined to Hume that he was now 'prepared to consider an alternative unarmed form of struggle to achieve Irish independence' and that if someone would outline such a course, he would not only be 'prepared to listen but prepared to work in that direction'.[14]

This engagement marked the beginning of what later became known as the Hume–Adams talks, facilitated and encouraged by Father Alec Reid, who had administered the last rites to the two corporals murdered by the IRA. Hume and Adams, with the added credibility of their both being Westminster MPs, agreed that to become an effective force for peace the nationalist/republican constituency had to be widened beyond the SDLP and Sinn Féin and the narrow politics of Northern Ireland. Adams was well aware that Sinn Féin was what its Irish name meant, 'Ourselves Alone', but that was not enough to end the conflict and bring peace. The result was what became a nationalist coalition embracing the SDLP, Sinn Féin, the Dublin Government and, critically, Irish America and the White House. Unionists, deeply suspicious, scathingly dismissed it as the 'Pan Nationalist Front'.

Such were the political currents that ran through the closing years of the 1980s. But, despite the progress made in uniting the different shades of Irish nationalism, there was no sign of any IRA ceasefire. The unremitting cycle of violence continued.

In the summer of 1988, to add to the bloodshed of the previous months, the IRA dealt the army two heavy blows. On 15 June it planted a bomb under an unmarked military vehicle waiting to take soldiers home after a charity 'Fun Run' in Lisburn. Six soldiers were killed. On 20 August another IRA bomb, placed in a drainage culvert near Ballygawley, County Tyrone, killed eight soldiers and injured twenty-eight. The soldiers were returning to base in a bus at night, having been on home leave. Both bombs contained Semtex explosives from Libya. One of the first to arrive at the aftermath of the bomb was a part-time UDR soldier and local councillor, Sammy Brush. He told me what he saw as he swept the scene of devastation with his torch.

> There was glass, blood and bodies and young soldiers badly
> mutilated but still alive. It was a scene of carnage that I would never
> want to witness in my life again. All you could do was to try and
> comfort them and do your best for them. It was a terrible incident,
> terrible to think that another human being could blow up other
> human beings.[15]

Ten days later the SAS ambushed three IRA volunteers preparing to kill an off-duty UDR soldier. The SAS fired 220 rounds. The IRA fired sixteen.[16] There were suspicions that the three IRA volunteers had been involved in the Ballygawley bus bomb, although it was never proven. The tabloid press was jubilant. The *Sun* proclaimed 'SAS rub out IRA rats'. The *Star* was more specific. 'Revenge! SAS kill three bus bombers'. Whatever the truth or otherwise of their involvement in the Ballygawley bus bombing, the three had been under surveillance for some time before the attack. Six weeks later, Mrs Thatcher responded by having the Home Office introduce broadcasting restrictions that meant that the voices of members of proscribed organisations and their associates, republican and loyalist, could not be heard on television or radio. It was not so much an anti-terrorism measure as a gesture designed to reflect the Government's and the public's abhorrence of the media allegedly giving 'terrorists' and their supporters what Mrs Thatcher described as 'the oxygen of publicity'.

The last months of the violent decade ended as they had begun – in violence. On 22 September 1989, the IRA bombed the Royal Marines' School of Music in Deal, killing ten bandsmen and injuring twenty-two. The bomb went off at breakfast time as the bandsmen were in the canteen and rest room before beginning morning rehearsals. The Marines' Commandant General, Lieutenant-General Sir Martin Garrod, referred to the IRA as 'thugs, extortionists, torturers, murderers and cowards – in fact, the scum of the earth'. The mother of one of the dead bandsmen echoed Sir Martin's words. 'Instead of putting them in prison, which does no good, they should be put up against a wall and shot.'[17]

The decade ended in stalemate with the SAS and the security forces hitting the IRA hard, thanks to the penetration of its ranks by MI5, GCHQ, RUC Special Branch and in particular by military intelligence, whose top-secret Force Research Unit (FRU) ran high-level agents within the IRA such as the agent codenamed 'Stakeknife'.[‡] The IRA remained undeterred by its losses and showed increased capability, thanks to Semtex and Colonel Gaddafi's munificence. At the same time, the loyalist paramilitaries intensified their offensive, now targeting known republicans, assisted by the collusion of some sections of the police and others with loyalist sympathies. It seemed as if the conflict would never end. But the British and the IRA – and the loyalist paramilitaries too – knew that at some stage it would have to, and end in a settlement that would have to be acceptable to all sides. Things were about to change.

[‡]'Stakeknife' was alleged to be Freddie Scappaticci, who was believed to have worked for the FRU since being recruited in the late 1970s. Over time he rose to be head of the IRA's internal security unit, colloquially known as 'the nutting squad', which rooted out and 'executed' IRA members suspected of working for the British. His position meant that 'Stakeknife' could also tip off his handlers about danger to its agents within the IRA.

21

Big Changes

The close of the decade was marked by two important changes in the political landscape. The most significant was the resignation of Prime Minister Margaret Thatcher. Having failed to win an outright victory in the Conservative Party's leadership election, she stood down on 22 November 1990, after eleven years in power during which she had symbolised resistance to the IRA from the hunger strike to the unleashing of the SAS. She was visited by Tory Party grandees, the 'Men in Grey Suits', who told her that her time was up. The unpopularity of the poll tax – which had resulted in violent street demonstrations – and growing divisions over Europe were among the reasons for her ousting.* A week later, she was succeeded as Prime Minister by John Major, who was the antithesis of Margaret Thatcher. Major was a conciliator and a pragmatist. He told me that when he walked into Number 10 he drew up a list of priorities for his Premiership. Top of the list was Northern Ireland. The mood music from the Northern Ireland Office, orchestrated by the Northern Ireland Secretary, Peter Brooke, had already begun to change a year before Mrs Thatcher's resignation.

---

*The poll tax marked a change in the way local government was financed. The rates, a tax on the value of property – strongly opposed by Conservatives in particular – were replaced by a standard tax placed on individuals, known as the Community Charge, with the amount being set by each local authority. In 1991 John Major, who succeeded Mrs Thatcher, abolished the Community Charge and replaced it with the Council Tax based on property values, listed in different bands.

On 2 November 1989, in interviews with journalists to mark his first hundred days in office, Brooke was asked if he could ever envisage a British Government talking to Sinn Féin. The standard answer, echoed repeatedly through the 1980s by Mrs Thatcher, was that HMG would not talk to the IRA and those who supported its violent campaign. Sinn Féin steadfastly refused to condemn the 'armed struggle'. In his answer, Brooke changed the tune, saying it was difficult to envisage 'a military defeat of the IRA' but pointed out that the scenario might change under certain conditions.

> If the terrorists were to decide that the moment had come when
> they wished to withdraw from their activities, then I think the
> Government would need to be imaginative in those circumstances
> as to how that process should be managed. Let me remind you of
> the move towards independence in Cyprus [following a violent
> campaign by EOKA[†] 'terrorists']. A British minister stood up in the
> House of Commons and used the word 'never'. Within two years
> there had been a retreat from that word.[1]

Brooke's words, uttered only five weeks after the IRA bombed the Royal Marines' School of Music in Deal, provoked a storm of protest from unionists, outraged that a British secretary of state would ever contemplate talking to the political representatives of those responsible for such an atrocity. On the other side, nationalists were relieved to hear of the possible change of policy and welcomed the fact that the Northern Ireland Secretary had mentioned the unmentionable. Peter Brooke later told me he had no regrets about what he had said.

> As the Troubles had been going on for twenty years and there was
> no particular reason at that moment to think that the security forces
> were going to make a sudden breakthrough which was going to lead
> to the IRA's defeat, I gave an honest answer to an honest question.

[†]EOKA, which means 'the National Organisation of Cypriot Fighters', was the Greek Cypriot paramilitary organisation that fought an insurgent campaign to end British rule in Cyprus and unite the island with Greece.

I was arguing that if you reach this kind of impasse, it was sensible to explore other ways of resolving matters.[2]

Brooke continued to elaborate on the same message, encouraging the IRA to talk, not kill. A year later, on 9 November 1990, he treated the unlikely audience of Canned Food Importers and Distributors at the Whitbread Restaurant in London to a dissertation on 'The British Presence'. What became known as 'the Whitbread Speech' was not what his bemused audience had been expecting.

> An Irish Republicanism seen to have finally renounced violence would be able, like other parties, to seek a role in the peaceful political life of the community. It is not the aspiration to a sovereign, united Ireland against which we set our face, but its violent expression.

He then added the words that had been seeded by John Hume as a result of his ongoing dialogue with the British Government:

> The British Government has no selfish, strategic or economic interest in Northern Ireland: our role is to help, enable and encourage. Britain's purpose … is not to occupy, oppress or exploit but to ensure democratic debate and free democratic choice. Partition is an acknowledgement of reality, not an assertion of national self-interest.[3]

The following month, in December 1990, the IRA declared its first Christmas ceasefire in eleven years. But it was of short duration. Six weeks later, on 7 February 1991, the IRA mortared Downing Street, almost wiping out John Major and his new Cabinet. They were discussing the Gulf War in the Briefing Room at 10 Downing Street, only a short distance from the transit van parked across the road in Whitehall from which the mortars had been fired. It was a clear sign that the IRA and the Armalite – and mortar bombs – were still very much in business.

Around the same time, Peter Brooke was also being informed about Brendan Duddy and the back channel, although Brooke never knew the names of those involved. Duddy was still known by the codename

'Soon'. Brooke knew only what he needed to know as a result of his regular weekly meetings with John Deverell, MI5's Director and Controller of Intelligence in the province. Deverell, like Brooke, was an undogmatic pragmatist. 'John and I would see each other with very great regularity,' Brooke told me, 'and it would be an entirely private occasion.'

> Although we had a particular agenda that we were pursuing on those occasions, there was ample opportunity for the conversation to range much more widely. We had bilateral discussions that went on for two and three-quarter years and therefore we had ample opportunity for testing this sort of subject [the back channel to the IRA leadership]. The need-to-know principle is, in my view, extremely important. Although I knew enough to know what I was doing, it was in my view better that I did not know every last dotted 'i' and crossed 't'.[4]

John Deverell knew the IRA had to be engaged if there was to be peace, as did Peter Brooke. The problem was how to reach that stage. 'The Mountain Climber' was about to make his final appearance.

At the end of the second hunger strike on 3 October 1981, Brendan Duddy and Michael Oatley, the latter now back in London, had agreed that the conflict was currently frozen as Mrs Thatcher had no intention of engaging with the IRA. Brendan had no doubt that at some stage the British would be back. He was right. Ten years later Michael Oatley returned to Derry. By then the political landscape had changed with Peter Brooke, now supported by the new Prime Minister, John Major, making it clear that the British were ready to talk once the IRA ended its campaign of violence.

During the decade that followed the hunger strike, the back-channel link remained in being and Oatley stayed in touch with Brendan, who intermittently kept his IRA contacts warm despite the chill outside, convinced that at some stage the deep freeze would thaw.

In February 1991 Oatley was about to retire from SIS and felt he would like to spend his final months in office making use of his long-standing connection with Brendan one more time to see if he could have any influence on the situation before he left the stage.

We still had an asset in Brendan Duddy in the existence of the
Link and the history of trust and discretion which had been created
[during the 1975 ceasefire and the near resolution of the first hunger
strike in 1980]. It seemed a waste to walk away and just forget all
that drama and the mutual confidence we had once shared while
bringing in the peat [for the fire in Brendan's 'wee parlour' in the
lead-up to the 1975 ceasefire]. I'd been continuing to keep in touch
with the situation and have conversations with Brendan from time
to time. It did seem, during 1990 and the early part of 1991, that
there might be a mood developing within the Provisional leadership
where a political strategy, as an alternative to violence, might be
something that they would consider pursuing. It was a personal
initiative. I hadn't asked permission to do it or got any political
clearance.[5]

Oatley got in touch with Brendan to test the water, to see if Martin
McGuinness would be interested in having an informal meeting.
Brendan agreed it was 'time that things moved on a bit' and that it was
an idea worth pursuing. He then contacted McGuinness either directly
(Brendan was often in personal touch with McGuinness) or through
the usual channels. One of those channels was Noel Gallagher, a friend
of both parties. Gallagher was about to play a significant role in what
was soon to evolve into 'Operation Chiffon'.

Gallagher, a Derry coal merchant and a child of the Troubles, had
grown up with Martin McGuinness in the Bogside and had been best
man at his wedding. He was well connected on both sides of the border,
a friend not only of McGuinness but also of Albert Reynolds, the leader
of Fianna Fáil who became Taoiseach in the crucial years of 'Operation
Chiffon' between 1992 and 1993. Reynolds and Gallagher had much
in common besides being teetotal and smoking the same cigarettes.
Gallagher was Reynolds' main contact in the North and Reynolds
valued Gallagher's friendship and opinion. Reynolds writes:

He was a dedicated Republican desperate to see an end to the
Troubles. He was very knowledgeable and well connected with
some of the leading figures in the IRA. Whenever he came down
to Dublin he would call in to see me for a cup of tea. He was a

regular visitor. We talked and talked and talked about the North.
Throughout my time as Taoiseach he was often a well-informed and
helpful link in introducing me to many people in the North, on
both sides, who would become very active in working with me to
make the peace process a success.[6]

The feedback that Brendan got from Martin McGuinness was that
he was interested in meeting Michael Oatley, having consulted the
Army Council who gave him the go-ahead but only on the basis of a
listening brief.

The agreed venue for the meeting was to be Bernadette Mount's
house. The scenario was so designed that, should Oatley be carpeted
for a highly unauthorised meeting with McGuinness, there would be
a credible defence to hand: that he just happened to be in Derry and
popped in to see Bernie for old times' sake, remembering how she had
smuggled IRA leaders across the border and provided B&B during the
1975 IRA ceasefire. Bernie also had a connection with McGuinness,
as one of his daughters worked in the dress shop in Derry that Bernie
managed for Brendan as part of his business portfolio.

Oatley was confident that McGuinness would be discreet about the
meeting. Both sides were acutely aware of the need for confidentiality,
which had been carefully maintained over so many years. McGuinness
and Oatley then adjourned to Bernie's living room for their private
meeting. Bernie, like Brendan, wasn't in on the privileged conversation
but thought, from her brief observation of their time together before
and after withdrawing to her living room, that they seemed to 'gel well
together.' Oatley was impressed by McGuinness.

> It was rather like talking to a ranking British army officer of one of
> the tougher regiments like the Paras or the SAS. I thought him very
> serious and responsible about the situation he occupied. I didn't see
> him as someone who enjoyed getting people killed. He managed
> to keep himself extremely well informed about politics and had a
> sophisticated view as to what was going on in British political life.[7]

McGuinness and Oatley talked privately for several hours while Brendan
stood by outside. Oatley, now face to face with McGuinness, was diplomati-
cally blunt.

I said I assumed he would recognise that he'd been a significant member of the leadership for a very long time and that the IRA hadn't really achieved anything for many years in terms of advancing its objective, although it continued to give the security forces a difficult time. A lot of people had been killed but nothing tangible had been achieved. On the side of the British Government, there was clearly a willingness to go on for ever, if necessary, with a policy of containment, which was being quite effective at that stage. I thought that perhaps he should recognise that, in the end, there would be a change of leadership in the republican movement and that there were only so many years left during which he would play a leading role. I pointed out there was a considerable change in the political circumstances in which we all found ourselves with the development of the European Union, and that if he was minded to pursue a political course, there might be things that the British Government could do to help. I emphasised that I didn't have any authority to offer anything, but he was quite happy to discuss these possibilities in a hypothetical way and in a very positive way.[8]§

Oatley had no illusions about McGuinness.

He was a likeable, strong and impressive man to meet, clearly honest and dedicated to his cause. He convinced himself that he was fighting the British establishment but very many innocent people who had nothing to do with the British establishment suffered as a result of his activities and his presiding over assassinations and torture.[9]

Brendan, who had arranged the meeting and set up the dinner with Bernie, was impressed by the relationship he saw unfolding, 'like a couple wanting to get together to enter a courtship' – perhaps said with a degree of exaggeration. The informal symposium was a watershed for both sides. Oatley wrote a detailed report of his conversation with

§The meeting with McGuinness happened well before Brexit, when the UK left the European Union on 31 January 2020, forty-seven years after joining what was then the European Economic Community on 1 January 1973.

McGuinness and on his return to London went to see Sir John Chilcot, the Permanent Under Secretary (PUS) at the Northern Ireland Office.

> My position, in discussing this with John Chilcot, was I had deliberately done this without authority – which was of course very naughty of me – but I wasn't sure that the NIO would have felt like making this initiative at this stage. I said the position which I observe is that there is an interest in pursuing the political course, though perhaps not very quickly, and that there is something either to encourage or discourage, and obviously what you do about it is up to you. The NIO's response was, 'Thank you. Interesting.' That was the end of the story and the end of my involvement.[10]

Oatley's report to Chilcot was to play a crucial role in the events that followed. At the centre of those events was Michael Oatley's successor, the former MI6 officer now working for MI5 whom I refer to simply as Robert. 'Operation Chiffon' was about to be born.

PART III

22

Robert: the Third Man

Robert was the Third Man in the trilogy of MI6 and MI5 officers – Frank Steele, Michael Oatley and now Robert. As I mentioned earlier, I first met Robert in the autumn of 1999 in the pouring rain in his farmyard many miles from London when he had simply, and rather convincingly, denied that he was the person I believed he was. It was a case, he said, of mistaken identity. It was over two decades later, in June 2021, that I received that astonishing letter, in which he wrote, 'for a variety of reasons, I could now give you some background which might fill some gaps – were you so interested'. Among those reasons were the deaths of his wife and Martin McGuinness.

There was a phone number on the letter so I hesitatingly picked up the phone and rang Robert. He sounded very different from the person I had met in the farmyard when he had denied everything. I thanked him for his letter and admitted my surprise at receiving it after so many years. I asked if I could come and see him and he agreed. He greeted me with a smile and a friendly handshake. He was relaxed, and looked fit and well for someone who must have been in his late eighties. There was no doubt that on this occasion he was pleased to see me, unlike on my last visit, which he remembered but may have preferred to forget. He said I had appeared 'like a genie out of the bottle' and told me how he had reacted to my sudden appearance.

> I couldn't believe it. I thought, 'Why? Oh dear! Oh dear!' I know what the orders are if approached by the press. You deny everything. I was merely following standard procedure. Never admit anything

and report it – which is exactly what I did. Yes, I was lying to you.
I lied about everything you asked to try and establish the truth.
I remember you leaving your *Provos* book. My neighbour must have
given it to me via our postman, who remarked on seeing its title
and cover (a photo of Adams and McGuinness carrying a coffin),
'Do you think our neighbour has been in the IRA?' My wife was
horrified! Absolutely horrified. It did distress her so. For her it
was like a ghost from the past. She hated the whole business of
Northern Ireland with me going across backward and forward. Yes,
it [your visit] was just a shock. I hadn't expected anything like that.[1]

Robert followed instructions to the letter and duly reported my visit,
noting that it had ended 'with a friendly handshake' and that it had been
'relaxed on both sides – on the surface'. The only point of divergence
in our memories of that encounter was the question of whether Robert
had invited me in out of the rain. I remembered being left on the back
doorstep. Robert's recollection was different.

I think what I might have done was to have left you at the kitchen
door and dashed in to get your *Provos* book, avoiding the kitchen
where my wife might have been. My study was the closest room
to the back door and also where I would have seen anybody on
business – not that I wanted your business at that stage. I have no
doubt whatsoever because I can remember that we stood facing
each other and you kept putting more questions to me. I think your
mind must have been on what question can you put next.

At our second meeting, in 2021, Robert said he was also keen to make
sure I didn't see the two authorised histories of MI5 and MI6 on his
bookshelves.* That was the first of a series of meetings in which he told
me his remarkable story. At the very beginning, I asked him why he
had decided to contact me. He said he was concerned about certain
glaring inaccuracies in the reporting of his role – the main one being

---

*Christopher Andrew, *The Defence of the Realm: The Authorised History of MI5*, Allen Lane,
London, 2009, and Keith Jeffery, *MI6: The History of the Secret Intelligence Service, 1909–1949*,
Bloomsbury, London, 2010.

that he had manufactured the highly controversial 'The conflict is over' message, alleged to have been sent from Martin McGuinness to the British Government.

> Increasingly I felt I'm never going to get justice. I had been accused, anonymously but in print, of making up an essential message from the IRA ['The conflict is over']. I'm never going to hear that it [the misrepresentation] has seen the light of day so people know what it was like for me, and how it came about, because it's all locked away in the files of the Security Service. I must get these things put right and the only person who can do it is you. You're the only person who has been in touch with me and who writes very knowledgeably. I'd also just seen your most recent BBC television documentary [*Ireland After Partition*, BBC2, 14 June 2021] and that jolted my mind. I thought that when I was dead, my son would be the one to give a eulogy in church. That's not much good then. I'm not going to be there. I'd like what I did to be remembered. People will get things wrong and they would place the wrong emphasis on things, but you wouldn't because you understand Northern Ireland. The more I thought about it, the more I thought I'd have to make contact with you.[†]

[†]The narrative that follows is based on interviews with Robert on 12 August 2021, 6–7 September 2021, 3–4 March 2022 and 25–26 July 2022.

23

Operation Chiffon

After Michael Oatley retired in February 1991, intense discussions ensued in London and Belfast about what was to happen to Brendan now that Michael Oatley was no longer working with him. The back channel was still known in Government only to Sir John Chilcot, the Permanent Under Secretary at the Northern Ireland Office. Around the time of his retirement, Oatley had circulated a full historical account of his dealings with Brendan, the back channel and Martin McGuinness for a strictly limited readership in MI6 and MI5. Senior ministers at Westminster were kept completely in the dark.

Chilcot feared the shattering political consequences should it ever become public knowledge that the Government was in contact with the IRA, given that the Secretary of State, Peter Brooke, had given assurances in the House of Commons, in particular to unionists like David Trimble, that there had been no meetings with the IRA. In the event of word leaking out, there was a Plan B – a carefully worded spin. Although Oatley was still working for MI6 at the time of his meeting with McGuinness, it could be spun that he had retired that week, which was true, although chronologically it was after the meeting in Bernie Mount's house.

Chilcot was said to have been 'fascinated' by Oatley's report that the IRA was interested in moving towards a political solution and a negotiated peace. There was, however, some scepticism in Chilcot's inner circle that Brendan could be the magic bullet to peace. Nevertheless on balance the inclination was to press on and arrange a replacement for Michael Oatley.

Following his retirement, Oatley was asked by the Security Service to introduce a successor to Brendan. Oatley strongly urged that John Deverell, the Director and Coordinator of Intelligence (DCI) in Northern Ireland, should be selected but Sir Patrick Walker, then Director General of MI5, turned this down as it would conflict with Deverell's official position. Oatley, loyal to SIS, wanted an MI6 officer to succeed him but the Security Service, MI5, wanted its own man. A tense tug of war ensued between Stella Rimington, then MI5's Deputy Director General, and Michael Oatley. Stella was furious when she heard that Oatley had met McGuinness in early 1991. In the end Oatley lost out.

Robert had reached retirement age, and was looking forward to spending time at home with his wife and living a less fraught and dangerous life, enjoying their hobbies of bird watching and walking in the English countryside. But those plans were shelved when he received an invitation from John Deverell, an old friend from his Oxford University and Colonial Service days, to join MI5. Robert accepted the offer.

On joining the Security Service in 1988 Robert had no idea of what lay ahead, although he was familiar with the Irish situation. It was also the period when he first became aware of Michael Oatley's role in dealing with Brendan, who Robert, erroneously, assumed was an agent and whose identity was kept secret in accordance with standard tradecraft.

John Deverell initially asked Robert to take on a job in security, which he did from 1988 until early 1991, unaware at the time of the sensitivities around finding someone to look after Brendan. Although Robert also knew Michael at SIS, he knew nothing of Michael's long history and relationship with Brendan. He was soon to find out when, in early 1991, a few weeks after Oatley's retirement in February, MI5's Director General, Sir Patrick Walker, asked him to look after Brendan. Robert was briefed on the history of the back channel and accepted the challenge.

By this time there had already been sea changes in the intelligence agencies' connections with Northern Ireland as a result of a turf war. It was decided that MI5, the domestic intelligence agency, should be responsible for the domestic problem of Northern Ireland and not SIS, the foreign intelligence agency responsible for overseas operations. It marked regime change, with MI5 now responsible for looking after Brendan Duddy and the back channel to Martin McGuinness and the IRA.

'Operation Chiffon' was born in 1991 shortly after Michael Oatley's retirement. It was a clandestine operation under the aegis of MI5, whose purpose was described in MI5's archive as 'to achieve a ceasefire and talks' with the Provisional IRA (PIRA).[1] 'Operation Chiffon' was the apogee of the work that Frank Steele, Michael Oatley and Brendan Duddy had begun in the early 1970s and would not have been possible without their groundwork carried out over nearly twenty years.

Robert remembers being called to a meeting with MI5's Director General, Sir Patrick Walker, in early to mid-1991 when Sir Patrick briefed his Deputy, Stella Rimington, on 'Chiffon'. At the time, she knew nothing about it, as 'Chiffon' was secret. Stella Rimington was appointed MI5's Director General later the following year and proved fully supportive of Robert, 'Operation Chiffon' and the back channel.

Robert's involvement in 'Chiffon' signified the beginning of a new phase and was marked by a change of operational codenames. 'Soon', as Brendan had been known for two decades, was binned. He was given a new codename and was to become the lynchpin of 'Operation Chiffon'.

With 'Chiffon' now up and running, John Deverell and John Chilcot decided that the Northern Ireland Secretary, Peter Brooke, had to be brought into the loop as he, like the rest of the Cabinet and, at this stage, Prime Minister John Major, had only a general idea of what was going on in the shadows. John Deverell arranged a private meeting with Peter Brooke, most likely with John Chilcot in attendance, and informed the Secretary of State about 'Operation Chiffon', although he would not have mentioned its codename. Deverell warned Brooke that if anything went wrong and the Government's unofficial contact with the IRA became public knowledge, he would be 'the first person in the firing line'. Brooke was presented with the options: to shut down the contact (Brendan) with all the attendant sensitivities and danger, or to give it a new lease of life in view of the encouraging noises that Michael Oatley had reported back from Martin McGuinness. Brooke favoured the latter. 'It would be silly to throw it away,' he said as he later told me in an interview; 'I was quite prepared to take the damage if anything happened.'[2] Brooke was prepared to throw his political weight behind 'Operation Chiffon' at considerable risk to his political career.

With 'Chiffon' now an MI5 operation, the copious volumes of files on Brendan were passed from MI6 to the Security Service, where they lay unopened until Robert took over. His first task was to familiarise himself with Brendan's back story as recorded in the 'Soon' files that stretched way back to the pre-ceasefire days of 1975. At one stage Brendan asked Michael Oatley if he could see his own files. The request was refused.

Robert's second and most crucial task was to devise a way of contacting Brendan and establishing a relationship as Michael Oatley had so successfully done over so many years. It wasn't going to be easy: Robert would be approaching him out of the blue without any personal introduction from Oatley, which Oatley had not been inclined to do as he (Oatley) was believed to have wanted to carry on working with Brendan himself. But as far as MI5 was concerned, that was not an option. Robert then spent the next two and a half months from February to mid-May 1991 planning his approach to Brendan and devising the best way to meet him on a credible pretext. Robert had the spy's tradecraft to fall back on, which he had been trained to use and employ over many years.

He knew from his own research, ploughing through local newspapers and the *Londonderry Handbook*, that Brendan was Chairman of the local Chamber of Trade. That, he decided, was the way in. He would devise a cover story, or, in intelligence terminology, a 'legend'. Robert's legend was to become 'Colin Ferguson', with a business card that described him as a representative of Euroassets, a business consultancy with an address in the West End of London. Euroassets was a shell company administered by an office, totally unconnected with MI5, which answered letters and phone calls on behalf of any absent company executives. In the case of the client 'Colin Ferguson', the messages would have been passed to a PO box. The mechanism was devised as an overt way of doing business that would not present problems were it to be penetrated by the IRA. The cover company's story was that it had been engaged by a leading German department store, anonymous in the legend for commercial reasons, to search for a site for a multi-million-pound retail development in Derry. The subterfuge was strengthened by a friend Robert had made in Düsseldorf who was prepared to vouch for Robert if Euroassets was ever traced.

Robert knew he was running a risk as he had no documents to prove that he was 'Colin Ferguson' and was therefore, against all intelligence practice, forced to use a double alias.

To help his bona fides Robert phoned and wrote to various Northern Ireland development agencies, of which there were many at the time, whose names would be useful in conversation with Brendan. The province was desperate for investment, with Catholic unemployment in Derry running at 40 per cent in the 1990s.³ Robert also needed to organise his own flights, hotels and car hire, which he did through the same business-address agency.

Legend apart, Robert needed authenticity, validation to show Brendan that he was working for the British Government. John Deverell obliged and got John Chilcot to sign a letter saying that Robert was the Secretary of State's representative and the Government wished to resume contact through him. On 23 May 1991, with his legend now in place, Robert was ready to drive the seventy miles from Belfast to Derry. Once in the city, he rang Brendan from a public telephone box.

Robert was nervous, despite such subterfuges being part of SIS's well-rehearsed playbook. He introduced himself over the phone and said he needed Brendan's advice for the investment report he was writing regarding a new retail centre that would bring desperately needed jobs to Derry. Brendan was hesitant, showing no sign of any great enthusiasm for the project. He remembers the phone call.

> He sounded a very polite, nice man. He said, 'I'm interested in
> bringing some employment to the City and I believe that you
> can help as you're Chairman of Londonderry Chamber of Trade.'
> I just sighed and said, 'I'm very busy at the moment.' Then he said,
> 'Can I come and see you? It would only take maybe half an hour.'
> I said, 'No.'⁴

Brendan finally gave in and agreed to meet. Robert was hugely relieved that his persistence and tradecraft had finally paid off. He had an appointment. The telephone box could almost have heard his sigh of relief. There was no Plan B. He had imagined that Brendan, being involved in property development, would have jumped at the welcome opportunity for his job-starved city, yet he had shown not the slightest interest: but at least he had agreed to meet. It was the opening Robert needed and had worked so hard to achieve. Brendan gave Robert directions to his house, which weren't necessary as Robert had already recced the area and identified Brendan's unpretentious post-war villa, tucked away in a relatively quiet, middle-class suburb, a short drive from the city centre.

Robert first did an anonymous pass of the house and was a little concerned to see a police car blocking the narrow entrance that opened on to a modest parking area that seemed to hold more cars than it had been designed for. He wondered, as I did when I later became a frequent visitor to Brendan's house, at the parking skills necessary to get them all in without damaging the paintwork. There were several RUC officers standing outside. Robert walked to the front door and rang the bell. He could feel the police officers' eyes 'boring into my back'. One of Brendan's two sons, Larry or Brendan Jnr, opened the door and asked Robert to wait as their father was in his study with an RUC officer.

Robert sat down on the well-worn sofa in the comfortably furnished entrance hall, straining his ears to hear what Brendan and his visitor were talking about. His anxieties were never far beneath the surface. Was Brendan about to be arrested? If so, Robert would have a serious problem in looking after him, as Brendan was not an agent but his security required a similar degree of care. The police and army knew nothing about 'Operation Chiffon' and Brendan's role in it. Which identity would he use when he was finally invited into Brendan's study? He sat there trying to appear as nonchalant as possible, reading and then rereading the popular local paper, the *Derry Journal*, his mind racing over what to do if his carefully arranged cover plan to meet Brendan face to face bit the dust. After a wait that seemed much longer than it actually was, the RUC officer emerged and one of Brendan's sons 'rather curtly' showed Robert into the study. 'At last,' Robert thought, but with some dismay he saw that Brendan's other son was already in the room with his father. Robert's plan was to have a private one-to-one with Brendan, for his ears only, given the sensitivity of what he was about to impart.

Robert now tentatively began to follow the script he had so carefully prepared. He started to explain his cover mission but was interrupted when, a few minutes later, one of the other sons came into the room.

Everything seemed to be going wrong. Robert could only reveal the real purpose of his visit when he was alone with Brendan. He said he thought of the TV commercial for Hamlet cigars which suggested that, when everything went wrong, the only thing to do was to relax and take a puff on a Hamlet. Meanwhile Brendan was rapidly losing interest, although he recognised the kind of person Robert was, describing him as being 'Very nice, very soft, very gentle. He starts talking and I'm switched off completely. My purpose was to get him in, be polite – never be rude – and get him out again.'

Fifteen minutes into the meeting, Robert, fearing that he could not keep on treading water for much longer as 'Colin Ferguson', finally got his break when first one and then the other son left the office to make coffee. The audience had gone. Robert seized the moment, leaped to his feet and, producing John Chilcot's letter of validation from his pocket, like a rabbit out of a hat, handed it over. 'I've come to you from the Secretary of State, Peter Brooke,' he announced to a startled Brendan Duddy.

Brendan looked stunned, read the letter, jumped up and shook Robert's hand enthusiastically – and then shook his hand again. Brendan remembers his reaction to the revelation. 'At that second, I knew it was all over. John Major and Peter Brooke would not be sending someone over to talk to me if it wasn't the beginning of the beginning.' Brendan instantly knew that the bamboo pipe, under new management, was up and running again, and was delighted that, even though Michael Oatley had retired, he (Brendan) was still at the heart of it.

But there was still the matter of identities. Robert explained that he wasn't 'Colin Ferguson' and that his real name was Robert. He gave no more detail, unlike Michael Oatley, who had worked with Brendan under his full name. It was only when Robert met Martin McGuinness and Gerry Kelly at a face-to-face meeting at Brendan's house two years later, in March 1993, that Robert realised that Brendan had given him the alias 'Fred'. As Brendan said, with a name like 'Fred' there was nothing to lose. 'Fred' was the codename by which the IRA subsequently got to know Robert.

Brendan and Robert then adjourned to Brendan's 'wee room', with the sofa, the easy chair and the peat fire smouldering in the corner, where, as Brendan said, 'peace was made'. Robert remembers his first meeting with Brendan as being incredibly long.

I made five trips to the loo to relieve myself of the endless cups of
tea. Brendan talked in an unending torrent in a way that was to
become all too familiar to me over the next two and a half years.
He told me his life's history and the essential part he had played
in trying to modify PIRA's policy. His special link was to Martin
McGuinness who, he said, privately wanted to stop the conflict but
didn't know how. Brendan was trying to steer him but McGuinness
said he needed British backing. I did not know how far I could trust
his judgement or accuracy, but all he told me at this initial meeting
fitted in with what I had read in his files and with what Oatley had
told John Chilcot about his own meeting with McGuinness at the
beginning of 1991.[5]

I knew at first hand that Brendan could talk for Ireland. In the course
of the largely one-sided conversation, Brendan wanted to know from
Robert what message he had brought from London that he was to pass
on to the Provisionals. Robert replied that the only message was that
the British were ready to listen to whatever they had to say but could
not engage in any dialogue until they stopped the killing. Brendan was
underwhelmed and said this was a negative response and a block to any
peace move by the IRA. Robert stressed that this was British policy, no
talks without there being a ceasefire first. On a personal and unspoken
level, Robert agreed with Brendan and was not convinced that the
British Government's current approach, with its categoric insistence on
the primacy of a ceasefire, would in itself be the means to the end of
the 'armed struggle'. Robert was to spend most of the next two years,
with an exhausting investment of determination, courage and subtlety,
trying to change Government policy so that it no longer insisted on an
IRA ceasefire before any face-to-face talks. Robert knew this was the
prerequisite for any movement towards peace.

Brendan then let off steam about John Hume, the SDLP leader
who was also working for peace in a more conventional way by
engaging with the Dublin Government and Gerry Adams, who in
turn was engaging with Catholic priests at the Clonard monastery in
West Belfast. The careers of John Hume and Brendan Duddy, both
Derry men, had been closely entwined from the days of the civil
rights movement in 1968. Brendan was envious of Hume's success and
high media profile, something Brendan could not enjoy because his

activities and connection with the back channel were inevitably and necessarily clandestine. He felt that Hume had gone on to become the leading Catholic politician in Ireland with all the limelight that went with it, whereas he (Brendan) had made his money through property, hotels, restaurants and shops. Brendan saw himself as an unrecognised political leader who had devoted himself to becoming, as he saw it, PIRA's political guru, with his own agenda of pushing the republican movement towards compromise and peace. Brendan was the secret peacemaker.

The conversation then moved on to Michael Oatley, with whom Brendan had worked since 1974. To Robert's surprise, Brendan told him about a particular disagreement he had had with Michael, despite the closeness of their relationship. He said Oatley had left SIS with a pension and a decoration, whereas Brendan was left with nothing except the abiding memory of all he had done to further peace and the personal risks he had taken to help advance it. He had expected a pension from MI6 but had never received one, which left him feeling aggrieved. Oatley, believing Brendan to be a successful and wealthy businessman, says Brendan had no need of one and insists the question was never raised. Brendan disagrees. However, when Brendan's business was suffering, not just because of the ongoing conflict but because of the time he was spending dealing with the back channel and going backwards and forwards with messages, Oatley arranged for substantial funds to be provided to make sure Brendan's business didn't go under.

Thinking quickly on his feet, Robert realised that that was something that he could probably arrange without too much trouble with his new masters in MI5. 'Having got the thing going, money would not have been an obstacle.' Money opened doors. John Deverell and John Chilcot knew how important Brendan's role had been so far and how much they depended on him to continue to push the peace process forward. Robert said he would see what was possible and later arranged a pension, to be paid when Brendan's work was done.

After Robert's first meeting at Brendan's house when Robert had produced the letter of authorisation from John Chilcot, the two men got down to business. Their first proper meeting lasted eight hours – from around 1 p.m. until around 9 p.m. – in which Brendan went over in exhaustive detail what he had done with Michael Oatley since the early 1970s and Robert set out what he and the British Government, given the renewed relationship, were hoping to achieve in the months and possibly years ahead. Robert was pretty wrung out at the end of the session but thought it had gone well. He then left Brendan's house and drove, 'in a slightly dazed state', to the outskirts of Derry where he pulled in by a phone box, and rang John Deverell. Deverell was relieved to hear that Robert was well and still alive and said he had been about to ask the RUC to call at Brendan's house on some pretext, in case Robert had come to harm. From the start, Deverell, knowing the risks that Michael Oatley would have taken, knew the risks Robert was taking.

From that first meeting Robert also knew that at such meetings he could glean valuable intelligence. Brendan was not an MI5 agent. His mission was not to be a spy but to do whatever was necessary to push the peace process forward.

> Without people like Michael Oatley and Robert, we would not have the peace process. The notion that every arm of the British Government is ambivalent towards Ireland is simply not true. Some of the most honourable men I have ever met have been members of the secret services.[6]

Brendan's mission was to do whatever was necessary to push the peace process forward. His debriefings with Robert were invaluable and helped paint a picture of the mood on the republican side. Robert was then able to write up detailed accounts which were read by the handful of top officials in the Northern Ireland Office responsible for framing policy and by Secretary of State Peter Brooke, now briefed on 'Operation Chiffon'.

In the ensuing two years, from 1991 to 1993, Robert wrote dozens of reports, the central theme of which was that the leaders of the IRA, principally Martin McGuinness and those close to him, wanted peace; that it was a genuine intention that might ultimately be supported by the Provisional Army Council, despite its factions of 'hawks' and 'doves'; and finally and crucially, that there was a need for a positive response from the British Government to show that it was sincere in wanting peace in order to help convince sceptics on the Army Council that 'Perfidious Albion' could be trusted. For the IRA that would be a huge ask, a gigantic leap of faith. Not surprisingly this was difficult because there was a long legacy of distrust, the bitter fruit of decades of the conflict that both sides were now seeking to end. Trust was in short supply, not least in the eyes of McGuinness and the IRA leadership who believed that the British had conned the republican movement into calling the ceasefire in 1975. This may have been convenient wishful thinking on the part of the Provisionals insofar as that may have been the end result of the ceasefire but it was never its initial intention: the British were genuinely trying to find a road to peace, even at that time. Above all, Robert had to trust Brendan himself.

> Was he telling me the truth or concocting stories? I believed, by checking his stories with what we already knew, he was telling me the truth, despite his personal, strongly held convictions.[7]

Robert was soon to find out the risks Brendan was running and how he put his life on the line.

24

Brendan: a Terrifying Interrogation

For the next six months the back channel was worryingly silent, perhaps because the ever suspicious Army Council was deliberating whether the 'Brits' were serious or whether it was being led into another carefully prepared trap, as its members were convinced had happened in 1975. Robert was also beginning to be concerned about the back-up he was receiving from the Northern Ireland Office. He found John Chilcot's Deputy, Quentin Thomas, sceptical about the value of Brendan. As for Chilcot himself, Robert found him a likeable, supremely polite and quietly spoken mandarin but not someone who was always easy to read.

> It was difficult to get a one-to-one with Chilcot. He was not sympathetic to the world of espionage and agents and basically disapproved. He wasn't interested in my show and was more interested in the broad and bigger picture of talks with the Dublin Government [and constitutional political parties on both sides of the border]. I was reliant on John Deverell. Perhaps I should have been making far more fuss.

Robert was also conscious of his personal relationship with John Deverell, his friend and mentor who had offered him a post-retirement job. Robert didn't wish to appear to be rocking the boat in difficult and dangerous political waters.

It was mid-July 1991 when MI5's duty officer rang Robert at around 7 a.m. one day to say that Brendan had rung during the night, saying 'It's urgent but don't wake him.' Robert had given Brendan a contact number, probably one that would always be manned. Robert returned the call later that morning to be told that Brendan was coming to Heathrow and needed to meet urgently. Robert was to go to the Athenaeum Hotel in Piccadilly. Being security conscious and still with a nagging feeling that Brendan might be under the IRA's control, Robert used an MI5 car and driver to take him to the meeting, tailed by a back-up car as insurance. It was clearly a critical meeting held before Robert was absolutely sure of his ground with Brendan. He could have secretly recorded it but thought it would be unwise and decided against it.

Brendan, Robert thought, was exercised about something. He wasn't his normal ebullient, garrulous self. He was clearly worried. He began with the dramatic announcement that this was probably the end of his long history of the British using him as the back channel to the IRA. He then explained why. He said he had told McGuinness a few weeks earlier about his eight-hour meeting with Robert at Brendan's house. McGuinness listened 'impassively', which was not a good omen. McGuinness was deeply suspicious.

A few days later, Brendan was instructed to be at a certain street corner in Derry at a certain time. He obeyed, no doubt with some trepidation. A car picked him up with a driver he did not know or recognise. The driver kept himself to himself as they drove across the border, only a few miles outside Derry, and then for around forty miles or so along country lanes into the hills of Donegal. The ominous silence in the car got Brendan worried. There was no small talk. Where was he being taken? For what purpose? And would he survive whatever lay at the end of the road?

The car stopped at a lonely farmhouse. Few words were exchanged as Brendan was led into a room where five people, one a woman, were sitting on one side of a table. The only person he recognised was Martin McGuinness. Brendan was told to sit in a chair facing his interrogators. A chilling two-hour session followed, conducted by McGuinness in ice-cold tones. The others asked only the occasional question. McGuinness was in absolute control. The atmosphere was hostile and Brendan was extremely frightened. He knew that, beneath McGuinness's charming and affable public exterior, the most powerful IRA leader in the North had the power of life and death.[1]

The focus of Brendan's interrogation by McGuinness was his relationship with Robert – or 'Fred' as the IRA now knew him, having been told by Brendan that it was the name by which he was known. Was 'Fred' working for British intelligence and, if so, was Brendan working with him? Robert remembers Brendan telling him that McGuinness wanted to know everything about that initial meeting in his house and everything that Robert had said. Others in the room suspected that Robert had come 'to sniff out their military positions'. Robert asked Brendan if, during his interrogation, he had revealed Robert's intelligence connections. Brendan said he had 'kept quiet' about that 'otherwise I [Brendan] would have been a dead man'.

Brendan survived the nerve-racking interrogation by the skin of his teeth and managed to avoid providing McGuinness with the confirmation that he was seeking, that Robert was working for British intelligence. Had he done so, it might well have been Brendan's death warrant and Robert's too. Brendan was then ordered by McGuinness to break off all contact with 'Fred' and get in touch again with Michael Oatley, whom the IRA leadership had trusted, believing that only Oatley could wield the influence with the British Government that mattered. It was a mark of McGuinness's respect for Oatley. But, for the British, Oatley was no longer an option, nor was it for Brendan despite the IRA's insistence on Oatley, as the NIO had ruled out any further dealings with Michael.

Having listened to Brendan's chilling account of his interrogation by McGuinness, Robert tried to stay 'as nonchalant as possible' while inside feeling 'cold and depressed' as he saw Brendan's involvement – and therefore his own – in 'Operation Chiffon' disappearing in the shadows of a remote farmhouse on a dark Donegal night. In an attempt to retrieve the position, Robert impressed upon Brendan the impossibility of Michael Oatley being recalled to deal with Brendan and emphasised the uniqueness of his own position. Again he stressed that the British Government was serious and that Brendan should leave the IRA in no doubt about that, while at the same time repeating the qualification that it would have nothing to say to the IRA until it ended the violence.

Robert and Brendan left the Athenaeum Hotel, with Robert depressed by what he had heard and Brendan relieved to have unburdened himself. The meeting had lasted three hours. They then said goodbye on the pavement outside. Brendan said it would probably be 'goodbye' for the last time. Inwardly Robert wondered how he could possibly regain the initiative. But at least Brendan was still alive.

In the days that followed, Robert turned his mind to how he might retrieve the situation, establish his bona fides with McGuinness and the IRA and convince them that he really was the Government's emissary, in effect the British Government Representative, as Oatley had been known, with specific instructions to work towards peace. He remembered that way back in 1972 when the IRA had declared a three-day Christmas truce[2] at the end of the bloodiest year in the conflict, the Northern Ireland Secretary, Willie Whitelaw, had agreed reciprocal confidence-building measures by using prearranged phrases in a radio broadcast. The IRA would be given details of the particular phrases in advance to indicate that the contact with the British Government was genuine. Robert suggested that John Deverell should ask the Northern Ireland Secretary, Peter Brooke, if he would be prepared to do something similar. Brooke agreed but felt the opportunity would have to wait until the autumn.

With the plan in place, Robert rang Brendan from a Northern Ireland Office phone at Stormont with news of the mechanism for a potential breakthrough that would hopefully get things back on track. At least, Robert thought, if the IRA was monitoring the NIO's phones, it would help establish his credentials.

To Robert's relief, he found Brendan very relaxed on the phone and he expressed surprise that Robert had not rung earlier. It was as if the disconcerting meeting at the Athenaeum Hotel had never happened. Brendan asked, stressing the urgency, if they could meet for lunch in two hours' time at the Waterfoot Hotel at the Belfast end of Derry's Foyle Bridge. Two hours, Robert thought, would just give him time to drive from Stormont to the bridge, known in Derry as 'John Hume's Bridge' as he had facilitated EU funds to finance it.

Robert told Deverell of Brendan's insistence and said he had to leave now and there was no time to arrange armed surveillance. Deverell had cause to be worried, conscious of the threat to Robert's safety in the wake of Brendan's interrogation in Donegal and his subsequent debrief by Robert in London. Brendan had assured Robert that the Waterfoot restaurant was secure as it was used by businessmen and was on the 'safe' side of the river, the side where the majority of Derry's Protestant/ unionist community lived. Robert said a quick goodbye to an anxious John Deverell, put his foot down and headed for the Foyle Bridge and Derry, wondering what Brendan wished to impart with such urgency.

To Robert's surprise, Brendan turned up more or less on time and was calm and measured as if his interrogation in the remote Donegal farmhouse or the exchange with Robert at the Athenaeum Hotel in London had never happened. Robert outlined the plan to which Peter Brooke had agreed. Brendan was encouraged and said it might do the trick. Over lunch Brendan expressed concern about knowing only Robert's Christian name in case at some stage he (Brendan) was pressed by McGuinness to provide his full name as proof that Brendan was not being duped by British intelligence. Robert compromised and gave Brendan his middle name, McLaren. Brendan later told the Provisionals that his British contact's name was Robert McLaren. The name was subsequently leaked by the Provisionals with the result that the media came to know, crucially lacking his real surname, that the British Government Representative was a man called Robert McLaren. Without his surname, Robert remained virtually untraceable by the media and also not confirmable by the IRA. Robert left the meeting at the Waterfoot in better spirits, knowing that Brendan was on board with Peter Brooke's plan and finally convinced that Brendan was not going to betray him to the IRA. The return of Michael Oatley to look after Brendan was now a matter of history.

More meetings followed over the summer and early autumn of 1991 when it became clear from Brendan's reporting that the IRA leadership now accepted that, through Brendan, they were once more genuinely in touch with the British Government. To Robert's disappointment there was no response from the IRA to his suggestion that Peter Brooke could include some key phrases buried in one of his speeches as a covert mechanism to establish Robert's bona fides. Later other intelligence did indicate that McGuinness suspected Robert was working for MI5 or MI6, but the fact that it was now accepted that his mission was to work towards peace cancelled out any life-limiting consequences. It was highly unlikely that McGuinness would order the 'execution' of his lifeline to peace. But the risks were still there for both Robert and Brendan.

25

Treading Water

Over the next six months leading into 1992, progress remained painfully slow. Robert felt he was treading water and grew increasingly frustrated. From the beginning of 'Operation Chiffon', John Chilcot had arranged for Robert to have regular briefings on the Government's Northern Ireland policy from his Deputy, Joe Pilling, who was in post at the time before leaving to become Director of Prisons. Robert went to Pilling's office at Stormont wearing his Northern Ireland Office pass. He liked Pilling. He was relaxed and easy to deal with but 'rather broad-brush in discussion'. Crucially Pilling, one of the 'doves' in the Northern Ireland Office, had faith in Brendan. He told Robert, 'When there's a solution in Ireland, I think it will come through Brendan's efforts, rather than from our attempts to find a solution via the Irish Government.' They were words that Robert was greatly reassured to hear. When Joe Pilling moved on, he was succeeded by Quentin Thomas. Robert noted the contrast. 'Thomas was more bureaucratic and agnostic about Brendan's influence with the IRA leadership.'

In the dog days of early 1992, Robert continued to report, based on communications with Brendan, now 'on even better terms with McGuinness', that the IRA was 'willing to stop fighting'. To his dismay and frustration, there was 'no parallel thinking or advice or encouragement from Quentin Thomas, nor from John Chilcot, who, although friendly, I rarely saw'.[1] Robert pressed John Deverell for a regular dialogue with Chilcot, 'whose man I was after all', but Deverell was 'unable or unwilling' to arrange anything. Robert felt increasingly isolated; the sense of direction that 'Operation Chiffon' had originally had appeared to have evaporated.

> I lacked any clear direction as to what I was supposed to be doing
> or saying. There was no strategy for using Brendan and no clear
> idea what we wanted to achieve. We had opened indirect dialogue
> with PIRA but we had no clear idea how to exploit the situation.
> Our only message was 'stop the killing and we'll talk face to face
> with you'. The PIRA leadership, according to Brendan, needed
> help to get off the hook of violence without losing control of their
> followers. I sensed I was dealing with an explosive situation.

Within the IRA's Army Council, there were the same kind of hesitations as within the Northern Ireland Office. Having given David Trimble and the unionists the assurance that the British Government would not talk to 'terrorists' until they ended their military campaign, the Northern Ireland Office was caught on a hook of its own devising, making an end to violence the *sine qua non* of any face-to-face talks with the IRA. Chilcot and Thomas attempted to calm Robert's anxieties by telling him, 'We can get away with your link because we're not in direct contact.' At this stage, this was technically true as it was Brendan who was in touch with the IRA and not Robert. Robert was still not happy and contrasted the way in which the South Africans and the Israelis handled their negotiations with 'terrorists' by dealing directly with Nelson Mandela of the African National Congress and Yasser Arafat of the Palestine Liberation Organisation.

> The factors that should have been present in the thinking of the
> British, in seeking an honourable way out of the situation, were
> totally lacking in the NIO. It existed to protect the Secretary of
> State and to protect his political position.

In March 1992, frustrated by the lack of any discernible progress, Robert seized the initiative and suggested to Quentin Thomas that although the British Government was not allowed to send the IRA any written message, perhaps there could be no objection to giving Brendan a briefing paper on what the British Government's position would be if the IRA were prepared to end the violence. Robert said he could leave it for the IRA leadership to read, although it would not be addressed to them. Thomas embraced the idea and, according to Robert, exclaimed '*Un bout de papier!*' The 'piece of paper' was duly written, signed off by Peter Brooke and handed over to Brendan by Robert. Brendan then delivered it to Noel Gallagher, one of his several conduits to Martin McGuinness. The subsequent feedback via Gallagher did not match the optimism with which the message had been sent. Word came back that it was 'dry like sandpaper, dry as dust and so carefully phrased that it was hard to understand'. Robert was disappointed but recognised that at least it was a start, 'like a puff of smoke from a fire that is hard to light'.

Robert's meetings with Brendan continued through the summer of 1992 at a house that Robert had rented on a six-month lease in County Antrim. An MI5 secretary was on hand to provide the participants with a light lunch and endless cups of tea during meetings which invariably went on for up to six hours. When the lease on the house ran out, Robert reverted to a house that was much closer to Derry and had previously been used by Michael Oatley for his meetings with Brendan. The distance may have been shorter but the meetings were not.

> When we met, Brendan would pontificate for hours, mostly a repetition of what he had said before, and a castigation of us for the lack of any initiative. I was able, however, to extract increasingly good intelligence from him – like the attitude of the PIRA leadership. He didn't reveal any names, claiming that if he knew no names, he could not be accused of revealing any secrets. I was aware that I was telling him detail too as he had to be in a position to speak authoritatively on the British position.

Robert had been authorised to do this as he'd been told the Northern Ireland Office had nothing to hide. This was true, as Robert recalled, but 'a bit of subtlety would have been of value'.

> There was no 'game plan' for what I was doing. I felt I needed guidance, discussion and political direction, instead of which I was left on my own, dealing at one remove with the IRA's leadership in the most crucial matter affecting Irish and probably British politics.

I knew I had to succeed and only consistency and patience would achieve this.

Robert's state of mind wasn't improved when John Chilcot reported a conversation he'd had with John Hume, who told him he knew Brendan Duddy was the British Government's secret link to the IRA, which meant the closely guarded secret, designed to protect Brendan and Robert, and the British Government's 'deniability', was no longer closely guarded. A worried Robert was angry and confronted Brendan with the breach of security.

> He was silent for several minutes. He finally admitted his folly
> and promised he would never repeat it. He had not been able to
> resist showing off to the man who had succeeded where he himself
> wanted to be – at the summit of Irish politics.

And Robert became increasingly depressed by the deteriorating security situation.

Throughout 1992, there had been no sign on the ground that the IRA was minded to temper its military campaign. It set the tone for the rest of the year by detonating a roadside bomb on 17 January that blew up a minibus carrying construction workers on their way home after repairing damage to an army base. The attack came at the Teebane crossroads in County Tyrone, a remote location between Omagh and Cookstown. Seven Protestants were killed and one died later in hospital. The bomb, detonated by a command wire, contained up to 500lb of home-made explosives and left a crater more than twenty feet wide and three feet deep.[2] The IRA claimed the victims were a 'legitimate' target as they had been working on a security-force base. The families of the bereaved and the Protestant community to which they belonged saw it as naked sectarian massacre. At the funeral of one of the victims, the Protestant Bishop of Derry and Raphoe eloquently voiced the feelings of his community:

> It is unthinkable that today's terrorist can become tomorrow's
> politician engaging in dialogue and seeking an acceptable political
> arrangement for this country. Those who plant a massive bomb by

the side of the road and murder innocent men returning home after a day's work have no part to play or contribution to make to the political and economic life of this society.[3]

Sectarian revenge was soon to follow. On 5 February 1992, two gunmen from the loyalist Ulster Freedom Fighters walked into Sean Graham's bookmaker's shop on Belfast's predominantly nationalist Lower Ormeau Road and shot dead five Catholics, including a sixteen-year-old boy and a pensioner. As the gunmen left, they shouted 'Remember Teebane!' One of those injured described the scene.

I just lay there and prayed that the shooting would stop. It seemed to go on for a lifetime. People were yelling out in agony. You could hardly see anything. The room was filled with gun smoke and the smell would have choked you. My life will never be the same again. The things I saw that day will follow me to the grave.[4]

In the Irish Republic the day after the slaughter, Albert Reynolds became the leader of Fianna Fáil and Taoiseach. He, too, was shocked by the killings and determined to do all he could, in partnership with John Major and conversations with his friend, Noel Gallagher, to try and end the bloodshed and bring peace. It was to become another axis of the process.

The SAS was soon in action again. On 16 February, four IRA men were shot dead in a carefully prepared ambush, again the result of precise intelligence. Minutes earlier they had opened fire on Coalisland RUC station with a 12.7mm Russian heavy machine gun, mounted on the back of a hijacked lorry. It was thought they were making an IRA propaganda video. They had then driven through the town waving an Irish tricolour on their way to a nearby church car park where the getaway cars were waiting. The SAS was waiting there too and shot them dead.

Two months later, John Major called a UK General Election for 9 April 1992, wishing to confer legitimacy on his Premiership which he had inherited following Margaret Thatcher's resignation in 1990. More significantly, his time as Prime Minister was nearing its end as the statutory five years between elections since Mrs Thatcher's landslide victory of 1987 was up. Major's hoped-for legitimacy was confirmed when he won with a majority of twenty-one seats. The SDLP increased its vote while Sinn Féin's share of the vote decreased slightly from 11.4 per cent to 10 per cent. Its biggest casualty was Gerry Adams, who lost his Westminster seat. It was probably a sign of the times, with events on the ground giving clear indication that the IRA showed no intention of ending its campaign.

The day after Major's election, the IRA sent the Government a violent reminder as it had done two months after he succeeded Margaret Thatcher in November 1990 by mortaring Downing Street. At 9.20 p.m., the IRA exploded a huge bomb packed inside a white Ford Transit van outside the Baltic Exchange in the heart of the City of London. It consisted of a ton of ammonium nitrate fertiliser and 100lb of Semtex. The explosion caused an estimated £800 million-worth of damage. It was the biggest bomb detonated in London since the Luftwaffe's attacks on the capital in the Second World War. The IRA phoned a warning twenty minutes before the explosion but gave the location as the London Stock Exchange half a mile away. Three people were killed, including a fifteen-year-old schoolgirl, Danielle Carter, who was on a trip to London with her father.[5]

Two days after the Baltic Exchange bomb, John Major, now Prime Minister for the first time as the result of a General Election – as opposed to an election within the Conservative Party – reshaped his Cabinet and brought in his old friend Sir Patrick Mayhew as Northern Ireland Secretary. Mayhew was a former Dragoon Guards officer and a patrician old-style Conservative in the mould of Willie Whitelaw twenty years earlier. He had been Attorney General since 1987, serving initially under Prime Minister Margaret Thatcher.

Mayhew got the call at home and did not know whether he was being summoned for a job or the sack. 'It was a lovely sunny day,' he told me. 'So I picked a camellia that was in flower and stuck it in my buttonhole.' And off he went to see the Prime Minister. It was good news. 'I'm afraid I didn't say any of the solemn things people are supposed to say on these occasions. I simply said, "Whoopee!"'[6] The Baltic Exchange bomb was a grim and timely reminder to the new Northern Ireland Secretary of what lay ahead.

Once in office, Mayhew was briefed on 'Operation Chiffon' and the link via Brendan to Martin McGuinness. He was appalled and was tempted to shut the back channel down. It was unconscionable to deal with the IRA after the Baltic Exchange bomb – added to its mortaring of Downing Street when Mayhew, as Attorney General, was a member of the Gulf War Cabinet. Dealing with the IRA, however distanced, went against all the principles in which he believed.

It's not surprising that Mayhew remained unconvinced of the IRA's sincerity with the devastation of the Baltic Exchange coming three months after the Teebane bomb. He thought the IRA was simply playing games. Nevertheless, by the end of 1992, despite his scepticism about the back channel and the encouraging noises coming back from it, Mayhew was prepared to send a public message to the IRA in a speech in Coleraine, under the guise of its somewhat anodyne title, 'Culture and Identity'. It was partly intended to test the Provisionals.

> Unity cannot be brought nearer, let alone achieved, by dealing out death and destruction. It is not sensible to believe that any British Government will yield to an agenda for Ireland prosecuted by violent means ... provided it is advocated constitutionally, there can be no proper reason for excluding any political objective from discussion. Certainly not the objective of a united Ireland through broad agreement freely and fairly agreed ...
>
> ... in the event of a genuine and established cessation of violence, the whole range of responses that we have had to make to that violence could, and would, inevitably be looked at afresh.[7]

Again the condition was 'a genuine and established cessation of violence'.

Towards the end of 1992, as the mood music began to change, there were signs that Robert's patience and persistence might be beginning to pay off. The Northern Ireland Office gave him a document for Brendan to pass on to McGuinness. It spelt out for the first time that, if the IRA stopped fighting, Sinn Féin could be one of the participants in the future government of Northern Ireland: the document stressed however that the majority veto still applied and it was up to republicans to persuade the unionists to accept a new concept of running the country, which crucially could include a thirty-two-county united Ireland. Sinn Féin sent a positive response but with a proviso.

> The document is interesting but the present method of communications is totally unsatisfactory. A more satisfactory means

of discussion must be found if there is to be any hope of forward movement.[8]

What the IRA wanted was face-to-face talks, but the British Government steadfastly refused to agree without a ceasefire. The stalemate continued into 1993 with neither side trusting the other. The breakthrough finally came as the result of Martin McGuinness's speech at Sinn Féin's annual conference, Ard Fheis, on 20 February 1993, held at a community hall in the Dublin suburb of Ballyfermot. It was a clear public statement from McGuinness and the republican movement intended for the British Government and the British people – and unionists in particular.

> We are quite prepared to be open and flexible to serious proposals which can lead to a realistic agreement. We must allow each other room for manoeuvre. This places a considerable onus on everyone including ourselves as Irish Republicans to apply new and radical thinking to the predicament Unionists find themselves in ... to guarantee and protect their interests in any new arrangements which will be needed to resolve the conflict.[9]

For the British it rang all the right bells, although it fell short of promising a ceasefire that would enable face-to-face talks.

Two days after Sinn Féin's Ard Fheis, things began to move at unaccustomed speed. Brendan got in touch with Robert, saying they had to meet urgently and he was coming to London to give him potentially exciting news. Robert was encouraged by Brendan's sudden enthusiasm. Perhaps there had been a breakthrough? They arranged to meet at a hotel near Heathrow where Brendan imparted the news. He said that McGuinness and another unnamed Army Council man had driven to Derry to see him after Sinn Féin's conference and McGuinness's speech. The three talked for two hours in the course of which, according to Brendan, McGuinness said, 'The conflict is over but we need the British to tell us how to make peace.' Robert, surprised but delighted and relieved at the news, assuming that Brendan's account was accurate, asked him if he could report this to the Northern Ireland Office. He hesitated but then said, 'Yes. McGuinness meant it for you.'

Robert duly reported the message to John Deverell and John Chilcot, using Brendan's words, although he suspected he was taking a risk by

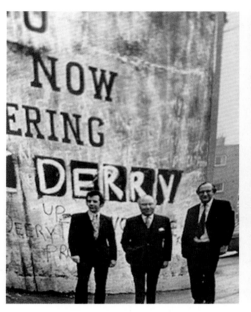

MI6 Officer Frank Steele, right, with William van Straubenzee, Minister of State NIO, centre, in 'Free Derry', roughly 1972. The man on the left is unidentified.

William Whitelaw was the British Government's Secretary of State for Northern Ireland from 1972 to 1973. On 7 July 1972, he negotiated with the Provisional IRA leadership at Cheyne Walk.

Belfast IRA Commander Seamus Twomey confronts British troops in Lenadoon Avenue in Belfast, prior to the breaking of the IRA ceasefire, 9 July 1972.

Brendan Hughes, senior IRA commander in West Belfast and leader of the first hunger strike in 1980.

Peter Taylor and the Thames TV crew are attacked by loyalists during the
breaking of the IRA ceasefire on Lenadoon Avenue, 9 July 1972.

Brendan Duddy, the Derry businessman who for almost twenty years
was the key link in the back channel to the IRA. His identity remained a
closely guarded secret until 2008 when he agreed to be named.

Michael Oatley, the MI6 officer who was the British end of the back
channel, working endlessly for peace with Brendan Duddy.

Billy McKee and Proinsias Mac Airt in Belfast's Crumlin Road Gaol, early 1970s. On their release in 1974 they helped negotiate the 1975 ceasefire with Michael Oatley.

The Reverend Ian Paisley at the 'Ulster says NO' rally outside Belfast City Hall on 23 November 1985, addressing an estimated crowd of up to 100,000 Protestants protesting against the Anglo-Irish Agreement.

The last official photo taken of the Miami Showband, May 1975. Fran O'Toole, the lead singer, is second from left.

Roy Mason, the Northern Ireland Secretary from 1976 to 1979.

Provisional IRA press conference with Martin McGuinness, David O'Connell, Seán MacStíofáin and Seamus Twomey in Derry, 13 June 1972. The book's jacket photo depicts them waiting outside the conference in 'Free Derry'.

Father Alec Reid gives last rites to a British Army corporal murdered by the Provisional IRA in Andersonstown, West Belfast, 19 March 1988. The corporal's face has been obscured for reasons of privacy.

4. The conflict is over but we need your (British) advice on how to bring it to a close. We wish to have an unannounced cease-fire in order to hold dialogue leading to peace. We cannot announce such a move as it will lead to confusion for the volunteers because the press will misrepresent it as surrender. We cannot meet Secretary of State's public renunciation of violence, but it could be given privately so long as we were sure that we were not being tricked.

The seminal 'The conflict is over' message as allegedly verbally relayed by Martin McGuinness to Brendan Duddy in Derry on 20 February 1993, and by Brendan Duddy to Robert near Heathrow the following day. Robert wrote it down longhand.

Gerry Adams, Albert Reynolds and John Hume meeting in Dublin, signifying the 'Pan Nationalist Front', 1994.

Gerry Adams and Martin McGuinness announce the IRA ceasefire in West Belfast, 31 August 1994.

President Bill Clinton meeting Gerry Adams on the Falls Road on 30 November 1995 during Clinton's visit to Belfast.

Bertie Ahern, George Mitchell and Tony Blair at Stormont for the final negotiations of the Good Friday Agreement, 1998. At the time they were the Taoiseach of the Republic of Ireland, the US's Special Envoy for Northern Ireland and the British Prime Minister, respectively.

Martin McGuinness, as Deputy First Minister, shakes hands with the Queen in Belfast, 27 June 2012. The First Minister, Peter Robinson, is centre.

Peter Taylor with Brendan Duddy at Duddy's granddaughter's
wedding reception at the City Hotel in Derry, April 2013.

The coffin of Brendan Duddy leaves St Eugene's Cathedral
in Derry after the funeral service, 16 May 2017.

stretching its interpretation and its provenance. This was later to have disturbing repercussions, as Robert was to recognise.

> What McGuinness had not said was, 'Tell the British it is from the PAC [Provisional Army Council]. I gave it that authority as I felt that was McGuinness's intent – not precisely but by implication – and without it the Northern Ireland Office would lend it insufficient credence.

Robert was wary, not doubting that McGuinness had said it – given what he had been assured by Brendan – but equally sure it was not an authoritative message from the Army Council to the British. To have conveyed it as such would have entailed extremely serious problems for both McGuinness and Brendan. Nevertheless, Robert presented it 'strongly and starkly' as being an authoritative message from the republican movement just as Brendan had transmitted it to him. He was convinced that the IRA genuinely wanted to stop fighting and that one side had to make a move towards the other.

When Robert got home that night, he sat down and wrote a four-paragraph report, in longhand, that summarised the message Brendan said McGuinness had given him in person. Robert had to take what Brendan told him on trust. At this stage he had no doubts. He wanted to get the message down on paper while it was still fresh in his mind. The key section of Robert's aide-memoire was the fourth paragraph that summarised the oral message that McGuinness had given first hand to Brendan and that Brendan had then passed on to Robert.

> The conflict is over but we need your [British] advice on how to bring it to a close. We wish to have an unannounced ceasefire in order to hold dialogue leading to peace. We cannot announce such a move as it will lead to confusion for the volunteers because the press will misrepresent it as surrender. We cannot meet the Secretary of State's public renunciation of violence but it could be given privately as long as we were sure that we were not being tricked.[10]

The following day, 23 February 1993, an emissary from Martin McGuinness's inner circle flew over from Belfast to join Brendan and meet Robert, knowing how sensitive the next move would be. Robert showed the emissary paragraph four of his aide-memoire, saying it was a summary of the message from Martin intended for the highest level of the British Government. Robert asked the emissary directly, 'Did McGuinness actually say this?' 'That's the least of what he said,' Robert says the emissary replied.

> That's why I was so convinced that the message was genuine and they weren't just concocting it. The emissary wouldn't put words into McGuinness's mouth. I didn't doctor it, I didn't lie. It was exactly what they had said. I didn't really care about the Army Council because after all McGuinness was head of the IRA's Northern Command and he wouldn't have been saying this into the wind. I thought I was quite safe in phrasing it in such a way.

But Robert was still uneasy about ascribing McGuinness's message to the IRA's supreme body. In the past, such messages had invariably been in writing and not just passed orally. He was fighting within himself but was happy if the reader of the message thought it came from the Provisionals' Army Council. Nevertheless, he began to get slightly cold feet. What if Brendan was being economical with the truth? If that were the case, Robert would be breaking one of the intelligence services' golden rules: never exaggerate or fabricate. The thought continued to haunt him.

> I thought perhaps McGuinness is going out on a limb and I can't afford to lose him. I suggested to Quentin Thomas that perhaps we needed to emphasise that McGuinness might be putting this forward as his personal view. I was trying to backtrack a bit. I was concerned that the Government would overreact and McGuinness was going to get into trouble. The message was a game-changer. Even Quentin Thomas, who had previously been agnostic about the value of the back channel, got excited. Chilcot certainly did. I knew I'd put a bit of a spin on it. I implied that a message like this would have had to have had the approval of the Army Council. Mayhew was sceptical at the beginning but I think he also got excited as did everybody on the British side. I then said to Quentin Thomas, 'Easy on. This may be McGuinness speaking slightly out of turn and he can get into trouble over this.'

Quentin Thomas always firmly believed the message from McGuinness to Brendan was genuine, not least given what McGuinness had said at Sinn Féin's Ard Fheis. John Chilcot's reaction to the message, however, was typically more measured and cautious:

> John Deverell brought me the much argued-about message late
> one evening, ostensibly emanating from Martin McGuinness or at
> any rate the IRA leadership. Now where that really originated from
> is open to question, I think. Probably somewhere in between ...
> I think it fair to say it didn't matter so much whether it was a true
> bill coming straight from the IRA as that it opened the door a little
> bit to constructive dialogue and response. So we in effect decided to
> take it as if it was valid; it didn't matter that much whether it was or
> not because, provided it wasn't rejected out of hand and publicly by
> the IRA, it had its own value.[11]

John Major received the news just as dusk was falling on what he told me was 'a pretty miserable, dreary, dark day'.[12] He was working in the Cabinet Room when his Private Secretary came in with the message. Major, like Mayhew, was encouraged but not over-excited. He told me he had no doubt that McGuinness was a member of the Provisional Army Council. If he couldn't deliver the IRA, there was no point in talking to him. But he was conflicted about the possibility.

> The angry part of me said I would never sit down [with the IRA].
> The pragmatic part of me, of course, would have done so had
> I thought there was going to be an outcome from any such meeting
> that would carry the process forward.[13]

Both Major and Mayhew took advice from John Deverell, their point of contact for matters related to the back channel, and were assured that the message was genuine. After all, Deverell knew at first hand from Robert where it came from. Mayhew's initial scepticism about Brendan was now softened as progress, in the form of the message from McGuinness, seemed to be producing results. As Mayhew told me, he was pleased that the message had come and he definitely wasn't expecting it.

I certainly didn't regard it as a white flag. I wanted to regard it as a
recognition that, contrary to the IRA's belief over many years, the
British Government was not going to be shoved away from the
principle of consent and democracy by violent attacks, whether
in Northern Ireland or the City of London. If it was that, then
I wanted to sustain that conversion to politics and abandonment of
violence.[14]

Robert believes he did not have the opportunity to give his account
of the message's provenance to John Chilcot, as he had to John Deverell,
since he did not have a close enough relationship with him. Perhaps
Deverell did not communicate the reasons why Robert initially had
no doubt that the message was genuine and that it did come directly
from Martin McGuinness – although perhaps not with the Army
Council's blessing. When the Government later made the message
public, McGuinness was incandescent and vehemently denied he had
sent it. On a technicality, McGuinness was right. The message was an
oral communication allegedly delivered by McGuinness to Brendan,
and then passed on by Brendan to Robert, who subsequently wrote it
up – by hand. Sinn Féin said the message was 'bogus' and written by the
British Government. Although the message may – or may not – have
been 'bogus', it was summarised by Robert, and therefore technically
'written by the British Government'. The line that perhaps did most
damage to McGuinness and Sinn Féin was 'we need your advice on
how to bring it to a close' – contentious words that suggested surrender.

To maintain the momentum of the 'conflict is over' message, on 24
February 1993 Robert met Brendan at a Heathrow hotel and gave him
the British Government's written response to the message it had been
assured came from Martin McGuinness. This is Sinn Féin's written
account of the British Government's response.

The British Government Representative [Robert] ... was very
upbeat about the possibility of delegation meetings. He and his
colleagues had been working on this for years. The Republicans
will have to grasp the opportunity while it exists. Events on the
ground will bring an enormous influence to bear. The IRA needs to
provide the space to turn the possibility of meetings into a reality.
A suspension is all that is being required of them.[15]

Things now began to move quickly. At last it seemed the dialogue with McGuinness and the republican movement was gaining traction. Two days later, on 26 February, Robert sent another message via Brendan setting out the British Government's position. It said the Government had agreed to talks with Sinn Féin; there would have to be a 'no violence' understanding during two to three weeks of private talks – although the understanding would not be made public. As a result, the Government believed it could convince Irish republicans during the talks that 'armed struggle' was no longer necessary.[16]

On 1 March 1993 Robert gave Brendan an oral message that a date and venue had been agreed for an exploratory meeting to discuss logistics for delegation talks. The agreed date was 23 March and the venue was to be Brendan's house. The reply came back four days later that Sinn Féin welcomed the possibility of a meeting and said that Martin McGuinness and Gerry Kelly would be its nominees.[17]

The stage was set. At this point there was no precondition of a ceasefire as the meeting was designed to be purely 'exploratory'. 'Operation Chiffon' was beginning to bear fruit, although its full ripening was to take time.

26

Talks about Talks

On 19 March 1993, four days before the scheduled exploratory meeting at Brendan's house, a detailed outline of the Government's position was sent to McGuinness in the form of a Nine-Point Plan. It said, to summarise, that there was need for a healing process as no one has a monopoly of suffering; any dialogue could only follow a halt to violent activity; no objective, advocated by constitutional means, could be excluded from discussion; and in the event of a genuine and established end to violence, the whole range of responses would inevitably be looked at afresh. Finally, the document stressed, the Government was aiming for an agreed accommodation, not an imposed settlement, but there could be no prior objective of ending partition. For Sinn Féin the following was the crucial paragraph:

> the eventual outcome of such a process could be a united Ireland
> but this can only be on the basis of the consent of the people
> of Northern Ireland. Should this be the eventual outcome of a
> peaceful democratic process, the British Government would bring
> forward legislation to implement the will of the people here.[1]

The Nine-Point Plan was sent with an oral message from the British Government via Robert. It warned that the process was fraught with difficulties and all acts of violence hereafter could only exacerbate those difficulties, quite conceivably to the point when the process would be destroyed and a potentially historic opportunity squandered.[2]

The warning was grimly prophetic. The following day, 20 March 1993, tragedy struck in Warrington, Lancashire. The IRA had planted bombs in two litter bins in a crowded shopping precinct which exploded when the town centre was packed with Saturday shoppers. The bombs killed two young boys, Johnathan Ball, aged three, and Timothy Parry, aged twelve. Johnathan was out shopping for a Mother's Day present. He died at the scene in the arms of a nurse. His father, Wilf Ball, was devastated.

> He was what made me live. He was great. My life is just shattered
> now, absolutely shattered. A child of three years and ten months
> and they took his life. He has done nothing to anybody. In my
> heart I don't think I can ever forgive them. I don't think I shall ever
> forgive them.[3]

The IRA said it had given a warning. The police said it was imprecise. In a letter to Northern Ireland's *Sunday Life* newspaper Johnathan's parents, Wilf and Marie, wrote: 'If these initiatives lead to peace in Ireland, we shall be better able to bear our pain, if not Johnathan's death is a meaningless blasphemy.'[4]

The other young victim, Tim Parry, had been going to buy a pair of football shorts and suffered severe head injuries while fleeing the impact of the first bomb in the litter bin. He never regained consciousness and died in hospital five days later, with his parents, brother and sister at his bedside. Messages of sympathy poured in. His father, Colin, said, 'We produced a bloody good kid, one of three. He had his moments. He could be a cheeky, impudent little pup, a good kid. The IRA – I have no words for them at all.'[5] Colin Parry and Wilf Ball went on to form a Peace Foundation in their sons' names.

The Warrington bombings provoked universal condemnation, akin to that after the Enniskillen Remembrance Day bombing six years earlier. Ironically, both tragedies helped galvanise the drive for peace.

The day of the Warrington attack, Robert met Brendan at the Dunadry Inn, near Aldergrove airport outside Belfast, to discuss a message to McGuinness about the proposed meeting scheduled for three days later. They knew nothing about the Warrington bombs until Robert rang John Deverell and asked him to come to the Dunadry Inn to sign off the message. Deverell then broke the shocking news about

Warrington and asked if the message to Brendan had been handed over. Robert replied that he was with Brendan at that moment. The message was put on hold. Deverell rushed to the hotel and told Robert and Brendan that Whitehall had decided that, after the enormity of the Warrington bombs and the public outrage that followed, the exploratory meeting with McGuinness and Kelly could not go ahead. 'There had been a lot of fuss in Downing Street and they wanted to pull out,' Robert remembers. 'The PM was anxious and wanted to call the whole thing off.'[6] John Chilcot had initially told Deverell that the message should be passed on as quickly as possible, presumably because he recognised that the bombing made it all the more imperative that the planned meeting on 23 March should proceed. Understandably, Robert was appalled by the bomb and the deaths of the two young boys, but, not meaning to be callous, was phlegmatic, recognising this was the way the republican movement operated, with Sinn Féin talking peace while the IRA carried on killing. All the more urgent therefore, he reasoned, probably also reflecting Chilcot's view, that the meeting should go ahead in the hope of making Warrington the last of such atrocities.

The day after the Warrington bombs, with the headlines and news bulletins leading with the horror of the atrocity, as an exhausted Robert was getting ready for bed, he received a phone call at home from Brendan at around 9 o'clock that evening. He said McGuinness and Kelly were coming to Derry because of the Government's message of 19 March, the day before the Warrington bombing, and it was crucial that they should meet 'Fred', who should be accompanied by a second British official. Such a configuration (two on two) was necessary if they were 'to cement a possible cessation of violence'. Robert, who admits to being impulsive, said 'OK. I'll fix it.' John Deverell, he reasoned, would be the ideal second person and, as his boss, would add weight and authority to the British side.

Robert rang Deverell the next morning, on 22 March, and asked the key question: 'I need somebody to come with me, will you do it?' Deverell was cautious, said he would think about it and would get back with his answer that evening. He duly returned the call and gave Brendan the answer he had expected and hoped for. 'OK, I'll do it,' Deverell said, while making it clear he wasn't keen. Robert knew his boss and his friend – and wasn't disappointed.

I didn't think he [Deverell] could resist the bait. He came like me
from the Colonial Service in Africa where he knew we had to act
quickly – and like me he'd been in the army. We were from a different
background from a lot of people in the Security Service. I was used
to taking decisions, taking them on my own and getting on with
it. I knew he was the same make-up as me and, like me, would be
excited at the prospect of meeting antagonists such as these.

All seemed set for the meeting. Robert spoke to Deverell again the
following morning (23 March) and said he was going for a break to
get some fresh air before the potential game-changing encounter that
evening. He said he would be back in the MI5 office at Stormont Castle
around teatime.

He drove to a scenic spot in County Down in the beautiful countryside
not far from Stormont's doorstep. He needed valuable time to turn
things over in his mind in the peace and tranquillity around Strangford
Lough that made the daily violence of the conflict seem a million miles
away. He mulled over what he had done, what was at stake and the
potential dangers it held. There was no turning back. He just hoped
that John Deverell would keep his word and be there with him. But he
knew the enormous political risks he was taking: 'I wasn't frightened of
the IRA. They wanted a meeting and that was fine but it was a meeting
that hadn't got approval and was against British Government policy.'
There had not only *not* been a ceasefire but the Warrington bombs had
just exploded. Robert was conflicted as he considered the implications
of what he was about to do. He was, and always had been, a man of
strong Christian faith.

I'd never done anything like this in my life. I knew I was doing
something that could bring down all hell on my head if it went
wrong. That's when my heart pains began. That's when I felt this
thing at the back of my throat. Vaguely I recalled this could be
the start of a heart attack, brought on by anxiety. [He was later
diagnosed with a medical condition.] I have a strong faith and had
no doubt that God would answer my prayers positively. I felt my
heart and prayed that I be allowed to go through with the meeting
and then if I had to die, it would be at home with my wife. Right,
I thought, I'll test myself out and climbed the hill in front of me.[7]

He drove to the Castle Espie Wetland Centre, a wildfowl and wader reserve by Strangford Lough, and then to a café where he had lunch and a beer. The weather was calm, a condition he hoped to emulate too. With time to think and unwind a little, he gradually began to feel better and the pain dissipated. Relieved, he eventually headed back to Stormont where John Deverell had called a meeting for 4.30 p.m. Before going through the door, Robert reminded himself that the agreed subterfuge for the meeting with McGuinness that evening was that the only person present on the British side was Brendan, thus covering for Robert and Deverell to maintain the fiction that no British official had met the IRA.

Duly refreshed and feeling better, Robert walked into the room to see John Deverell sitting with a Northern Ireland Office official and another MI5 officer. Neither was across the subterfuge. Deverell began by saying that he'd just come from a meeting with John Chilcot and Quentin Thomas. He repeated what Chilcot had said: if the IRA leaders tell us they would stop the violence at, say, midnight on a certain day, we would take their word for it and agree to speak to them at one minute after midnight. Robert reminded the two officials in the room that Brendan was meeting the IRA leaders that evening. They had no idea it was a cover story and that it was Robert and Deverell who were planning to meet the IRA. One of the officials asked whether offering immediate talks after a ceasefire was now British policy, and could Brendan actually say this to the IRA leaders? Deverell was emphatic that he could. He added that at his earlier meeting with Chilcot and Thomas there had been a discussion as to whether at this stage an intelligence officer could meet McGuinness. At this point Robert held his breath. The reply was disconcerting. The feeling was that this would be unwise, in particular after Warrington. Having brought Robert and the two officials up to speed, the meeting ended. Deverell and Robert were now alone.

To Robert's consternation, because of Chilcot and Thomas's decision that the involvement of any intelligence officer would be 'unwise', Deverell told Robert the evening's meeting with the IRA could not now take place. Robert suspected, in retrospect, that it was likely that Deverell had raised the question in order to give himself the escape route he wanted. Robert recognised that while his own career was coming to a close, Deverell's career was still on the rise and helping bring peace to Northern Ireland would be his crowning achievement and likely to elevate him further. Robert feared that if things went wrong, he, Robert, would be finished, as would be the close relationship between MI5 and the Northern Ireland Office.

Robert was angry and felt let down. He told Deverell it was an appalling decision to take at this late stage. He rang Brendan from Deverell's office in an anonymous annexe at Stormont, to warn him that he, Robert, would now be coming on his own and that John Deverell wouldn't be with him. Brendan was furious that Deverell could consider pulling out at the eleventh hour. 'The men are in town,' Brendan said, with the ominous warning that there would be serious repercussions for the peace process if there were not two British representatives at the meeting as was agreed at the previous discussions. The IRA would be convinced that the 'Brits' were not in earnest and could not be trusted, confirming the Provisionals' long-held, deepest suspicions.

Most worryingly, Brendan claimed – rightly or wrongly – that a bombing in London had been postponed because of the forthcoming meeting and the operation would now be likely to go ahead. Robert ended the conversation, considering it highly unlikely that McGuinness or one of his surrogates would ever have imparted such sensitive operational information to Brendan, but concerned that if it was true, and the bombing did go ahead and there were deaths and casualties, they would be on his head. While on the phone, out of the corner of his eye, Robert noticed that Deverell was playing a video game – 'Battleships' or 'Noughts and Crosses' – on his office computer. He couldn't remember which.

> I thought, John, how can you be so detached and I'm here sweating blood? Here I am at the end of this phone arguing with this nearly berserk Brendan. He was getting more and more excited, worse things were going to happen if I didn't come. 'You'll lose the chance,' he said. 'And you'll lose me.' He repeated the IRA leaders would expect *two* British representatives and would back out otherwise. He was throwing everything into it. Anyway I said to John Deverell, 'I'm sorry. I'm going to go.' John was not turning a blind eye. He'd given me categoric instructions that I was *not* to go. I said it was me or nothing and he reluctantly agreed. I thought, right, that's it and off I went.[8]

Robert got into his hire car, rented under his alias, and set off, yet again, on the long journey to Derry, trying to collect his wits on the way, and forcing himself to think positive thoughts. At least events were moving on and there was no time to worry about heart attacks or being sacked.

Brendan, typically, having said 'the men are in town', had insisted that Robert be with him in one and a half to two hours – and that was probably some thirty minutes ago. He watched the speedometer rise on the first of the few stretches of new motorway between Belfast and Derry and then glanced at the petrol gauge and saw that he was almost running on empty. He pulled into a petrol station a few miles along the dual carriageway, filled up and then realised he didn't know how to start the rented car. 'It was one of those silly starters where you have to press the button.' He managed to get someone from inside the petrol station to show him how to do it. It was all eating up precious time. Back in the car, Robert began to feel excited. The adrenaline was now racing. John Deverell had said all the right things institutionally and done his duty – while covering himself. Now Robert was on his own.

27

Out on a Limb

Robert arrived at Brendan's house around 8 p.m. There were two people there with Brendan. One was Noel Gallagher. The other was Denis Bradley, a charismatic and silver-tongued former priest who was close to the McGuinness family. Brendan nicknamed Bradley the 'Star' because of his quick mind and way with words. Brendan introduced Robert as 'Fred'. It was the first time Robert had heard of the codename that Brendan had given to the IRA. Robert liked Bradley the best. 'I found him by far the easiest of the trio and the most likeable. Unlike Brendan he had a sense of humour as well as a sense of proportion – and, having left the priesthood, was now happily married.'[1] Brendan's shortcomings in the humour department were probably the result of his mission being deadly serious. There was not a lot to be light-hearted about.

Brendan's contemporary notes of the evening reveal that he gave all the participants codenames for security reasons. Denis Bradley was 'Star', Noel Gallagher was 'Tax', bizarrely Brendan was 'June' (the month of his birthday) and Robert was 'Fred'. McGuinness and Kelly were to be known as 'Walter' and 'Campbell' respectively. John Deverell, who had been expected to accompany Robert, was referred to as 'James'.[2]

Robert was shown into Brendan's modest boardroom, set out formally for a conference, with each place having a pencil and paper and a copy of the Northern Ireland Office's Nine-Point Plan at the side. Two places awaited the arrival of McGuinness and Kelly. Brendan told Robert that they were down in the Bogside, a short drive away, waiting in McGuinness's mother's house. Noel Gallagher went off to fetch them. Robert fortified himself with two glasses of Brendan's good malt whiskey and felt much better, refusing to accept Brendan's dismal assessment of the situation, while still wondering at the back of his mind if he was walking into an IRA trap. Nevertheless he was here and the imperative was now to get on with the job. With Noel Gallagher away on his mission to pick up McGuinness and Kelly, Robert explained to Brendan and Bradley that John Deverell had been ordered to fly urgently to London with the Secretary of State, Patrick Mayhew, and that was why he, Robert, was here alone. He also made it clear that he had no authority to be at the meeting. Brendan and Denis Bradley, alarmed at the admission, warned him of the danger of saying that he had no authority to be there. 'I accepted however their advice that I would have to purport to have it.'

After about twenty minutes, Noel Gallagher returned but minus McGuinness and Kelly. He reported that neither man would meet Robert as they had been promised two 'visitors' and one alone was unacceptable. Without a moment's hesitation, Brendan intervened and proposed that Robert go down into the Bogside with Denis Bradley and persuade them to come. Having got to this critical stage, Robert knew he had no choice, while pointing out to Brendan that he was like Field Marshal Haig sending his troops over the top while he (Brendan) remained safely behind. Robert, fortified by Brendan's whiskey, no longer felt apprehensive. 'My thoughts were that, having come so far, I was going to see it through.' Robert had been frightened before, not surprisingly given the nature of his job, but not on this occasion. 'I was often scared but not that evening. I no longer thought that PIRA could kidnap and interrogate me. I had come to negotiate peace.'

Robert got into Bradley's 'ramshackle' car and, leaving Brendan's more prosperous suburb behind, headed down the hill into the dark, narrow, terraced streets of the Bogside. Seeing soldiers ahead, with headlights on, checking vehicles, Bradley made a quick detour before arriving at Mrs McGuinness's house in a deserted dark and narrow street. He advised Robert to move crabwise with his back to the wall to avoid being seen. 'It was like the Resistance in France at the end of the Second World War,' Robert told me.

Bradley knocked on the door several times, with Robert 'almost holding on to his coat tails'. McGuinness half opened the door, not expecting another visitor. Bradley apologised for intruding and introduced 'Fred'. Robert found himself in a sitting room where his eyes met an alarmed-looking Gerry Kelly, the former London bomber, Maze escapee and IRA gun-runner. A white-haired Mrs McGuinness was sitting watching a BBC TV programme about intensive abdominal surgery, possibly, and ominously given the circumstances, a repeat of the long-running series *Your Life in Their Hands*.

The room was full of school photos of family and grandchildren and what Robert assumed to be a photo of Martin's father, William, hanging on the wall. So as not to intrude further on his mother's viewing, McGuinness led Robert and Bradley through the sitting room into a small, cramped kitchenette. Gerry Kelly followed. By now, Noel Gallagher had driven down to join them. McGuinness and Kelly spoke briefly to each other in Gaelic. McGuinness then took the lead, turned to Robert and asked him firmly but politely who he was and what he wanted from them. 'Oddly I felt in control. I believed in my own concocted cover story and sensed that I could win the coming verbal contest if there was to be one.' Robert was not lacking in self-confidence.

> As with my initial meeting with Brendan, I pitched my role as
> high as I could and summoned up every bit of authority I could
> pretend to have – when, in fact, I had none. I said I came from the
> Secretary of State because it was time for the bloodshed to end.
> McGuinness tested my story, saying 'You must be MI5 or MI6
> or something? Why did you use two different names? [Brendan
> had told McGuinness about Robert's pseudonyms during his
> interrogation in Donegal.] Why did you come alone?' We went
> backwards and forwards on the last question and there was a point
> when I felt I cannot get any further. I'm losing this one. Eventually
> McGuinness said, 'Well, we've waited twenty years for this moment
> and we can wait a bit longer. You should go away and come
> back with a colleague later in the week. Then we could talk, but
> not now.'

Robert knew he was beaten. Gallagher had spoken very little and was almost an invisible presence. Then, for the first time, Denis Bradley spoke up. He had officiated at the marriage of McGuinness and his wife, Bernadette, and was the former confessor and priest to the McGuinness family. He asked if he could speak to McGuinness and Kelly alone. Robert and Gallagher adjourned to the sitting room where Mrs McGuinness switched off the TV and chatted happily with Robert. He found they had something in common, the border town of Strabane, fifteen miles south of Derry, where the McGuinness family initially came from and where, in an extraordinary coincidence, Robert's parents had spent the first night of their honeymoon. They were on their way to Donegal but had not realised that the border closed at 6 p.m. so fell back on staying the night in Strabane. Mrs McGuinness was clearly enjoying the story and the coincidence. Robert thought to himself, 'Great, she'll like this.' At least he was getting Mrs McGuinness onside, if not yet her son. That was going to be more difficult.

After about fifteen minutes Bradley emerged and asked Gallagher to come in. Robert chatted merrily with Mrs McGuinness for a few more minutes before Gallagher reappeared. 'Get into Denis's car,' he told Robert. 'It's on.' As they pulled away, some local boys shouted out there was a puncture in one of the tyres. Bradley, with time rapidly slipping away, said they would get there on the rim as they rattled back to Brendan's house.

Shortly afterwards, Gallagher arrived with McGuinness and Kelly. There were no smiles, handshakes or small talk. It was all very business-like. They were ushered into the boardroom and took their places at the table opposite Robert. Brendan, Bradley and Gallagher sat behind him. Brendan remembers that the meeting began within three minutes of McGuinness and Kelly's arrival. Brendan chaired the meeting, setting out the simple rules: any party could ask for an adjournment at any time and there was no time limit to the discussion.

McGuinness began by continuing the interrogation of Robert he had begun in Mrs McGuinness's cramped kitchenette. Where did he come from? Was he MI5 or MI6? Robert, now having already faced the interrogation, was not fazed and, on the spur of the moment, invented a story that he was working for the Cabinet Office. He thought this was the cover that Michael Oatley had used in his dealings with the IRA in the early 1970s. He said he was there with the full authority of the British Government (which he was not) and his mission was to enable the beginnings of a dialogue to take place. McGuinness asked who he wished to talk to. 'The heart of the republican movement,' Robert replied, 'the people who make decisions,' knowing full well that he was facing two of them. He added that the Nine-Point Plan, resting beside them on the table, was both the private and the public policy of the British Government. He was asked if 'Mr C.' would be present (presumably John Chilcot). Robert replied that that was a matter under discussion.

McGuinness and Robert dominated the discussion with Kelly, the minute-taker, assiduously scribbling away, taking notes and throwing in the occasional question. McGuinness was also intently taking notes to make sure, Robert believes, that the record of the meeting was 100 per cent accurate. Brendan, Bradley and Gallagher were keenly listening observers.

'Fred' (Robert) stressed time and again that the British were looking for an agreement to end the Provisionals' campaign in Ireland and England and that everything was up for discussion, including the future of the North and South of Ireland. He emphasised there would be no declaration of intent by the British Government to withdraw from Ireland, that is 'Brits Out', but this did not preclude an agreed solution emerging. Robert had got into his stride.

> I was used to being on the stage and playing a part. I'd acted in *Romeo and Juliet* with me as Juliet. It was an all-boys school. I was fourteen at the time. I then went on to play Gloucester in *King Lear*, who had his eyes put out in that charming Shakespeare way, and Caesar in *Julius Caesar* [who met an even bloodier end]. That stood me in good stead and gave me confidence. The difference was now it was two people I was performing to rather than two or three hundred.

Robert was on a roll, confident he would avoid the fate of Shakespeare's characters, but the key moment that was to swing the discussion and potentially lift the barrier to an IRA ceasefire, the prerequisite of any talks with the British, was still to come. It was the exchange I first became aware of in 1994 when I read Sinn Féin's account of this highly contentious moment in the meeting, in its document *Setting the Record Straight*. The section is based on the detailed minutes taken by Gerry Kelly and Martin McGuinness of what Robert had said.

> Mayhew had tried marginalisation, defeating the IRA, etc. That's gone. Mayhew is now determined. He wants Sinn Féin to play a part, not because he likes Sinn Féin but because it cannot work

without them. Any settlement not involving all of the people
North and South won't work. A North/South settlement that won't
frighten unionists. The final solution is union. It is going to happen
anyway. The historical train – Europe – determines that. We are
committed to Europe. Unionists will have to change. This island
will be as one.[3]

During a short break for both sides to consider the situation. Brendan
grew increasingly excited, congratulating Robert on his performance. 'I
think you've done it,' he said. 'I think you've got a ceasefire.'

Kelly's contemporary minute was written in a different political climate,
twenty-seven years before Brexit and the UK's decision following a
referendum to leave the European Union.[*] I could not imagine that
any British official would ever spell out Britain's long-term thinking in
such a startling and unequivocal way. I later asked those present at the
meeting – Martin McGuinness, Gerry Kelly and Brendan Duddy – if
it was true that 'Fred' had really said this. All of them assured me he
had. I also talked to Sir John Chilcot a year before he died in October
2021. In a Chilcotean way, he came pretty close to confirming it – but
without actually doing so. I asked if there was any British record of
what was said at the meeting. Sir John said there was not.

At midnight, McGuinness asked for an adjournment. Brendan noted,
'tea and cake was enjoyed by all'. It sounded a bit like 'Church teas' on
a Sunday afternoon. Brendan had been growing increasingly worried
that, in being so positive, Robert might be overstepping his brief in his
anxiety to get the dialogue going. During the break, Brendan expressed
this concern. Robert replied he had already overstepped his brief by
coming to the meeting in the first place but said that all of his answers
to questions were as had been agreed by his superiors. Brendan pressed
him a second time. Robert replied that all of his answers were within his
instructions and that he never exceeded his brief – and by nature and
experience he tended to be conservative.[4]

---

[*]The result of the Brexit referendum on 22 June 2016 was 52 per cent in favour of leave and 48
per cent in favour of remain. Significantly the vote in Northern Ireland went heavily the other
way, with 56 per cent voting to remain and 44 per cent to leave.

The mystery remains why 'The final solution is union' section does not appear in Brendan's account of the meeting, dictated and typed up shortly after the event.

When the meeting resumed, McGuinness asked 'Fred' when the dialogue would begin. 'Fred' said immediately a decision was made on halting the violence. McGuinness pointed out it would require ten days for the republican movement to give an answer about its position. McGuinness then asked what if there was no agreement over the suggested five to ten days of discussion. 'The Irish problem must be solved either now or tomorrow or later, next week or next month,' Robert replied. 'The British Government would be back again.'

The closing moments of the meeting became more informal and relaxed. Robert had discussed the various locations where the Government had suggested a meeting with Sinn Féin might take place – Norway, Denmark and Scotland were all mentioned – and the Government would provide a plane and cover the costs.[5] McGuinness said if there was to be a meeting, he would prefer it to be on home ground in Northern Ireland. Robert felt he had now established a relationship with McGuinness. 'I was over the moon. I couldn't believe it.' McGuinness then raised the question of the British Government's likely response to any IRA attack in the lead-up to talks about a ceasefire and a political settlement. Robert gave his answer.

I said if the slates come off a police station as the result of a bomb, they'd accept that but the worst thing would be an attack on London. 'Yes,' McGuinness said, 'we know that.' That brought me back to reality. I thought you're still a killer and I mustn't forget it.

But I still needed confirmation from the lips of Robert himself that he had said, 'This island will be as one.' It took me nearly thirty years to get it.

When I interviewed Robert in the summer of 2021 and pressed him on what authority he had said the words recorded in the Sinn Féin minute, he explained that they simply reflected what Michael Oatley had told Martin McGuinness at their meeting in Bernie Mount's house just before Oatley retired in 1991. Oatley had written up the meeting in a report for John Chilcot which Robert told me he had seen and read several times. I put this to Michael Oatley. He says he doesn't deny saying to McGuinness, 'Ireland will be as one,' but doesn't remember saying it. 'If Robert says that it is my account of the conversation, to which I do not have access, then of course I said it. Probably in terms of a supposition.' Robert is categoric about what Michael put in his report in his debrief to John Chilcot.

> I have no doubt at all that that was what I was drawing on. That was my reason for saying it. It gave me authority. I would never have thought of saying that otherwise. I wasn't making it up as I went along. That I drew from the Oatley account, thanks to his good, clear write-up. All the things he had said, I repeated. I thought it having been said once [by Michael Oatley], it could be said again.

The meeting with McGuinness and Kelly at Brendan's house lasted for around five hours, with breaks, from 8 p.m. until well after midnight. Robert had arranged to stay that night at John Deverell's house. He drove there, still on a high. 'I was so happy, pleased and proud.' He stopped off at the first telephone box to ring Deverell to tell him he was all in one piece. Back on the road, he ran into an RUC roadblock. The officer looked at his driving licence and was very polite. 'Are you here on business or pleasure, sir?' he asked. Robert probably thought it was a bit of both, the pleasure being the consequence of the business. He was on a high and felt elated. 'Everyone thought we were going to get a ceasefire.'

Deverell was relieved to see him and showed him into the drawing room. Nursing a welcome glass of whiskey, Robert told him all about the meeting and said he (Robert) should go and debrief John Chilcot in the morning. Chilcot, under the impression that it was only Brendan who had gone to the meeting, had no idea that Robert had defied orders and attended. Deverell immediately put paid to that idea, adamant that any such move would be highly unwise. 'That would destroy our whole position here,' he said. 'Chilcot would never trust our Service again.' They then fabricated a cover story making the source Brendan and not Robert. Robert was too tired to contradict his boss. Thus the fiction remained, known only to Robert and John Deverell, and of course to Brendan and the others at the meeting – Martin McGuinness, Gerry Kelly, Brendan Gallagher, Brendan Duddy, Noel Gallagher and Denis Bradley. Robert and John Deverell got to bed around 3.30 a.m. and were up early to send a telegram to the

Northern Ireland Office saying the meeting had been a success. Deverell congratulated Robert. 'I think you've pulled it off,' he said.

When Robert flew back to London the following morning, he hadn't noticed that John Chilcot, still having no idea that Robert had been at the meeting with McGuinness, had been on the same flight, until he recognised him walking to the terminal across the tarmac at Heathrow. 'Well, we're there, aren't we,' Chilcot said, recognising Robert. 'Very good. Brendan has done very well.' Robert said nothing to disabuse him of the fiction.

Later that morning, when the Northern Ireland Office digested the telegram, there was general excitement that Brendan had spoken so well and brought the IRA to the point of considering a ceasefire. Deverell's intention now was to take one bridge at time: to achieve a further meeting with the IRA leadership as a preliminary to a full plenary meeting with delegations from both sides. Robert's meeting with McGuinness was to be regarded as something that had never happened. Robert was dismayed by the labyrinthine workings of Downing Street and Whitehall.

All the action and initiative within the next few weeks was taken by the Security Service. The problem was that we had no say in policy and did not have the ear of the Secretary of State, nor any concept of decision making in Downing Street that would be needed before a ceasefire could be accepted. Secrecy was so compartmentalised and the different layers of government so cut off from each other that nobody could appreciate how the layer above would react. Even the Prime Minister, John Major, could not give a definitive answer without consulting his Cabinet. In fairness, the vital fault lay with me in holding an unauthorised meeting and in John Deverell not allowing me to tell the truth at once of what I had done. I had been too impulsive, and he had been initially carried along by me instead of being a restraining hand – as his position required him to be.

Robert returned home to England for a much needed break after his exhausting and nerve-racking meeting with McGuinness and Kelly. He was met at the station by his wife, who was greatly relieved he was safely back, his undercover work in the province being a constant worry. 'I think I may have helped bring peace to Northern Ireland,' he told her. But cementing that peace was still many years away.

28

Getting Ready

The widespread fiction in Whitehall continued to be that Brendan was the hero of the hour. Logistical preparations, overseen by the Security Service, went ahead for the delegation meeting that was anticipated to take place between the British and the Provisionals, represented by Sinn Féin, in the not-too-distant future. No time was lost. By mid-April 1993, within three weeks of Robert's meeting with McGuinness and Kelly, MI5 had purchased a large bungalow. The couple who helped get things ready knew who they were working for but did not know the purpose for which the bungalow was intended. Within a week, they had everything equipped and furnished. A meeting room and two adjacent anterooms were prepared. The preparations even extended to providing a tray, decanter and glasses, and no doubt something to pour into them, in the hope of celebrating success.

Transport logistics were also in place. The plan was, on the appointed day of the meeting, to ask the Provisionals' delegation to meet at Brendan's house from where they would be driven to the specially prepared bungalow. A van had been equipped with seats in the back and would be driven by the SAS, with Robert next to the driver at the front, over a route that one of his colleagues from MI5's Irish Section had checked and timed. The bungalow would be guarded by the SAS. Inside would be secure telecommunications manned by the Security Service, which the Provisionals were free to use should they so wish. There were facilities for the two sides to eat or drink together if so minded. Two Security Service secretaries volunteered to do the catering. According to Robert, all these arrangements were pushed through with precision and calmness by Stephen Lander, then head of the Irish Section and later to become MI5's Director General.*

Around the time the preparations for the meeting between the British Government and the republican movement were being made, Brendan had been trying to reach McGuinness but without success. McGuinness finally came to see Brendan and explained that he had been away from home for long periods – something he had warned about at the meeting with Robert in Brendan's boardroom. Brendan assumed he had been consulting his foot soldiers and their commanders about a ceasefire and the conditions for it. It was one of the reasons why the IRA's decision to call a ceasefire took so long. Brendan finally reported that McGuinness's consultations with the IRA leadership and its rank and file had been successful but there was one stipulation: the Provisionals wanted one more preliminary meeting before agreement on a final full session. That proved to be the major obstacle standing in the way of putting the bungalow and its contents to the use for which they had been purchased.

Robert broke the news that the IRA wanted a further preliminary meeting to John Deverell in his office at Stormont. It came as a serious blow. Deverell, Chilcot and Thomas had all assumed that having agreed to the exploratory meeting at Brendan's house on 23 March – a meeting agreed without a ceasefire being in place – that was it as far as preliminary meetings were concerned. The next step was intended to be a full meeting, after a 'suspension of operations' or a ceasefire, as the Government had outlined in its communications down the back channel. Deverell rang Quentin Thomas to break the news. Thomas was adamantly against another preliminary meeting without an IRA ceasefire.

Robert was bemused that Thomas was heartened that a breakthrough to a ceasefire was on the horizon and yet was not ready to go the last mile to advance the prospects for peace. Thomas remained wedded to the cardinal principle that no British official could meet the Provisionals until the IRA had actually called a ceasefire. He, like John Chilcot,

*Sir Stephen Lander served as MI5's Director General (1996–2002). He then went on to become Chairman of the UK's Serious Organised Crime Agency (SOCA), which became the National Crime Agency in 2013.

was still under the impression that it had been Brendan who had met McGuinness and Kelly – not Robert. According to Robert, who was in the room listening to John Deverell's phone call to Quentin Thomas, Thomas was adamant that there could be no second meeting. Deverell kept his temper but Robert lost his. Everything was keyed up for a meeting to take place as the next stage in the process – the bungalow, the transport and security were all ready, as were the tray, decanter and glasses. When Robert broke the news to Brendan, that Quentin Thomas had vetoed a second meeting, Brendan was devastated: it had been phenomenally difficult to get to this stage and the Provisionals had gone as far as they could. 'Operation Chiffon' was in danger of falling apart.

Later that day, Deverell, another MI5 colleague and Robert trooped up to Stormont Castle for a meeting with Chilcot, Thomas and Patrick Mayhew's Private Secretary. Mayhew was away in his south of England constituency, Tunbridge Wells. According to Robert, Deverell spoke 'firmly and well' but Chilcot, with his typically courteous and obliging manner, followed Thomas in rejecting the Provisionals' request for another face-to-face meeting prior to a full session – without the prerequisite of a ceasefire. Robert felt frustrated and angry.

> The fact that the opportunity for which we all had been working for months was now there and could, if not dealt with positively, disappear seemed not to concern them. The meeting ended in a mood of gloom on our side. We felt that whereas we really wanted to achieve peace, the Northern Ireland Office adhered to the fiction that we did not deal with terrorists who had not renounced violence.[1]

That evening, Robert had supper with John Deverell and his wife at their home. The two men ate without enthusiasm, the cloud of the depressing meeting with Chilcot and Thomas still hanging over them. It was a pleasant early spring evening in April, with daffodils in bloom. Supper over, Deverell and Robert adjourned to the drawing room for a post-prandial whiskey. Then, outside, a marauding cockerel was spotted in the garden, stripping Mrs Deverell's carefully tended spring border and decimating her daffodils. Deverell leaped to his feet, grabbed a log of wood from the basket by the fireplace, dashed to the open French windows that looked on to the garden and hurled it at the predatory bird crying, 'Take that, Quentin Thomas.' Spirits immediately rose. Robert and Deverell felt they had got it out of their system, by fighting back and achieving something, if only saving Mrs Deverell's precious border.

Robert's gloom was soon intensified when on 24 April 1993 the IRA pulled off another 'spectacular' as it had done the year before when it bombed the Baltic Exchange. An Iveco tipper truck was stolen in Newcastle-under-Lyme, Staffordshire, repainted and then loaded with a ton of ANFO high-explosive mixture (ammonium nitrate and fuel oil) smuggled in from South Armagh, the same origin and the same mixture as the devastating Baltic Exchange bomb. In London an IRA Active Service Unit drove the truck into Bishopsgate, in the heart of the City, and parked up outside the headquarters of HSBC. Warnings were then delivered from a public telephone box traced to the village of Forkhill in South Armagh, around an hour before the explosion. The police immediately started evacuating the area. At 10.27 a.m., the bomb exploded, leaving a fifteen-foot-wide crater in the street and damaging buildings up to half a mile away. The cost of the damage was estimated to be around £500 million.[2][†] Forty-four people were injured and one person was killed, a *News of the World* photographer, Edward Henty, who had ignored police warnings and was trying to get closer to the bomb to get a better picture and a possible scoop. The bomb also severely damaged the medieval church of St Ethelburga which had survived the City of London fire in 1666. The explosion was followed by a message from the IRA leadership, with a warning to 'the British establishment … to seize the opportunity and to take the steps needed for ending its futile and costly war in Ireland. We again emphasise that they should pursue the path of peace or resign themselves to the path of war.'[3]

The Government's response to the bomb was to establish a 'ring of steel' around the City as a defence against future IRA bombs and by installing thousands of CCTV cameras. Meanwhile its response to the IRA's warning to 'pursue the path of peace' was put on hold as the Bishopsgate bomb was hardly a sign that the IRA was ready for peace

---

[†]Estimates of the damage range from £350 million to a billion pounds. I follow Toby Harnden, author of *Bandit Country: The IRA and South Armagh* (Hodder & Stoughton, London, 1999).

or an indication that a ceasefire, the Government's prerequisite for talks, was in the offing. Robert and John Deverell knew it was all part of the IRA's tactic of pursuing the war until the eleventh hour before announcing a ceasefire and a halt to military activities. Prime Minister John Major made the Government's position clear.

> Frankly, we thought it was likely to bring the whole process to an end. And we told them repeatedly that that was the case. They assumed that if they bombed and put pressure on the British at Bishopsgate or with some outrage or other, it would affect our negotiating position to their advantage. In that judgement they were wholly wrong. Every time they did that, they made it harder not easier for any movement to be made towards a settlement. They hardened our attitude, whereas they believed that their actions would soften it. That is a fundamental mistake the IRA have made with successive British governments throughout the last quarter of a century.[4]

After the stressful weeks and months that followed the meeting at Brendan's house, during which Robert and John Deverell perpetuated the subterfuge that it had been Brendan who had met McGuinness, Robert took a much needed break in May 1993 – a walking holiday in Austria with his wife. He knew it would be a risky time to be away but felt he owed her a holiday and could not afford to procrastinate any further. To make sure nothing was missed, he asked one of his colleagues to keep in touch with Brendan. When he returned home on 24 May, his colleague was waiting with a message from Brendan. It was good news. The Provisionals had sent a message saying that they had agreed to a two-week suspension in response to the Government's Nine-Point Plan. The message, dated 19 May, said:

> Though it will be of short duration, [the suspension] underlines the sincerity of those involved and their faith in us. It is clear that we are prepared to make the essential move if a genuine peace process is set in place. We now wish to proceed without delay to the delegation meetings.[5]

Once Robert had returned from leave there began a waiting period that was to last several long, lonely and anxious weeks. The IRA appeared ready to declare a ceasefire but the Government seemed disinclined to respond. Robert's frustration grew.

> When I came back from this holiday, every day I was thinking,
> what the heck's happening? Is a ceasefire still on the rails?
> I envisaged another meeting somehow or other. I remember when
> I reached the age of retirement, if you were still going to be in the
> civil service, you had to have a medical. That's when I described my
> symptoms to the doctor and she said it was a medical condition –
> and warned me against future stress. What would happen if I took
> a risk that I had to take and it made me scared? The doctor said
> I shouldn't do it. And I said, 'Well, I may have to.' I was still
> thinking in those terms. I've got to find some way through to
> McGuinness to reassure him the thing is still on the rails.[6]

Robert believes that what he achieved in talking to McGuinness was convincing him that he (Robert) wasn't a liar and wasn't trying to deceive him. With this in mind, he decided the best course of action was to write a personal letter to McGuinness and ask Brendan to pass it on. For Robert these were desperate days, when he was ready to risk anything to regain a brief moment of ascendancy. This is what he wrote – in coded language as if the letter came from a bank about a loan:

> There is depression and anger here at our failure to respond to
> your brave and straightforward offer. None feel it more than I do
> for obvious reasons. I appreciate – as do all those most closely
> involved – the position this puts you in. It also contrasts with all
> that you have heard earlier. You have my word that all that was
> conveyed was done so honestly and accurately at the time.
> The present position is that the local Chairman [Sir Patrick
> Mayhew] had accepted your offer, but such a vital economic
> issue [the IRA's offer of a suspension] had to go to the Board [the
> Government]. We had miscalculated in assuming that the National
> Chairman [John Major] would simply give it the nod of approval.
> Recent economic events [IRA attacks] have made him nervous
> of bold steps and your unfortunate headline events of April [the
> Bishopsgate bombing] have made acceptance of your offer much

more risky for him. You and I may think this should not matter, but the fact is that it does and it is that which is holding things up – if you like, human characteristics rather than anything more sinister.

We all hope that you and your colleagues can bear with the situation – you are certainly being asked for a lot, but there is will on both sides to complete the loan [the ceasefire] and we must succeed. We have our struggles and pressures from individuals as perhaps you do ... our wheels turn far too slowly, but that is the way of the Bank [the Government], not any notion of stringing the other side along.

I can only ask for patience for all our sakes. You will carry out your own financial policy [the IRA's campaign] and it would be impertinent for me to suggest anything otherwise (as well as being counter-productive); but in economic terms headline stuff [IRA 'spectaculars'] knocks us back because the National Chairman [John Major] is then wary of proceeding and it gives support to those who are against such a step.

I hope you will not mind me ending with a new meaning to Tiocfaidh ár lá [Irish for 'Our day will come'].[7]

The Irish sign-off, although well meaning, was controversial as it used the signature language of Gerry Adams. The letter and its tone were to haunt Robert when everything was finally revealed and the game was up.

29

Robert Comes Clean

Despite the good news about the ceasefire, Robert couldn't stop thinking about the implications of what he had done, implications for himself, the British Government and the IRA. The Government didn't know he had met Martin McGuinness and the IRA didn't know he hadn't told the Government he was at the meeting.

> I had deceived my own side by meeting the Provisionals without authority and having done so had had to make slight alterations to the ensuing communications between the Northern Ireland Office and the Provisionals in order to conceal my role. I had also given McGuinness clear indications that we were ready for a ceasefire. If my side discovered my deception I would be in trouble. If the Provisionals believed I was a liar or deceiver then the peace process was finished and Brendan might be in danger. At the risk of sounding pathetic, I felt entirely alone and was carrying a heavy responsibility for British policy with high political risk and no prospect of support because I had acted without orders and things had now gone wrong.[1]

The situation in Northern Ireland was getting worse and there were real concerns that civil war might be looming. The new cycle of tit-for-tat violence began on a Saturday afternoon, 23 August 1993, on Belfast's loyalist Shankill Road. The IRA was not only attacking the British establishment by bombing the City of London, it was also targeting the loyalist paramilitary organisations in Northern Ireland who were conducting a campaign of assassinating not only known or suspected members of the IRA but innocent Catholics too. The IRA's prize target was Johnny Adair, alleged to be the commander of the Ulster Defence Association's 'killer wing', the Ulster Freedom Fighters, the organisation responsible for many of the killings of republicans, nationalists and Catholics. The IRA had received intelligence that Adair and other members of the UFF's leadership were meeting that Saturday in a room above Frizzell's fish shop in the heart of the Shankill. It had been used for some time as the headquarters of the UDA's West Belfast Brigade. For the IRA it was a target too good to miss.

Two young IRA men, Sean Kelly and Thomas Begley, from the neighbouring republican enclave of Ardoyne, entered the fish shop dressed in white coats as delivery men. Begley was carrying a 5lb bomb in a holdall. They thought the meeting of the leadership of the UDA and UFF was going on in an upstairs room.[2] The IRA did not know the meeting was over and Adair and his comrades had left. Begley was about to plant the bomb on the fish counter when it exploded prematurely. It had an eleven-second fuse. It was thought the IRA's intention had been to give a warning to clear the shop before the explosion but the bomb exploded first. Ten people were killed including the owner, John Frizzell, and his daughter, Sharon McBride. John had owned the fish shop for twenty-seven years. More than fifty people were wounded. Thomas Begley (aged twenty-three) was killed, blown up by his own bomb. Sean Kelly (twenty-one), the other bomber, was seriously injured and was dug out of the rubble along with many others when the building collapsed like a pack of cards. He was sentenced to nine terms of life imprisonment. The judge at his trial, Lord Justice McDermott, described the bombing as 'wanton slaughter' and 'one of the worst outrages to beset this province in twenty-five years of violence'. Kelly was released, along with up to 500 republican and loyalist prisoners, under the Good Friday Agreement of 1998.

Gerry Adams, fully aware of the now stalled moves in the background towards an IRA ceasefire and talks, was reported to have been 'shocked and horrified' by the Shankill bombing.[3] In its immediate aftermath he was faced with an agonising dilemma: should he attend Thomas Begley's funeral, knowing that attendance would have been seen as support for the bombers? Non-attendance would be seen by the IRA as betrayal of two of its foot soldiers by one of the leaders of the republican movement.

Adams not only attended the funeral, he was one of those who took a turn carrying Thomas Begley's coffin. Not to have done so would have risked losing the support of the IRA's rank and file, to which Begley and Kelly belonged. Losing the support of the IRA's grass roots risked in turn being terminal for McGuinness and Adams's efforts to keep the IRA onside in the delicate back-channel manoeuvres to effect a ceasefire and could well have finished Adams's role as a leader of the republican movement. Billy 'Twister' McQuiston, a senior member of the UDA and former loyalist prisoner who happened to be on the Shankill Road when the bomb went off, reflected the intensity of loyalist reaction to the bombing at the heart of its community. 'Anyone on the Shankill Road that day from a Boy Scout to a granny, if you'd given them a gun they would have gone out and retaliated.'[4] McQuiston, probably like the majority of his fellow loyalists, was outraged at the sight of Gerry Adams carrying Begley's coffin while professing the wish for peace. Additionally, the Shankill bomb brought home to the British Government that a loyalist ceasefire was also an inseparable part of the peace process.

And the carnage was just beginning. A week later, on 30 October 1993, the UFF took savage sectarian revenge for the Shankill bomb. Its target was a Halloween party being held at the Rising Sun pub in Greysteel, a village ten miles up the coast from Derry.[5] The planners of the attack probably thought there would be minimum security-force activity in a remote spot far from Belfast. Three men in boiler suits and balaclavas walked into the bar and opened fire after one of them had shouted 'trick or treat'. Six Catholics and two Protestants were gunned down. The bar floor was covered in blood, glass and bodies. The attackers then made their escape in a getaway car driven by a fourth member of the UFF waiting outside. The four were arrested shortly after the attack and sentenced to life imprisonment. They too, like the surviving Shankill fish-shop bomber Sean Kelly, were released under the Good Friday Agreement. A plaque was later placed at the Rising Sun pub with the message 'May their sacrifice be our path to peace'.[6]

Brendan had been overseas during the dreadful slaughter of that week and returned to Derry devastated by the bloodshed, fearing the peace process was in a tailspin. He was determined to do all he could to stop the slide into a feared civil war. He moved swiftly, and on 2 November 1993 met Martin McGuinness, probably at Brendan's own house. Robert reports that Brendan told him that McGuinness said the republican movement was ready to end hostilities and open a dialogue with the British. The gist of the message was written as follows:

> You [the British] appear to have rejected the Hume-Adams situation … Now we can't even have a dialogue to work out how a total end to violence can come about. We believe the country could be at the point of no return. In plain language, please tell us as a matter of urgency when you will open dialogue in the event of a total end to hostilities. We believe that if all the documents [i.e. the respective position papers] are put on the table – we have a basis of an understanding.[7]

In echoes of the 'conflict is over' message, Brendan told Robert the message was intended for the British government – and again sent with McGuinness's blessing. Robert hoped Brendan was telling the truth. Once more, as with the 'conflict is over' message, he harboured nagging doubts. 'I hoped Brendan was right. The stakes were already incredibly high and if, as I suspected, he was playing a game by himself, he had to live with these people [i.e. McGuinness and his close circle] and would be killed if he fabricated their responses.' Robert passed on the message. The Government responded quickly, and around 4 November Brendan and two of his colleagues met Robert, John Deverell and another MI5 officer at the Dunadry Inn. Robert told me what happened: 'John Deverell was spokesman for our side. We handed over a typed response from HMG to Brendan and his two colleagues. They took it away to discuss if it could be "sold to the IRA". The three came back and said it could be. There could never have been any discussion on the text.' The substantive British response to McGuinness's message was therefore accepted and given to Brendan to pass on to McGuinness. This was HMG's response:

> If, as you have offered, you were to give us an unequivocal assurance that violence has indeed been brought to a permanent end, and that accordingly Sinn Féin is now committed to political progress by peaceful and democratic means alone, we will make clear publicly our commitment to enter exploratory dialogue with you.

Our public statement will make clear that, provided events on the ground are fully consistent with this, a first meeting for exploratory dialogue will take place within a week of Parliament's return in January [1994].[8]

Brendan now believed that this response could be sold to the republican movement and hopefully bring about a ceasefire. Significantly, the response included HMG's oft-repeated proviso:

There can be no departure from the constitutional guarantee that Northern Ireland's status as part of the United Kingdom will not change without the consent of the majority of its people.[9]

This was to be the last ever exchange of messages via the back channel. Although on the face of it, all seemed set fair to make genuine political progress, there was a serious problem, also reminiscent of the fallout from the 'conflict is over' message. When McGuinness was apprised of what Brendan purported McGuinness had said at the meeting in Derry with Brendan only a few days before the Dunadry meeting, he was again incandescent, vehemently denying he had ever said such a thing. It seemed like *Groundhog Day* all over again. McGuinness suspected Brendan might be playing a double game as a suspected British spy. Shortly afterwards, four senior IRA men arrived at Brendan's house, ordered him into an upstairs room and subjected him to a frightening interrogation. Brendan would not tell me who the four men were, but it's reasonable to assume McGuinness and Gerry Kelly would have been among them. Brendan feared for his life, thinking he might be about to be killed. He narrowly survived the ordeal.

They questioned me upstairs for four solid hours. The questioning […] wasn't abusive, but very intense. They were the bosses. Let me put it this way, if I had been guilty of anything, I wouldn't have liked to have been sitting in that room. At the end they went out of that room with two thoughts in mind: first of all the Link [Brendan and the back channel] is finished and second that I did not send the message. They accepted that quite fully. But they also said that the time had come […] to begin dialogue [with the British] themselves. They wanted to be doing their own business.[10]

Margo watched Brendan come downstairs, 'ashen-faced'. The back
channel was dead but Brendan was still alive. Robert thinks that
during the four-hour interrogation Brendan probably blamed him for
the message and made him the scapegoat – as Robert was probably,
and erroneously, blamed for the 'conflict is over' message. No wonder
Brendan was 'ashen-faced' after what he had just been through. Brendan's
final interrogation at the hands of the four IRA 'bosses' marked the end
of an era, as Robert reflected in a personal note:

> Brendan was no longer trusted by the Provisionals or by the NIO –
> a sad fate as it was through him that the peace process had been
> brought as far as it then had. As would have been expected [in my
> Service], I then broke off all contact with him.

What does Robert make of these conflicting stories? It took me back
to his explanation as to why he got in touch with me in 2021 after
more than twenty years of silence. He said he wanted to set the record
straight as he had been portrayed as having fabricated both messages –
which he did not. 'I was made the scapegoat,' he says. 'Brendan had
grossly miscalculated and obviously escaped [an unwelcome fate] by
blaming me for everything.' Robert believes Brendan was right to do
so for two reasons: to save his own life and to push the peace process
forward, which was always his main aim. If that was his ploy – and there
is no way of proving it, as Brendan has died – it was for the best possible
motive, to bring peace to Ireland. A week after the Shankill bomb and
three days after the Halloween massacre, Prime Minister John Major
addressed the House of Commons and expressed his visceral loathing
for the IRA and all its works. He was referring to the issue of engaging
with the IRA.

> If the implication is that we should sit down and talk with Adams
> and the Provisional IRA, I can only say that that would turn my
> stomach and those of most Honourable Members. We will not
> do it. If there is a total ending of violence and if and when that is
> established for a significant time, we shall talk to constitutional
> parties that have people elected in their names. I will not talk to
> people who murder indiscriminately.[11]

To recap, at this stage John Major still did not know that Robert had met Martin McGuinness.

Robert knew how precarious the back channel was, with each IRA atrocity lending credence to the scepticism of those in Whitehall who had little faith that the process would deliver peace. The Shankill bomb and John Major's reaction to it only added force to their view. Robert was aware that Major telling the House of Commons that it would 'turn my stomach to sit down and talk with Adams and the Provisional IRA' came only eight months after he, Robert, had sat down and talked to Martin McGuinness, although no one, apart from John Deverell and Brendan Duddy, knew.

The secret was the sword of Damocles hanging over Robert, who feared that at some stage the truth would come out. It was the nightmare that he had lived with for months. In November 1993 it was to end in the most unfortunate of circumstances when new intelligence suddenly came to light indicating that a British official had met the IRA.

It was a light-bulb moment. Stephen Lander, who was under the impression that all the information about the meeting with McGuinness had come from Brendan, immediately put two and two together to identify Robert. When confronted by Lander, Robert admitted, 'Yes, it was me,' and proceeded to tell him the 'sorry tale'.[12]

The revelation that Robert had met McGuinness came as a bombshell for MI5, the Northern Ireland Office and the Government and greatly concerned John Deverell since he was intimately involved in the lead-up to the meeting with McGuinness and Kelly, although at the last minute he had forbidden Robert to go and Robert had disobeyed orders. Deverell now feared the potential damage the revelation might do to the sensitive relationship between MI5 and the Northern Ireland Office. He was anxious to have his name kept out of it, fearing for his career. He suggested Robert tell MI5's Director General, Stella Rimington, at the inevitable meeting when Robert had to face the music, that she should not tell the Northern Ireland Office's John Chilcot and Quentin Thomas that Robert had involved him (Deverell). Robert agreed it was a sensible idea. 'The less blood on the carpet the better,' he said.[13]

Having lived with the burden of his subterfuge for seven months, Robert was greatly relieved that at last things had come out into the open. He had always known the news was likely to break in some way – it was never a question of 'whether' but 'how' – but this was not the way that he would have wished it. At home, he awaited his fate, fearing execution.

John Deverell rang him in the evening and said that John Chilcot was thinking of resigning. Robert decided that there was only one principled course of action: to fall on his sword himself.

> I decided I could not honourably remain in the Service. So many
> things had gone wrong. I was at the basis of trouble for others
> and responsible for John Chilcot talking about resignation, so the
> correct and honourable thing for me to do was to resign myself.
> I saw Stephen Lander the first thing the next morning and said
> I was resigning and gave him the reasons why. He said it was a pity
> but quite understood – and that was that. I just wanted to disappear
> from official sight. I did so not with a heavy heart but with relief.
> I'd no regrets about what I had done. I should have been pleased
> because the nightmare was over, thank goodness.[14]

After Robert handed his resignation to the Security Service on 16 November 1993, his thoughts turned to retiring to the farm he had bought to rear sheep in the time he would now have to do so. He was enormously grateful for the way Stephen Lander and Stella Rimington, the Director General, had treated him when he had been expecting the worst.

> I saw Stella Rimington twice. The first time was when news of my
> meeting with the IRA broke. She said that I had correctly reported
> it to John Deverell and had very decently taken the whole blame
> on my shoulders. She said there was no question of making me a
> scapegoat. I left quite cheered as I'd been expecting dismissal from
> the Service. The second time was before MI5's internal inquiry into
> all that had happened. Again, she was very kind and I felt fortunate
> to have her as my DG. I had known her for some years but she
> could easily have made me a sacrifice for the Service's sake.[15]

She did however take him to task for the injudiciously worded letter he had sent to McGuinness with the Gerry Adams sign-off, 'Tiocfaidh ár lá' – 'Our day will come'. And there was further embarrassment on the horizon. Brendan had warned Robert that Adams and McGuinness were talking about publicly revealing McGuinness and Kelly's meeting with Robert and what he had said, to get their side of the story out first.

On Sunday 28 November 1993, news of the secret talks finally broke when the *Observer* ran a sensational front-page scoop, delivered by the terrier-like Belfast journalist Eamonn Mallie, about the Government's secret contacts with the IRA and how there had been a meeting between the two sides only three days after the atrocity of the Warrington bombs. The scoop was dynamite, not least because the Government had consistently denied that any such meetings had taken place – excusably because at the time the Government was not aware that Robert had met McGuinness and Kelly, although it did know that Michael Oatley had held an unauthorised meeting with McGuinness in Derry in February 1991.

Sinn Féin then called a press conference at which McGuinness revealed the meeting with 'Fred' and the position papers leading up to it that had been exchanged by both sides. The Northern Ireland Secretary, Sir Patrick Mayhew, was acutely embarrassed – as was the Government. It immediately tried to turn the tables by referring to the 'conflict is over' message and attacking the IRA for not ending the violence. Not surprisingly Sir Patrick, being the minister responsible, was on edge at the prospect of entering the lion's den as he went to parliament to face the music, underestimating the mood of MPs. To his astonishment, when he walked into the chamber, he received a rapturous reception from both sides of the House, relieved that it appeared that finally the Government was going the last mile to try and achieve peace in Ireland to end the carnage. Mayhew was delighted. The reception dispelled his misgivings as, with renewed confidence, he set about explaining the Government's position, based on 'the conflict is over' message from McGuinness. It was a bullish performance.

> It is clear that that message was consistent with our declared
> policy: namely, that if such people [the IRA] wanted to enter into talks
> or negotiations with the Government, they first had genuinely to end
> violence not just temporarily, but for good. If they did, and showed
> sufficiently that they meant it, we would not want, for our part, to
> continue to exclude them from political talks. That remains our policy.
>   We must never lose sight of the fact that it is the terrorists
> who must answer for the deaths, destruction and misery of the

past twenty-five years. It lies therefore with the IRA, and with it
alone, to end their inhuman crimes. It is for them and those who
support and justify them to explain why they have wickedly failed
to do that ... I promise the House and the people of Northern
Ireland that, for our part, we shall not cease our efforts to bring
violence to a permanent end. Peace, properly attained, is a prize
worth risks.[16]

Sir Patrick had held a press conference the day before he addressed
the House of Commons at which he had said that his account of
these events 'represented the truth, namely that nobody has been
authorised to conduct talks or to carry on negotiations on behalf of
the British Government with Sinn Féin or the IRA'. Far from being
an excuse, his words reflected the truth. Michael Oatley's meeting
with McGuinness in early February 1991 and Robert's meeting with
McGuinness and Kelly in March 1993 had both been unauthorised.
Despite McGuinness and his colleagues now dropping Brendan from
the peace process following his interrogation, the leadership carried on
engaging directly with the Government in the hope of bringing peace
closer. The Reverend Ian Paisley, the Honourable Member for North
Antrim, was not convinced. 'The people of Northern Ireland today
demand that the Secretary of State explains why he issued falsehoods
himself, got officials to issue falsehoods and got Downing Street to
back up those falsehoods.'[17] The Speaker of the House of Commons
bridled at the use of the word 'falsehoods', saying the word meant
one thing, 'lies', and asked Dr Paisley to rephrase what he was saying.
Dr Paisley refused. 'I stand by what I said. It was a falsehood: it was
worse, it was a lie.' The Speaker then banned him from parliament for
the rest of the day.[18]

Sir Patrick said Michael Oatley's meeting with McGuinness in early
February 1991 was 'unauthorised', but Sir John Chilcot later certainly
became aware of it because Oatley wrote a detailed account for him,
in addition to providing a full verbal account at a face-to-face meeting.
With regard to Robert's crucial meeting with McGuinness and Kelly in
March 1993, which lay at the heart of the controversy, the Government
denied any involvement because at the time it knew nothing about it.
Only Robert, John Deverell, Martin McGuinness and Gerry Kelly knew
that it had happened – along with the others who were present. The

world was soon to know too when on 5 January 1994 Sinn Féin published the minutes of the meeting and its antecedents – the communications on both sides that had led up to it – in its document *Setting the Record Straight*. The minutes of the meeting which had been taken by McGuinness and Kelly were now in the public domain, including the toxic words, 'The final solution is union…This island will be as one.'

But for Robert there was a surprising and soothing balm to the wound from an unexpected quarter. Having handed his resignation letter to Stephen Lander on 16 November 1993, he was now due to leave the Service by Christmas. Eleven days after facing the House of Commons, Sir Patrick Mayhew sent Robert a handwritten letter, dated 10 December. It began, 'Dear Fred …':

> I do not want to allow your career to conclude – and I know it
> has been distinguished by great dedication and courage – without
> expressing to you my personal admiration and thanks for your
> service. Great events frequently claim casualties as those who try
> to play a part in shaping them come to realize. It is important not
> to permit them to distort the true perspective of their enterprise
> in which they are sustained – and especially so when the casualties
> include ourselves.
>
> In time I am confident that peace, properly attained, will come to
> Northern Ireland: and that is what matters most of all to all of us.
>
> With my best wishes
> Yours sincerely
> Patrick Mayhew[19]

That letter from the Secretary of State helped ease the pain that Robert had gone through.

His retirement present was not a gold watch or even a rolled-gold Cross pen but the decanter, glasses and tray intended for the first full meeting between the British Government and the republican movement.*

Other letters from colleagues also gave him comfort, echoing what Sir Patrick had written.

---

*Michael Oatley had presented his IRA interlocutors on his departure after the IRA's 1975 ceasefire with rolled-gold Cross ballpoint pens. See p. 109.

Dear Robert

I felt I had to write to express my personal sadness that you have decided to resign following the recent disclosures. The case has been an exceptional one and I believe the progress made is due to a significant extent to your skill and experience. I am only sorry that, so far, we have not achieved the desired result.

For my part, I regard it as a privilege to have worked closely with such an honourable, astute and capable colleague. Please don't lose sight of your undoubted achievements in this current turbulent period. I wish you well for the future and hope that if we do eventually achieve the desired result, you will sit in your garden content in the knowledge that you played a significant role in its achievement.[20]

And he received support from other friends in Government, alluding to Sir Patrick Mayhew's letter:

We were very pleased to hear the heartfelt tribute to outstanding courage and persuasiveness in very difficult circumstances – richly deserved. It was an invaluable contribution to the development of the process and it is good that it has been recognised.[21]

Another colleague believed Robert had been 'hung out to dry' – presumably because he had covered for his MI5 superior, John Deverell, who had told him [Robert] not to notify John Chilcot that he had just met McGuinness.

Robert wrote letters too. On 15 December 1993, days before he left MI5 headquarters, Robert, ever the gentleman, wrote a farewell letter to Sir John Chilcot:

Dear John

As you know I resigned at the beginning of the month and as I will be leaving at Christmas I was anxious to write to you before I did so. First of all I wanted to thank you for the consideration you have shown me in the past few weeks. It has been a pretty awful time for all of us and as one revelation followed another I have felt keenly how badly I have let you down. You have been given various papers and reports on how and why things happened, but I wanted to say personally how sorry I was to have caused, in particular, such problems.

I count myself lucky to have had your support and understanding throughout the last two and a half years and this has always meant a great deal to me.

I hope that your continuing efforts to achieve a proper settlement are successful – I will read about them avidly.

With every good wish for the future.

Yours sincerely

Robert

Robert's *mea culpa* letter to John Chilcot and the letters of support he received from Sir Patrick Mayhew, colleagues and friends, helped assuage the guilt of his deception and the political fallout it had caused.

Eight months after Robert left MI5, on 31 August 1994, Gerry Adams announced that he had met the Provisional Army Council and had been informed that the IRA would declare 'a complete cessation of military operations' from midnight that evening. It was the goal of 'Operation Chiffon' for which Robert and John Deverell had laboured. Robert was at home when he heard the news on the wireless that morning. 'I was delighted. Happy, pleased and relieved. A mixture of all those emotions.'

Tragically, John Deverell never got to see the culmination of 'Operation Chiffon' which he, Robert and Brendan had worked so long and hard to achieve. He died on 2 June 1994, three months before the IRA announced its cessation of military operations. He was killed along with twenty-nine other intelligence officers, the cream of British intelligence, on their way to a security conference in Scotland, when their RAF Chinook helicopter crashed in atrocious weather conditions on the Mull of Kintyre. No doubt one of the items on the conference agenda would have been the ceasefire that the IRA was soon expected to declare, the aim of 'Operation Chiffon' that Robert, in the end, had helped make possible, completing the work that Frank Steele, Michael Oatley and Brendan Duddy had pioneered. But the IRA ceasefire was only the beginning of the long road to peace.

30

Peace Comes Dropping Slow

Watching from afar on his sheep farm, and feeling strangely detached, Robert saw more obstacles emerging on the road to a ceasefire and, it was hoped, the ultimate prize of peace. The first obstacle was Anglo-American relations, with John Major becoming incandescent when President Bill Clinton granted Gerry Adams a 'limited duration' visa on 29 January 1994 so that he could fly to the US to reassure Irish America, for years the IRA's munificent paymaster, that there would be no sell-out. At this stage there had been no IRA ceasefire. Major was furious and at one point refused to take the President's phone calls.

> Here we were, well on the road towards a settlement, and there were
> principal Sinn Féin figures going to America where they were going
> to raise more money. We knew what that money was being used
> for. It would have been used for arms. So, of course, we were very
> peeved. We thought it was a bad signal to give at that time.[1]

The Prime Minister feared that the optimistic words he'd used in his speech at the Lord Mayor's Banquet in London two months earlier, on 15 November 1993, might sound empty with the American President apparently kowtowing to the IRA before there was any ceasefire – the British Government's all-too-familiar red line:

> There may now be a better opportunity for peace in Northern
> Ireland than for many years. There are several important elements
> coming together. First, there is the burning desire on each side

of the community for peace, not a peace at any price but peace that is fair and just. No one wants to continue living with death and terror and fear for another twenty-five years. Second, the Irish Government have shown a new understanding of the rights and concerns of Unionists. They are willing to reach out to them and I believe to make constitutional change a part of an overall settlement. They accept, rightly, that it is for the people of Northern Ireland freely and democratically to determine their own future.[2]*

The good news was that the ill-feeling didn't last. The Prime Minister and the President made up and the White House became an enthusiastic champion of the peace process, with Clinton visiting Belfast on 30 November 1995, where he 'just happened' to run across Gerry Adams on a corner of the Falls Road, affording a photo opportunity complete with a handshake.

So why did the IRA ceasefire and the subsequent talks that culminated in the Good Friday Agreement and peace – the endgame of 'Operation Chiffon' – take so long? In the words of the great Irish poet William Butler Yeats, it was because 'peace comes dropping slow'.[†] After Robert's seminal meeting with Martin McGuinness at Brendan's house in Derry in 1993, it was to be almost eighteen months before the IRA declared its historic ceasefire in 1994 and then another four years before the Good Friday Agreement was finally signed in 1998.

Granting a visa to Adams was a small gesture that had huge political implications. After the brief spat with Downing Street, the White House and Irish America were to become fully signed up members of the peace process. I remember filming in the Maze prison at the time of Adams's visit to America and watching ecstatic IRA prisoners in their crowded H Block kitchen, drinking tea and eating mountains of

---

*The constitutional change was Dublin agreeing to amend Articles 2 and 3 of the Irish constitution. The Articles originally claimed Northern Ireland as part of the national territory, a claim that had always infuriated unionists. In 1999, following the Good Friday Agreement, the claim was amended to grant the right to be 'part of the Irish Nation' to all people born on the island of Ireland; the revised Articles also expressed a desire for the peaceful political unification of the island, subject to the consent of the people of Northern Ireland and Ireland.
†'The Lake Isle of Innisfree' (1890) by William Butler Yeats.

buttered toast, shouting, cheering and banging saucepans and anything else they could lay their hands on, when the TV news showed Adams in America, being feted like a visiting celebrity.

The prisoners, many serving life for murder, were representatives of the IRA's rank and file, although behind bars. I got the impression that they were 100 per cent supportive of what Adams and McGuinness were trying to achieve. On 23 February 1994, on his return from America, Adams received a rapturous reception at Sinn Féin's Ard Fheis, attacking the British Government for making the decommissioning of IRA weapons the prerequisite of any political engagement. To loud applause, he asked, 'Does anyone really expect the IRA to cease its activities so that British civil servants can discuss with Sinn Féin the surrender of IRA weapons after we have been decontaminated?'[3] The toxic subject of decommissioning – toxic, that is, to the republican movement – was first raised by the Northern Ireland Secretary, Sir Patrick Mayhew when he mentioned it had been referred to on 15 December 1993 in the Downing Street Declaration. The Declaration was signed by the British and Irish Prime Ministers, John Major and Albert Reynolds, and affirmed the right of the people of Ireland to self-determination with the crucial proviso that Irish unity could only be achieved by peaceful means and with the consent of the majority of the people of Northern Ireland. The Declaration was one of the essential building blocks of peace. Mayhew pointed out that, although the Declaration had not mentioned 'decommissioning' as such, it was clear from the wording – 'peace must involve a permanent end to violence' and 'a commitment to exclusively peaceful methods' – that decommissioning was implied even though not explicitly stated.[4] The issue of decommissioning was to loom over the decade that followed.

Although Michael Oatley had by now retired, he maintained contact with Brendan and kept a close eye on the progress – or lack of it – towards the peace that he had helped nourish over so many years, not least by his unauthorised meeting with Martin McGuinness at Bernadette Mount's house in February 1991, just before he retired from the Secret Intelligence Service.

> I think where decommissioning first came into the limelight was when it was included as an aspect of the Downing Street Declaration in 1993. My own view is that it's a very harmful

ingredient because I would have thought that the Government should, by then, have been aware that it was an unacceptable condition to suggest to the IRA.

Decommissioning means handing over your weapons which is the traditional mark of defeat. In the history of Irish rebellion, this is not something you do. If you decide to end your campaign you stick your gun somewhere in the roof and continue to lead a peaceful life, but you don't go and hand it in to an occupying power. There is a deep-rooted objection within the republican movement to any idea of handing in weaponry.[5]

Robert also made it clear that decommissioning never featured at any stage during the back-channel exchanges and certainly was never mentioned at his meeting with McGuinness and Kelly.

It was never discussed in my dealings. It was a wrangle that later went on and on and on. We were only at the beginning of the process. Decommissioning lay further down the road. And I thought the IRA was never going to agree to destroy its weapons.[6]

Meanwhile in the months leading up to the ceasefire the IRA was still using its formidable variety of weapons against soldiers and policemen, including attacks from 'barrack buster' homemade heavy mortars and shoulder-held RPGs, many smuggled in from Libya as part of the vast consignments imported in 1985 and 1986. The IRA offensive included three separate mortar attacks on Heathrow airport over five days in March 1994 which resulted in serious traffic disruption and some areas of the airport being closed. Coded telephone warnings were given. The IRA's intention was to launch attacks that would have maximum publicity impact but with minimal risk to life. And in the first three months of that year, there were firebombs in London's Oxford Street in addition to daily attacks in Northern Ireland. Although there were few deaths over the period, the offensive was relentless, as the chronology indicates.[7] It was the IRA's way of sending a message to the 'Brits' that, without a settlement, it had the capacity to carry on its 'Long War' indefinitely. On 5 April 1994, the IRA declared a three-day ceasefire. It was intended to be a timely reminder to the British Government that it was serious about peace, and a reminder to the people of Northern Ireland and politicians at Stormont and Westminster of what peace could be like. John Major was not impressed. On a visit to Northern Ireland on the day of the IRA's ceasefire announcement, he was dismissive and stuck to his familiar red line: 'What the people of Northern Ireland want is not a ceasefire over two or three days but a permanent end to violence.'[8]

The following months mirrored the back and forth on the back channel towards the end of 1993 when a message from the Government, conveyed to Brendan by Robert in his final days before retirement, clearly set out, at Sinn Féin's request, the consequences of 'a total end to hostilities'. The message was dated 5 November.

> If, as you have offered, you were to give us an unequivocal assurance
> that violence has indeed been brought to a permanent end, and that
> accordingly Sinn Féin is now committed to political progress by
> peaceful and democratic means alone, we will make clear publicly
> our commitment to enter exploratory dialogue with you ...
> Provided events on the ground are fully consistent with this, a first
> meeting for exploratory dialogue will take place within a week of
> Parliament's return in January [1994].[9]

The Government was effectively offering 'exploratory dialogue' within three months of the announcement of a cessation of violence. It didn't happen then because events got in the way. The Downing Street Declaration didn't go down well in republican circles and hard-liners on the Army Council were bitterly opposed to it, reflected in the day-to-day intensification of the military campaign through much of 1994. It seemed we were back to stalemate. John Major decided to break the impasse, the difference being that the exchanges were now conducted, not in the secrecy of the back channel, which was now dead, but openly in an exchange of letters between Gerry Adams, who sought 'clarification' of the Downing Street Declaration, and John Major, who stood his ground on no talks before a ceasefire. For Adams, the repeated request for clarification, while genuine, was also a convenient delaying mechanism while McGuinness and other senior IRA commanders prepared the IRA for the giant step of a ceasefire that would satisfy John Major and his Government.

To break the stalemate, Major repeated the offer made via Robert and the back channel on 5 November 1993 with 'our detailed offer of an exploratory dialogue within three months of a cessation'.[10] The republican movement welcomed the offer, despite misgivings by some hardliners who remained on board in order to avoid a long-feared split. While the wrangling over the small print in the Downing Street Declaration continued, as did IRA operations, there were other grave concerns on the security front. With talk of an IRA ceasefire in the air, the loyalist paramilitaries of the UDA/UFF and UVF, fearing that a secret deal was being done to pull the plug on Northern Ireland, responded as they had done in the wake of the ceasefires of 1972 and 1975: they intensified their attacks, not only on innocent Catholics but increasingly on actual and suspected members of the IRA and Sinn Féin. In 1994, the UFF and UVF 'out-killed' the IRA, with loyalist paramilitaries killing thirty-seven people to the IRA's nineteen.[11] The familiar pattern of tit-for-tat killings returned, now involving the Irish National Liberation Army (INLA), the bitter rival of the (Provisional) IRA, whose joint histories were punctuated by a series of bloody internecine feuds.

At lunchtime, on Saturday 16 June 1994, Trevor King, a senior UVF commander, was talking to two other UVF men, Colin Craig and David Hamilton, close to UVF headquarters on the Shankill Road. It seems they had just emerged from a meeting. An unmasked INLA gunman walked up, pulled out a handgun and shot the three loyalists in the head and neck. He then made his escape in a waiting Ford Sierra. Craig died almost immediately, Hamilton the next day and King, the INLA's prime target, three weeks later. On 18 June, the UVF took shocking sectarian revenge. It was the evening Ireland were playing Italy in the 1994 football World Cup. Two UVF gunmen walked into the Heights Bar in Loughinisland, a mainly Catholic village close to Downpatrick, and opened fire with a Czech-made rifle and an AK-47 automatic. Their victims were sitting watching the match with their backs to the door. Six Catholics were shot dead, including eighty-seven-year-old Barney Green, one of the oldest people to have been killed in the Troubles. He had put on his best suit for the Big Match. It looked like the Greysteel pub massacre the previous year all over again. Sir Patrick Mayhew scathingly called out the killers.

I suppose some of you have families. Let's just picture a future conversation you may have with your daughter, who asks you,

'What did you do in your so-called war, Daddy?' And you will say, 'I killed a man of 87. He was sitting with his back to me. He was watching the World Cup. I shot him dead.' She won't think that the record of a hero, will she?[12]

Loughinisland and the spate of loyalist killings brought it home to the British Government, as if it needed any reminder, that an IRA ceasefire was not the only component of the axis of peace, although it was the critical one from which everything else that 'Operation Chiffon' intended would follow. Loyalists too had to be encouraged to lay down their arms. For much of their leadership and many of the rank and file, it seemed fairly straightforward. Since the early days, the loyalist rationale had always been that loyalist violence was a reaction to IRA violence and that if the IRA stopped killing, they too would stop. It would make no sense to carry on and would make a mockery of the loyalist paramilitaries' professed raison d'être that they were 'soldiers' fighting the IRA. But as yet there was no IRA ceasefire, despite ever increasing rumours. The rumours were true. It was soon to happen.

On the morning of 31 August 1994, the long-awaited statement from the IRA finally came.

> Recognising the potential of the current situation and in order to enhance the democratic process and underline our commitment to its success, the leadership of Óglaigh na hÉireann [the IRA] have decided that as of midnight, Wednesday 31 August, there will be a complete cessation of military operations.[§] All of our units have been instructed accordingly ... We believe that an opportunity to create a just and lasting peace has been created ... A solution can only be found as a result of inclusive negotiations.[13]

That evening, hours before the ceasefire was due to begin, there were scenes of jubilation in West Belfast, with cars, bedecked with Irish tricolours, honking their horns in celebration as they drove past a large crowd gathered to hear the leaders of the republican movement,

---

[§]Óglaigh na hÉireann literally means the young men or soldiers/volunteers of Ireland. It came to mean the IRA, the Army of Ireland.

Gerry Adams and Martin McGuinness, hail the hoped-for peaceful and democratic future ahead. The event had all the appearance of a victory parade but, of course, it wasn't. Adams and McGuinness were at pains to avoid the impression that it was. Both knew there was a long way to go. The ceasefire was only the first step on the road to a political settlement and peace – the endgame of 'Operation Chiffon'. The terminology was crucial. The IRA, if not yet victorious, was 'undefeated'. John Major was sceptical about the IRA's long-term intentions, despite advice from MI5 that it was genuine and likely to last.

> There was no indication from them that satisfied me that they were really *not* going to return to violence if things didn't go their way. It wasn't a conviction in my heart that it was definitely going to be permanent. I didn't believe that it was but I believed we had to roll with that particular tide and see if we could turn what looked like a temporary but welcome cessation into something that was continuous.[14]

The morning the ceasefire was declared, Robert's telephone rang on his farm. He wasn't aware of the IRA's announcement and, since his retirement, Northern Ireland with all its anxieties and pressures had been far from his mind – to his relief, and his wife's too. The calls came as a complete surprise because that morning he was probably thinking about sheep and not the IRA.

> In a way it brought it all back. I got three phone calls, all in one morning, saying, 'Congratulations. This is the culmination of all that you did.' One was from a senior MI5 colleague, one from Stephen Lander and then one from Eliza Manningham-Buller. She said, 'It's Eliza. Are you happily settled?' I said I was and I could see the sheep on the hill. They all called me because of the ceasefire that had just been declared. How did I feel? I felt very pleased, delighted. Did I feel vindicated? There was quite a long gap [of almost a year and a half] between what I had done and said and the ceasefire, so I wasn't able to say that it was because of what I did. I was surprised that everyone else seemed to think it was.[15]

Robert was being typically self-effacing.

Shortly after the ceasefire, I remember talking to John Chilcot over breakfast in the Victorian splendour of Oxford's Randolph Hotel, anxious to know his thoughts on what was likely to happen during the next stage of the peace process and how long it would take before a final settlement might be reached. In his usual measured way, he said it would take about five years. I was surprised, not at the time being privy to all that had gone on before. I had optimistically expected around a year to eighteen months. Sir John, as he became in the 1994 New Year's Honours' list in recognition of his work on the peace process, was only one year out, with the Good Friday Agreement being signed in 1998.[16]

The next challenge was to get a ceasefire by the loyalist paramilitaries in place to test their contention that if the IRA stopped killing, they would stop too. Work was already well underway thanks to the groundwork by the UVF's David Ervine and Billy Hutchinson and the UDA's Davy Adams and other loyalists at grass-roots level. They were supported in their endeavours by Protestant clergymen including a Belfast Presbyterian minister, the Reverend Roy Magee, and Archbishop Robin Eames, the Primate of All Ireland, who had a hotline to John Major. For the purposes of peace, the UDA and the UVF put their traditional rivalries aside to come together beneath the paramilitary umbrella of the Combined Loyalist Military Command (CLMC) under the leadership of the legendary Augustus 'Gusty' Spence, the founder of the modern UVF. In 1966 Spence had been sentenced to life for the second murder of the Troubles.[**]

It was fitting, given his journey from war to peace, that on 13 October 1994, six weeks after the IRA ceasefire, Gusty Spence, as head of the CLMC, read out the statement announcing the loyalist ceasefire. He was flanked by Gary McMichael, David Adams and John White of the UDA's political party, the Ulster Democratic Party (UDP), and David

---

[**]Spence had been convicted of the murder of a teenage Catholic barman, Peter Ward, on 26 June 1966 as he left the Malvern Arms pub on the Shankill Road. It was while serving time in jail as the UVF's commander in Long Kesh in the 1970s that he renounced violence and encouraged an end to the conflict, beginning with a ceasefire. He was released on licence in 1984 after eighteen years behind bars. (David McKittrick, Seamus Kelters, Brian Feeney and Chris Thornton, *Lost Lives: The Stories of the Men, Women and Children Who Died as a Result of the Northern Ireland Troubles*, Mainstream Publishing, Edinburgh, 1999, pp. 26–7.)

Ervine, William 'Plum' Smith and Jim McDonald of the UVF's political party, the Progressive Unionist Party (PUP). Spence, unlike the IRA in its statement, apologised on behalf of all the loyalist paramilitaries, expressing deep regret for all they had done.

> In all sincerity, we offer to the loved ones of all innocent victims over the past twenty-five years abject and true remorse. No words of ours will compensate for the intolerable suffering they have undergone during the conflict. Let us firmly resolve to respect our differing views of freedom, culture and aspiration and never again permit our political circumstances to degenerate into bloody warfare. We are on the threshold of a new and exciting beginning ... so that together we can bring forth a wholesome society in which our children and their children will know the meaning of true peace.[17]

Despite the progress being made towards the end of 1994, with both the IRA and the loyalist ceasefires now in place, the British Government was still insisting that the IRA should give an assurance that its ceasefire was 'permanent', which caused deep unease in IRA ranks, as did Sir Patrick Mayhew's insistence on decommissioning. Nevertheless despite these widespread Cabinet and unionist misgivings, the Government decided to push ahead to maintain political momentum and the confidence of the leadership of the IRA and Sinn Féin. John Major always knew it was a gamble.

31

The Road to Good Friday

On 9 December 1994, the Government stuck to its promise of exploratory talks three months after a ceasefire. It was to be a historic day. I'd previously spoken to Martin McGuinness, who agreed to let me accompany him on the journey to Stormont's Parliament Buildings where the talks were to take place. He was planning to get to Belfast ahead of time to finalise things with Sinn Féin's 'kitchen cabinet' in order to be ready for the following day. The last time a British government had openly and formally talked to the IRA was in 1921 when the Prime Minister, David Lloyd George, met the IRA's military leader, Michael Collins, in Downing Street to sign the Anglo-Irish Treaty. (All the other meetings, like Cheyne Walk, had been secret.) Apprehensively, Collins put pen to paper, and while the ink was still drying, remarked, 'I may have signed my actual death warrant.'[1] His words were prophetic. He was shot dead the following year in an ambush by anti-Treaty IRA forces in the civil war that followed the Anglo-Irish Treaty.*

---

*With partition already a fait accompli earlier in the year, the Treaty signed on 6 December 1921 gave a degree of independence to the Twenty-Six Counties of the South, known as the Irish Free State, by granting it Dominion Status within the British Empire. The fact that the Free State government had to swear allegiance to the Crown proved too much for hard-line elements of the IRA. They accused Collins of betrayal, leaving the island partitioned and the Free State still connected to the British Crown by the oath of allegiance. The result was a fratricidal civil war that lasted for almost a year between 1922 and 1923.

I met McGuinness at his house in the Bogside early in the morning and sat beside him on the back seat of his car so we could talk while his driver headed to Belfast. I asked if he feared the fate of Michael Collins as the republican movement had already fractured over the ceasefire. The fracture wasn't widespread but was enough to pose a threat to McGuinness's life, so strong were anti-ceasefire feelings among a minority of his comrades. He shook his head and said it was not a thought that had crossed his mind. Clearly the immediate present and the future were occupying his thoughts, not the distant past. He dropped me off in Belfast as he left for a last-minute briefing with his colleagues.

The December morning of the first official meeting between Sinn Féin and British officials dawned cold, sunny and bright. I stood at the bottom of the broad steps of Stormont's Parliament Buildings in an area cordoned off to accommodate the large group of journalists ready to record history. I watched Martin McGuinness and Gerry Kelly arrive in an armoured black taxi and walk into Parliament Buildings through a side entrance with the Sinn Féin negotiating team, briefcases in hand. It was the final outcome of the meeting they had held with Robert, or 'Fred' as the IRA knew him, almost two years earlier when Robert had uttered the game-changing words, 'The final solution is union. This island will be as one.'

The meeting was, as advertised, 'exploratory', with both sides getting to know each other in a way that had only been done previously at second- or thirdhand via Robert, Brendan and the back channel. Quentin Thomas, the Northern Ireland Office's Political Director, tried to make the meeting as relaxed as possible. It was civilised and amicable with the occasional flash of humour. At one stage, McGuinness is reported to have cheekily asked Quentin Thomas, 'How is "Fred"?'[2] I doubt McGuinness would have received an answer. The IRA had no idea 'Fred' was now raising sheep. Sinn Féin denied it had any connection with the IRA and insisted it should be included in all-party talks on the basis of its democratic mandate, with Sinn Féin increasingly close to challenging the SDLP as the largest nationalist party in Northern Ireland. McGuinness and his delegation set out their political shopping list: the release of prisoners, the recognition of the Irish language and the fundamental reform of justice and policing by abolishing the RUC.[3] For their part, the British continued to raise the toxic issues of 'decommissioning' and the 'permanency' of the ceasefire, but there was no walk-out by Sinn Féin. It had travelled too far for histrionics.

The problem was that the British saw the meeting for what it was, 'exploratory'. Quentin Thomas described the process as being about 'the progressive adjustment of expectations'.[4] McGuinness, Kelly and Sinn Féin saw it as a means of expediting all-party talks and their inclusion in them. Further meetings followed, but the two sides were pursuing different agendas.

Peace continued to come 'dropping slow'. Throughout 1995, the deadlock continued, with Sinn Féin insisting on meeting ministers and being included in all-party talks and with John Major and Sir Patrick Mayhew insisting on decommissioning as a prerequisite of Sinn Féin's inclusion in such talks and any political settlement. And there was an additional problem. Major became increasingly dependent on the votes of unionist MPs at Westminster to sustain his Government. Unionists were utterly opposed to doing business with Sinn Féin, which they regarded as part of a terrorist organisation, consistently referring to it as 'IRA/Sinn Féin'. Major was caught between a rock and a hard place – between two lots of hard men.

> You were asking unionists and others to sit down at a table with people who had an Armalite and a bomb underneath the table, which, if the talks got to a sticky phase, they would take out and use. We were trying to get them into talks in a way that other people would talk to them. If 'the conflict is over', as the Provisional Army Council said, what was the need for weapons?[5]

The impasse over decommissioning and the government's need to secure unionist votes at Westminster were not conducive to peace. The IRA was getting restless. I met Martin McGuinness in the basement of a hotel in Dublin's O'Connell Street towards the end of 1995 – the first year in which, due to the ceasefire, no British soldier was killed. He was not happy. He asked me what I thought the British were up to. I explained that Major's room for manoeuvre was constrained by his dwindling parliamentary majority and his dependence on the support of unionist MPs. To McGuinness it was simply another excuse – the use of the unionist 'veto' yet again. The charm was gone. The eyes hardened. He warned that the British had better be careful.

McGuinness's words flashed across my mind when, a couple of months later, on 9 February 1996, the IRA exploded a 1,000lb bomb at South Quay, in the heart of London's Docklands. The damage amounted to an estimated £150 million. Two men who worked in a newspaper kiosk were killed. The IRA had given a warning but the area could not be cleared in time. The IRA ceasefire, which had lasted for seventeen months, was over. The IRA issued a statement shortly before the explosion, demanding 'an inclusive negotiated settlement'.

> Instead of embracing the peace process, the British government
> acted in bad faith with Mr Major and the Unionist leaders
> squandering this unprecedented opportunity to resolve the conflict.
> The blame for the failure thus far of the Irish peace process lies
> squarely with John Major and his government.[6]

Michael Oatley, although retired since 1991 after meeting Martin McGuinness at Bernie Mount's house in Derry, kept abreast of what was happening across the water. The Docklands bomb, triggered by the impasse over decommissioning, came as no surprise.

Robert, again watching from afar on his farm, was shocked by the breaking of the 1994 ceasefire and sorry that he was no longer in touch with the IRA, McGuinness having consigned the back channel to history and turned to dealing directly with the Government. By 1996, MI5 was out of the picture, at least as far as secret contacts were concerned. Robert harboured a feeling of regret.

> We were only at the beginning of the process. The IRA broke the
> ceasefire and it was back to the war. I was depressed. I thought,
> no, it's not going to work. There wasn't the opportunity to talk to
> McGuinness. The image of McGuinness and me fishing together
> and talking together flashed through my mind. There were so
> many things we could have talked about. But we never got to
> that stage.

Robert had been out of the picture for nearly three years.

For John Major, keeping the unionists on board was the priority. It was *Realpolitik*. Doing so while keeping the IRA in play was an almost impossible circle to square. Oatley had no doubt where the blame lay for the collapse of the ceasefire.

> I was quite appalled by the Conservative Government's reaction to the possibility of pursuing a peaceful negotiation or a peaceful dialogue which would, one hoped, lead the IRA into adopting a political programme rather than a violent programme. It seemed to me that, from the very beginning of the announcement of the 1994 ceasefire, the reaction of the Government was to slap the IRA leadership in the face. This wasn't a very helpful response and I have referred to it as picador politics. When you keep on sticking spears into the beast, it may eventually charge. And the beast did charge in Docklands because I think that the leadership felt that the whole dialogue that had been going on to that point was simply leading it into a trap and that the response of the Government was dishonest and disingenuous and was not consistent with the messages that it had been receiving. More and more barriers and difficulties were constructed.[7]

John Major's role was almost over. He had nurtured the fragile peace process since putting Northern Ireland at the top of his agenda the day he entered Downing Street in 1990. His final historic contribution was to set up the long-promised all-party talks, to be chaired by the US Senator George Mitchell, a politician noted for his fairness, independence and experience in conflict resolution. All parties who entered the talks first had to commit to six principles of non-violence, known as the 'Mitchell Principles', with all affirming their absolute commitment:

1. to democratic and exclusively peaceful means of resolving political issues;
2. to the total disarmament of all paramilitary organisations;
3. to agree that such disarmament must be verifiable to the satisfaction of an independent commission;
4. to renounce for themselves, and to oppose any effort by others, to use force, or threaten to use force, to influence the course or the outcome of all-party negotiations;
5. to agree to abide by the terms of any agreement reached in all-party negotiations and to resort to democratic and exclusively peaceful

methods in trying to alter any aspect of that outcome with which
they may disagree; and

6. to urge that punishment killings and beatings stop and to take
effective steps to prevent such actions.

But the problem was that the talks weren't 'all-party'.

After the Docklands bomb, the IRA had renewed its campaign
both in Northern Ireland and in England with a 1.5-ton bomb that
devastated Manchester's shopping mecca, the Arndale Centre, on 15
June 1996. These attacks automatically excluded Sinn Féin from all-
party talks. Major regretted the party's absence but made it clear why it
had come about: it was up to the IRA first 'to declare a genuine end to
this renewed violence'.[8] Sinn Féin delegates tried to get into the talks at
Stormont but were confronted by locked gates. It was frustrating but it
was also a propaganda gift on a plate.[9]

Fifteen months after the Docklands bomb, John Major lost the
General Election of 1 May 1997. He was defeated by Tony Blair, who
had become leader of the Labour Party and leader of the opposition
three years earlier, following the death of his predecessor, John Smith.
Blair's rebranded 'New Labour' won a landslide victory with a massive
majority of 179 seats. Blair told me he put Northern Ireland 'high up on
my list of priorities'. He planned to take over where John Major had left
off and a fortnight after becoming Prime Minister began by making it
clear to unionists gathered at the Balmoral Agricultural Show, a 'must'
in the unionist calendar, exactly where he stood.

> From the outset I had it in mind that we should really try both to
> revive the ceasefire and then put in place a proper peace process. The
> first substantial speech I made as Prime Minister was on Northern
> Ireland at a very unionist' gathering to make it clear to unionist
> opinion that they weren't going to be railroaded into something that
> was going to undermine their basic status. It was important to begin
> with a statement, not just that I accepted the union, but I supported
> it for as long as the majority of people want it to remain.[10]

Having made his policy clear to unionists, Blair now needed to do the
same with Sinn Féin. On 11 December 1997, he invited Adams and
McGuinness to a meeting in Downing Street. Politically the invitation

was made easier because in the recent General Election Gerry Adams had been re-elected as MP for West Belfast, having previously lost his seat to the SDLP's Joe Hendron; and Martin McGuinness had become MP for Mid Ulster. Five days later in district council elections in Northern Ireland, Sinn Féin underlined its electoral mandate by winning 74 seats, with almost 17 per cent of the vote, closing the gap on the SDLP which won 120 seats, with just over 20 per cent of the vote.[11] Sinn Féin was on the rise. The hunger strike was paying long-term political dividends.

Blair's Downing Street meeting with the leaders of the republican movement was a historic occasion, with powerful echoes of the past. There were more cameras outside Number 10 than there were after Blair's election.[12] Inside the Cabinet room, Tony Blair and his entourage were waiting: his Chief of Staff and Chief Negotiator, Jonathan Powell; his forthright official spokesman, Alastair Campbell; and his irrepressible Northern Ireland Secretary, Dr Marjorie 'Mo' Mowlam. Outside in the hall, the lights on Number 10's Christmas tree twinkled as the Government delegation stood by with an understandable degree of apprehension. Jonathan Powell told me what happened when the Sinn Féin delegation entered the room.

> Martin McGuinness wanted to break the ice so he said, 'This was where all the damage was done then?' We were absolutely horrified, thinking he was referring to the IRA's mortar attack on Downing Street. And he said, 'No, no, no. I didn't mean that. I meant this is where Michael Collins signed the treaty.' They were even sitting in exactly the same chairs Michael Collins and his delegation sat in while Lloyd George and Winston Churchill were sitting where we were. The parallels of history were really eerie.[13]

The meeting was relaxed and friendly, despite covering the toxic ground of decommissioning and the permanency of the ceasefire. The encouraging sign was that Blair offered immediate talks with British officials if the IRA called another ceasefire, warning that 'the settlement train was leaving the station'. Adams then told the journalists waiting eagerly outside in Downing Street that it was 'a significant step' and 'a good moment in history'. McGuinness suggested that the next step was for the unionist leader, David Trimble, to meet with Gerry Adams. 'That would be a gigantic step forward in the search for a peace settlement,' he said. Trimble was reportedly even keeping from going into the toilets at Stormont if McGuinness was inside, to avoid standing next to him.

Unionists were outraged by the Downing Street meeting, saying it was a disgraceful betrayal of all the families of the IRA's victims. Ian Paisley was the loudest critic of all, accusing Tony Blair of forcing the unionists to surrender. From the beginning Paisley had been bitterly opposed to the all-party talks and shunned them – warning, as ever, that they meant a united Ireland was just around the corner.

The republican movement decided it didn't want to be left standing at the station and took Blair up on his offer. On 27 July 1997 the IRA declared its second ceasefire in three years, after the one of 1994. Its statement stressed, lest HMG forget, that it remained 'committed to ending British rule in Ireland' and made its wishes clear: 'We want a permanent peace and therefore we are prepared to enhance the search for a democratic peace settlement through real and inclusive negotiations.'[14]

The Government's insistence on decommissioning before admission to all-party talks was dropped – on condition Sinn Féin signed up to the 'Mitchell Principles'. Sinn Féin ultimately signed. The all-party talks, now including Sinn Féin and the political representatives of the loyalist paramilitaries, began at Stormont on 15 September 1997. They lasted for an intensive, tumultuous and, not surprisingly, at times acrimonious seven months, with George Mitchell skilfully holding the ring to make sure all parties stayed the course and none walked out. Although both IRA and loyalist ceasefires were in place, there was a spate of murders on both sides – of drug dealers and others – that led to the temporary exclusion of the loyalist Ulster Democratic Party, the political front of the UDA/UFF, and the suspension of Sinn Féin whose delegates were excluded for seventeen days. There were no expulsions. It was more like being ordered to stand outside the classroom door.

Trying to reach an agreement that both sides could live with – and that would last – was a superhuman task. David Trimble's Ulster Unionists needed the assurance that the union was secure and the SDLP's John Hume and Sinn Féin's Martin McGuinness and Gerry Adams needed reassurance that a united Ireland was the ultimate direction of travel. The conflicting aspirations seemed incompatible but George Mitchell helped ensure that both sides gained a degree of satisfaction, with each side taking what understanding it needed from the Agreement that was in the process of being reached. Unionists got the guarantee, several times over, that the union was secure as long as that was the wish of the majority. Nationalists and republicans got a promise from the British Government that it would institute a border poll – a referendum in Northern Ireland to assess support or otherwise for Irish unity – should demographics change and a nationalist/Catholic majority emerge. But there was a proviso. In this event, the Northern Ireland Secretary had to be convinced that the new majority favoured a united Ireland. This was by no means axiomatic as not all Catholics were nationalists. An unspecified number wished to remain part of the United Kingdom. In the end interpretation and implementation of any border poll, should such circumstances arise, was to depend on the judgement of the Northern Ireland Secretary and the British Government.

As Easter 1998 approached, and with agreement appearing within touching distance, Mitchell set a deadline to concentrate the minds of all the parties involved. The deadline was midnight on Thursday 9 April, the eve of Good Friday. It was touch and go. I was at Stormont covering the last lap of the talks and waiting for the denouement. It didn't arrive on the appointed date but all the signs were that it would appear the next day – Good Friday. I spent the night trying to sleep on the unforgivingly hard floor of the press tent with dozens of other journalists. At one stage I managed to nod off only to be awakened by the booming voice of Ian Paisley, who had invaded our canvas sleeping space to warn us all that treachery and infamy were afoot under our very noses.

The sun rose on a freezing cold Good Friday morning to reveal Adams and McGuinness taking a relaxed stroll behind the wire that separated the offices set aside for the negotiating parties from the press tent and the rest of the world. They chatted amicably to journalists on our side of the wire but gave nothing away. They then retreated inside. For the next few hours we watched such comings and goings as we could see through the windows of the offices of each party in the drab conformity of the office block in which they were housed. There was considerable movement between them. The feeling spread that a deal might be on.

Meanwhile Tony Blair, accompanied by Jonathan Powell and Alastair Campbell, was going backwards and forwards trying to iron out remaining disagreements between the parties that might torpedo the whole

Agreement. As Alastair Campbell recorded in his diary, the air sometimes turned blue as Blair rushed around, mollifying, cajoling and persuading.

> I had a real sense that I was recording history. It was an extraordinary time, and felt like it. It showed TB [Tony Blair] at his infuriating best. Once he got the bit between the teeth, and decided to go for it, he always knew best. He was like a man possessed. He would pace up and down. He would ask to see someone and then ten seconds later, shout out, 'Where the fuck are they? I need them NOW!'[15]

The stress was beginning to tell on everyone. The price of failure hardly bore thinking about.

The Good Friday Agreement – or Belfast Agreement as it was officially called – was finally reached by all the parties at 5.30 p.m. on Good Friday after Senator Mitchell had received the crucial telephone call saying that David Trimble's Ulster Unionists were on board. Mitchell said he felt 'a sense of relief, gratification and really genuine happiness'.[16] The Agreement consisted of three key Strands.

> Strand One established the [devolved] Northern Ireland Assembly and Executive to make laws and decisions on most of the issues affecting everyday life in Northern Ireland.

> Strand Two established the North–South institutions – the North–South Ministerial Council and the North–South Implementation Bodies – that support co-operation between Northern Ireland and Ireland.

> Strand Three established the East–West institutions – the British–Irish Intergovernmental Conference and the British–Irish Council – that support co-operation between the United Kingdom and Ireland.[17]

The Agreement also set out a series of rights for the people of Northern Ireland, on identity and citizenship, and made commitments on decommissioning, security, policing and prisoners.

When Tony Blair arrived at Stormont for the last leg of the negotiations – as did the recently elected (1997) Irish Taoiseach, Bertie Ahern – to provide Prime Ministerial impetus to help reach the finishing line, he faced the waiting television cameras and memorably declared, 'A day like today is not a day for soundbites, but I feel the hand of history upon our shoulder.'[18] It wasn't a line that Alastair Campbell had written for Blair. 'It was a hell of a soundbite,' he wrote in his diary. 'The press loved it.'[19] The soundbite proved true.

The remarkable significance of the Good Friday Agreement from the republican movement's point of view – uncomfortable though it was, given its history – was that the IRA and Sinn Féin effectively accepted partition (which they had vowed they never would) by agreeing to take part in a devolved Northern Ireland power-sharing executive. They calculated, as Michael Collins had done in signing the Anglo-Irish Treaty in 1921, that the settlement provided 'the freedom to achieve freedom'. The leadership reasoned that acceptance of the unacceptable was a necessary prerequisite to ultimately achieving the long-term goal of a united Ireland. This was the underlying rationale of what Robert told Martin McGuinness and Gerry Kelly at the meeting at Brendan Duddy's house five years earlier: 'The final solution is union. This island will be as one.'

As far as unionists were concerned, they had won, although the penny hadn't dropped in every case. The guarantee that there would be no constitutional change in the status of Northern Ireland unless it was the will of the majority was reaffirmed. The union was safe – at least for the foreseeable future. That remaining uncertainty, given changing demographics, was what led Ian Paisley's Democratic Unionist Party (DUP) to boycott the all-party talks, with Paisley himself to trying disrupt them. He described the Agreement as capitulation to the IRA and 'the saddest day Ulster has seen since the founding of the province'.[20] He made it clear his opposition was implacable.

> The Agreement is not just flawed. It is rotten to the core. People may call me the wrecker. Well, they can say what they like about me. It'll not affect me or my eternal whereabouts. All I can say is that I'll not be changing. I will go to the grave with the convictions I have.[21]

Paisley was to eat his words.

On 22 May 1996, the Agreement was put to simultaneous referendums north and south of the border. It was supported by 71 per cent of the electorate in the North and by 94 per cent in the South.

Paisley and his followers voted against it. I asked Tony Blair for his assessment of the achievement.

> We could never have got peace without the Good Friday
> Agreement. It provided a framework for the future that was seen
> to be equitable and fair. That's its importance. You can't resolve
> a dispute like this unless you remember the past but you define
> the future differently. And if you don't put that future within a
> framework that's clear and balanced, then you live for ever with
> the history. What is also important to realise is the Good Friday
> Agreement was the start of the real process of peace and not the
> conclusion of it.[22]

Robert, not usually given to self-congratulation or hyperbole, was overjoyed.

> That was marvellous. It was fantastic what Tony Blair had achieved
> after he'd clearly made Northern Ireland the top of his agenda.
> The odds were certainly stacked against him. His achievement
> in putting it all together again was incredible. How on earth did
> he manage to do it – and do it quite quickly after the Docklands
> bomb? His reputation is now sullied by Iraq. I think people tend to
> forget the greatness of his achievement to pull off the Good Friday
> Agreement. For me it was a great moment.

Robert was at least prepared to admit that he had put a few bricks in the wall of peace. The Good Friday Agreement was the peace that Robert, Michael Oatley and Frank Steele had hoped for and strived for over twenty-five years with Brendan Duddy at the heart of it. Good Friday was the ultimate triumph of 'Operation Chiffon' – and Robert's role was central to it. As his MI5 line manager, Stephen Lander, agreed, without the back channel 'there would have been no peace process'.[23]

32

Endgame

There were two final acts to facilitate and underpin the peace. Both were highly contentious. The first was the release of paramilitary prisoners on all sides, regardless of the crimes they had committed or the sentences they had been given. To the IRA and Sinn Féin – and the loyalist paramilitaries – this was the *sine qua non* of their participation in the Agreement. It was tantamount to an amnesty, although the word never passed Tony Blair or Alastair Campbell's lips. The second was the decommissioning of all weapons held by both republican and loyalist paramilitaries, the issue that had held up the peace process for so long and in the end prompted the IRA's Docklands bomb.

Despite the enormous sensitivities, the issue of releasing prisoners, both republican and loyalist, was the easier to accomplish. Once Tony Blair had made the contentious decision, seen by the families of IRA and loyalist victims as a betrayal and a denial of justice, the gates of the Maze prison were gradually opened over a two-year period following the Good Friday Agreement. Sentence Review Commissioners were appointed to scrutinise each individual's release and assess whether the prisoner was likely to rejoin a paramilitary organisation and pose a further threat to society. There was a powerful incentive not to do so. Each prisoner was released with a licence that could be revoked if the Commissioners and the Secretary of State for Northern Ireland decided that they had joined a paramilitary organisation or supported paramilitary activities. The releases applied to 500 republican and loyalist prisoners sentenced before 10 April 1998, the eve of Good Friday. The final deadline for releases was to be 28 July 2000. That was when the last batch of seventy-eight prisoners emerged blinking from the gloom of the H Blocks, through the creaking turnstile gates and into the car parks and waiting areas for their families, separated to avoid possible clashes between old enemies. As loyalists emerged, there were no celebrations. Their welcome was muted. Republicans emerged to confetti and the popping of champagne corks. It was more like a wedding reception than a prisoner release. The IRA's commanding officer in the prison, Jim McVeigh, announced that his comrades were 'proud republicans, unbowed and unbroken'. He emerged having served sixteen years of his thirty-one-year sentence, passed in 1992 for conspiring to murder British soldiers. He'd joined the IRA at the age of sixteen. After his release, he went on to become a Belfast City councillor with a part-time job taking tourists on 'Troubles Tours'.[1]

Resolving the impasse of decommissioning was far less straightforward, although every bit as contentious – for the IRA, that is. The Good Friday Agreement established the mechanism for resolving it: the Independent International Commission on Decommissioning (IICD) headed by a Canadian army officer, General John de Chastelain. The UDA/UFF made it clear that they would only begin decommissioning their weapons once the IRA had started to decommission its own. To facilitate the process, the language was subtly changed to avoid any implication of surrender. Decommissioning became 'putting weapons beyond use'. Although the process was due to be completed within two years of the referendums on the Good Friday Agreement, it took seven years longer due to the complexity, sensitivity and utmost secrecy of the operation. The last IRA weapons were finally 'put beyond use' on 25 September 2005 after the IRA had publicly announced 'the war is over' two months earlier, on 28 July. The operation was overseen by senior IRA leaders and General de Chastelain accompanied by two of his colleagues on the International Commission.

How and where the IRA's arsenal of war was decommissioned has never been revealed. The silence of General de Chastelain and the IRA was absolute and has remained so to this day. What is not in doubt is that the majority of its weapons were 'put beyond use', confirmed by two independent witnesses, the Reverend Harold Good, President of the Methodist Church in Ireland, and the Redemptorist Catholic priest, Father Alec Reid, who had worked closely with Gerry Adams and John Hume on the early stages of the peace process. He had also administered the last rites to the two army corporals who had been murdered by the IRA after accidentally driving their car into an IRA funeral cortège. Father Reid later described, in a circumspect way, what they had both witnessed.

> I was surprised when we used to go to these sites and you would see all this war material, guns and explosives, all very carefully prepared, most of it with tags, all numbered by the IRA. Everywhere we went there was a man with a Kalashnikov [AK-47] and you could see it was loaded. In the end I picked up they were not only defending the site but the three Commissioners who were there to oversee the operation. They were a sort of bodyguard. In the very last act of decommissioning, the bullets were taken out of the bodyguard's gun and handed over to General de Chastelain by the senior IRA person in charge of the whole operation. It was a significant moment. This was the last gun and the man handing it over was quite emotional. He was aware, I think, that this was the last gun.[2]

General de Chastelain was as confident as he could be that the IRA had told him the truth as he recalled what he had seen at the sites where the weapons had been assembled prior to being 'put beyond use'.

> We are talking about flame-throwers, surface-to-air missiles, rocket-propelled grenades, commercial and homemade explosives and heavy machine guns. Of course we have no way of knowing for certain that the IRA hasn't retained arms but it is our understanding from discussing with them and our belief in what we had done, that they were sincere. When we said, 'Is this everything?', they said 'Yes, this is everything.'[3]

Following events from his farm, Robert was growing increasingly worried that the issue of decommissioning might torpedo the whole peace process, the last stages of which, with Brendan Duddy, he had been instrumental in getting underway with Martin McGuinness. He was delighted that, against all the odds, decommissioning had finally happened. He had been doubtful that it ever would. 'Looking back, I was able to rejoice,' he said. 'Yes, rejoice. An emotive word. Relieved and amazed.' Robert's predecessor, Michael Oatley, was equally relieved but not surprised, as he wrote in the *Sunday Times* on 31 October 1999, his interest in the evolution of the peace process that he had helped orchestrate in the early 1970s undiminished.

> The decision to cease the armed campaign was taken with trepidation by intelligent, ideologically committed individuals who had spent their adult lives in pursuit of what they regarded as a just war. They did not abandon their armed campaign because they needed a rest or thought it had become irrelevant. On the contrary, it was clear to them that it had put Irish constitutional issues higher up the political agenda than at any time since 1920. The suggestion of a ceasefire was furiously opposed within the IRA. Many feared that a move to political action would destroy its strength. Nobody was more conscious of this possibility than McGuinness and Adams, who had seen the damage done to the IRA by the 1975 ceasefire and had inherited the leadership of the republican movement as a result of it. But they decided to take a risk. I was a witness to their decision.[4]

Charles Moore, the former editor of the *Daily Telegraph*, the *Sunday Telegraph* and the *Spectator*, responded to Oatley's *Sunday Times* article with his acid pen in the *Daily Telegraph* the following day, telling readers, unflatteringly, that Oatley's article afforded 'a fabulous insight into the degenerate, post-imperial mindset of some of our secret servants'.

> Mr Oatley is clearly suffering from a spook's variant of the 'Stockholm syndrome' – whereby captives start to view the world from the standpoint of the kidnappers. Certainly, he is hostage to just about every republican myth about the 'peace process'. In Unionist eyes, Mr Oatley's remarks will validate the idea that talks on Ulster's new political structures are mere window dressing to conceal the fact that the province's future is really being carved up in secret between unaccountable secret servants and the Provisionals.[5]

Oatley and Moore shared no common ground. Two days later, Michael Oatley replied in the *Daily Telegraph* of 3 November.

I have not spoken to anyone in government about Irish matters since retiring from SIS in 1991 ... I believe that decommissioning is not an issue on which the Belfast Agreement should be allowed to founder; that the majority in both communities in Ulster do not wish it to be; that mainland voters have been misled as to its significance; that pressing republicans on the matter is counter-productive; that there are understandable reasons for this; and that identification of decommissioning as a yardstick of republican sincerity damages prospects for peaceful settlement. I believe that it has done so since the republican leadership first signalled interest in pursuing a non-violent strategy in 1991.

I believe that a disservice is done to the democratic process in the United Kingdom by presenting only one side of this coin. And that this also damages Unionism: Unionists will gain no credit with the mainland electorate by getting hung up on decommissioning while claiming a right to conduct arcane ceremonies around other people's backyards.

Once the IRA had started decommissioning, the loyalist paramilitaries followed suit. Ominously, however, the Commission's final report contained a sobering conclusion:

Decommissioning, as constituted, was as complete as it could be ... the process should suggest neither victory nor defeat ... [However,] it seems inevitable that some paramilitary arms remain un-decommissioned, either through loss or remaining in the hands of those who have never acceded to their leaders' direction.[6]

The Good Friday Agreement and decommissioning split the IRA, a split it had always feared and tried to avoid. IRA dissidents, including the so-called 'New IRA', were the nucleus of a future threat to the peace.

But the peace still had to be bedded down in the new political institutions established by Good Friday, with elections to the new power-sharing Executive at Stormont. Then a miracle happened. The Reverend Ian Paisley, who had done so much to wreck previous attempts at power-sharing and establishing closer ties with Dublin – and had excoriated dialogue with Martin McGuinness as sedition – suddenly underwent an astonishing Damascene conversion following a serious heart attack on

5 February 2012. He was hospitalised and was said to be close to death. Remarkably he recovered, saying the Lord had let him survive for one last task. Tony Blair confirmed what Paisley had told him.

> I was struck when Ian came out of hospital after his illness that he'd been through a near-death experience. He'd survived and it should be for a purpose. And if the purpose was peace, and that was God's will, then, then he should do that. Now that wouldn't mean to say for a single instance he would be deluded about the possibilities of it, but I sensed with him a different mission, after that period.[7]

Tony Blair was an Anglican who shared Paisley's deep faith. He converted to Catholicism two years after resigning as Prime Minister on 27 June 2007 – a resignation prompted by, among other things, his unpopularity over involving the country in the Iraq War.

Elections to the new Northern Ireland Assembly in 2007 produced a narrow result, with Paisley's DUP winning thirty-six seats and Sinn Féin close behind with twenty-eight seats. The new power-sharing dispensation meant that the two leading parties provided the First Minister and Deputy First Minister. The result was the almost unbelievable sight of sworn enemies since the outbreak of the Troubles sharing power in government, with Paisley as First Minister and McGuinness as his Deputy. It was a spectacle that few could have imagined, although I remember a senior MI5 officer telling me several months in advance that Paisley would 'do the deal' with McGuinness. As they laughed and joked together, they became known in Northern Ireland as the 'Chuckle Brothers' after a popular television comedy duo at the time. As McGuinness told me, the relationship was genuine on both sides.

> One of the great achievements of the last number of years was the process of trying to get the Democratic Unionist Party into government. Against all odds, we succeeded. Ian Paisley and I went into government together and we built up a good working and personal relationship which continued. Huge efforts have been made by myself and by Irish republicans to recognise that, as we go forward, we have to do it in a way in which everybody has ownership, everybody feels that their rights and entitlements are being respected.[8]

Robert could barely believe the 'Chuckle Brothers':

> I don't know which of them caused me most amazement. I found
> it quite incredible they were working together. I saw Paisley at
> a literary festival. He was relaxed and friendly and as large as
> life. The 'Chuckle Brothers'? Incredible. It was unimaginable.
> I'd seen McGuinness coming out of the chrysalis at our meeting
> at Brendan's house after initial hostility [during Robert's cross-
> examination in McGuinness's mother's house in the Bogside].
> Seeing them together now was quite incredible.[9]

When I asked Brendan Duddy about the sight of Paisley and McGuinness
working together, laughing and joking together and sharing power
together, it was too much for him. He choked and broke down.

> 'The Chuckle Brothers?' They were lovely. They enjoyed each other.
> My reaction? Delighted. Happy man. When you ask questions like
> that, I choke, I get emotional. I find it hard to answer. I had no
> choice except to do what I did. I had to do it.[10]

He coughed as he wiped away the tears, as he had when reading the
'com' from Bobby Sands.

The warm relationship between Paisley and McGuinness lasted but
the political relationship did not. A year later, Paisley stepped down, as
a result of hostile, personal attacks from his DUP colleagues who could
not stomach the sight of their leader, Paisley, who had founded the party
in 1971, sharing power with Martin McGuinness. Eileen Paisley, his
wife, accused the DUP of 'verbally assassinating him, leaving him with
no option other than to step down'.[11] Such was the intensity of feeling
on both sides. Paisley also claimed he was forced out as Moderator of
the Martyrs' Memorial Church in East Belfast that he had founded
in 1951. He vowed never to set foot within its doors again. It hurt the
family intensely but Paisley had no regrets. He had carried out the
Lord's work.[12]

Martin McGuinness carried on as Deputy First Minister, sharing
power with Paisley's DUP successors as First Minister: Peter Robinson
from 2008 until 2016 and Arlene Foster from 2016 until the Assembly
and the power-sharing Executive were suspended for three years in

2017 after Martin McGuinness resigned as Deputy First Minister over a political scandal that became known as the 'cash for ash' affair. Arlene Foster, who had initially overseen the initiative when she was Minister for Enterprise, Trade and Investment in 2012, refused to resign. McGuinness's resignation brought down the power-sharing Executive.* But the relationship between Arlene Foster and Martin McGuinness was never as warm as that between McGuinness and Paisley.

Arlene Foster had good reason not to warm to her Deputy.[13] She never forgot the day Martin McGuinness delivered a eulogy at the funeral of Seamus McElwaine, a notorious IRA gunman suspected by the intelligence services of multiple murders and of having tried to kill her father in 1986 on the family farm in Fermanagh. Arlene was eight years old at the time. Her father, John Kelly, was an RUC officer. He was wounded but survived.

Seamus McElwaine was later shot dead by the SAS as he prepared to ambush a British army patrol near Roslea, County Fermanagh. At his funeral, McGuinness described McElwaine as 'a freedom fighter murdered by a British terrorist'.[14] When Foster became First Minister in 2016, she was asked how she felt about sharing government with Martin McGuinness. She said she continued to find the personal connection 'difficult' but it wouldn't stop her working with him because the work was 'too important'. McGuinness echoed the sentiment.

> There is hurt on all sides and all of us have a responsibility to recognise that, if we are to consolidate peace and build genuine reconciliation. People like myself, Arlene Foster and all politicians, have a huge role to play by giving positive leadership in the work of reconciliation and coming to terms with the past.[15]

---

*The 'cash for ash' scandal was over the non-domestic Renewable Heat Incentive (RHI) designed to encourage businesses to switch from fossil fuels to renewable energy by burning wood pellets. The potential subsidising of the scheme was reported to run to almost £500 million. It transpired that the rate paid in the subsidy was greater than the cost of the fuel. Cost controls were lax and the cost spiralled. As a result the scheme was suspended and a public inquiry followed in 2020 that made no serious criticism of Arlene Foster. It concluded 'the vast majority of what went wrong was due to an accumulation and compounding of errors and omissions over time'.

The reconciliation of Martin McGuinness and Arlene Foster on Stormont's big political stage – although lacking the humour of the 'Chuckle Brothers' – was proof of how far the peace process had come in the two decades since the Good Friday Agreement and how it had bedded down. There were still bitter differences to be overcome, many of them arising from cultural issues like the Irish language and the safeguarding of historic traditions cherished by both sides which excited powerful emotions that were always simmering beneath the surface.

But on 27 June 2012 there was one act of reconciliation that was even more remarkable: the sight of Martin McGuinness, once the IRA's foremost commander in the North, shaking hands with the Queen, whose distant cousin Lord Mountbatten had been assassinated by the IRA. Mountbatten was also Prince Philip's uncle. Even more astonishing on 8 April 2014 was the image of Martin McGuinness, in white tie and tails, dining as Her Majesty's guest at a state banquet at Windsor Castle to honour the visit of the Irish President, Michael D. Higgins. McGuinness stood for the toast while the orchestra played 'God Save the Queen'. He had already been impressed by the way in which Queen Elizabeth had conducted herself on her state visit to the Irish Republic in 2011, the first British monarch to pay such a visit in a hundred years.

> I watched very carefully what Queen Elizabeth did in Dublin and the way she stood very reverently to honour those people who were rebels, Irish republicans who fought against the British army: her very powerful words where she recognised that things could've been done differently or not at all. I'm sure she was also speaking about Britain's participation in that process.[16]

In 2014 I interviewed McGuinness on the balcony of Stormont, overlooking the statue of Sir Edward Carson, the unionist champion who had organised Protestant resistance to Home Rule in 1912. Going to Windsor Castle and seeing the flags of his country flying side by side with the Union Jack made a great impression on McGuinness. He had no hesitation in justifying meeting the Queen.

> Queen Elizabeth has many reasons not to meet with me. I have many reasons not to meet with her. But the fact that we were prepared to engage in these encounters was an experience for me.[17]

Robert took a sanguine view of the encounter:

> Her Majesty was friendly and nice, as she always is. She's met all
> sorts of extraordinary people, mainly based in Africa, during
> the course of her reign but nobody quite so bloody-handed as
> McGuinness.[18]

McGuinness holding out the hand of friendship to Her Majesty did
not represent a change of heart or a rejection of the IRA's past but was
a calculated strategic decision designed to help win over unionists.
It was a clear sign that McGuinness and the IRA leadership had
finally taken on board what Frank Steele, Michael Oatley, Brendan
Duddy and latterly, Robert, had been telling the IRA for more than
forty years: that there could only be a united Ireland with unionist
consent. McGuinness dining at Windsor with the Queen set the seal
on 'Operation Chiffon'.

When I talked to McGuinness on the balcony at Stormont in 2014,
three years before he died, I asked if he believed that one day there
would be a united Ireland. He was unequivocal in his response: 'I've
never been as convinced of anything in my life that at some stage in
the future there will be a united Ireland. Absolutely.' I pointed out that
Peter Robinson, then First Minister, assured me that a united Ireland
was never going to happen, a view shared – and hoped for – by the
vast majority of unionists. McGuinness dismissed what his partner in
government had said.

> I place my faith in the people who will decide this, and it won't be
> statements like that. What will decide this will be a poll, at which
> the temperature of the people will be taken. And I do believe that
> at some stage in the future we will be in a scenario where people
> will vote to bring about the end of the link with Britain. Even the
> British government in the Good Friday negotiations were prepared
> to accept that … The IRA were fighting to bring about equality and
> the unification of Ireland. I'm still fighting for that but I'm fighting
> for that politically.[19]

Gerry Adams, who had shared McGuinness's fight, shared his
optimism too:

The struggle isn't over. I believe we will get a united Ireland.
I believe it has to be a united Ireland in which unionism feels
secure. There was a war. It's been brought to a conclusion. The IRA
have left the stage. Sinn Féin is now the largest party in terms of
votes on the island of Ireland. The big achievement of the Good
Friday Agreement is the British government have signed up to
legislate for a united Ireland, if that's what the people want.[20]

Peter Robinson contradicted Gerry Adams with a pithy riposte.

Gerry's not going to get his united Ireland. Unionists are capable
of extracting defeat from the jaws of victory. And republicans and
nationalists are capable of gaining victory from the jaws of defeat.[21]

But Robinson was also a realist, acknowledging the threat that
demographics pose to the union.

The security we have within the United Kingdom comes at a time
when the percentage of the population that is Protestant, loyalist
and unionist is diminishing and the percentage of the population
that is Catholic, nationalist and republican is increasing.[22]

And that fear is shared by many Protestants. I recall a disconcerting
exchange with a loyalist bystander in the shadow of a towering bonfire off
the Shankill Road, soon to become an inferno to mark the anniversary
of 12 July, the date of the victory of the Protestant King William over the
deposed Catholic King James at the Battle of the Boyne in 1690. I put it
to him: wasn't the union as safe as it had ever been given the guarantee
of the Good Friday Agreement? So what was he worried about? 'They
[the Catholics] are breeding like rabbits,' he replied. 'So fifty years on
that may change.' If it changes because the majority want it to change,
wasn't that OK? The reply was a defiant 'No.'

The issue of a united Ireland is not going to go away. In the end,
it's demographics that may decide the future. At least, it is hoped,
the debate will be peaceful – thanks in no small degree to 'Operation
Chiffon'.

Epilogue: Funerals and a Final Farewell

Over the past decade I've attended the funerals and a memorial for three of the peacemakers whose stories run through this book: Ian Paisley, Martin McGuinness and Brendan Duddy.

The Reverend Ian Kyle Paisley died as Lord Bannside on 12 September 2014. He was eighty-eight. I attended his memorial service at the invitation of his widow, Baroness Paisley. It was held in the Victorian splendour of Belfast's Ulster Hall, the historic temple of unionism, attended by unionist royalty and guests including Deputy First Minister Martin McGuinness. I watched him share the Order of Service with First Minister Peter Robinson as they sang 'All People That on Earth Do Dwell'. A giant oil painting of Paisley stood at the front of the stage.

In her tribute Baroness Paisley said her marriage of fifty-eight years had not been a dictatorship but a partnership filled with laughter and love. In the years in which I knew Paisley and on the many occasions I interviewed him, I often saw his laughter – especially when he once bought me an ice cream while campaigning in his constituency of North Antrim and refused to take any money for it. To understand the man, it's necessary to appreciate the Christian faith that underpinned his beliefs, actions and attitudes, which were controversial to many, especially Roman Catholics. In her tribute, Baroness Paisley painted a picture of one of the most dominant figures who filled the stage from the beginning to the end of the Troubles. She stressed his deep religious faith.

His home was his castle and he was at his happiest and most relaxed there. It is the place he would have chosen from which to enter his heavenly home and God granted his request … he slipped quietly and peacefully into the presence of the Good Shepherd … leaving us with the feeling that we had walked with him right to the door of heaven and he had just stepped through. We knew that immediately when he breathed his last breath on earth his next breath was taken in heaven. Neither Ian nor I or any of our family could ask for anything more.[1]

I felt it would not have been proper had I not been present when Martin McGuinness was laid to rest on 21 March 2017. Over forty-five years I had known and interviewed both Paisley and McGuinness from the early days when McGuinness was a young IRA commander in Derry and Paisley was the merciless scourge of the IRA, the Catholic Church and Rome. The fact that the two men, implacable enemies for decades, became friends and political allies – not to mention the 'Chuckle Brothers' – is a miracle I never imagined I would see.

I decided to fly to Belfast and then drive to Derry the night before McGuinness's funeral as I knew that to drive the seventy miles to Derry the following morning was likely to be a nightmare, with hundreds of cars causing traffic jams as thousands of mourners from all over Ireland headed for the city.

I arrived at my hotel just before midnight. I'd heard on the radio that there had been huge queues of people all day wishing to pay their respects at McGuinness's wake, many waiting for up to two hours. I rang one of his close comrades to see if it would be appropriate for me to join the queue. He said the queues had now gone as it was so late and he would meet me there.

I drove into the Bogside with a degree of apprehension, not sure how the presence of a 'Brit' would be received. My car was flagged down by an IRA steward at the entrance to the narrow lane of Westland Terrace where McGuinness had lived for most of his life. He asked me for my keys and said he would park my car for me. I met my contact and he was right. The two-hour queues had long gone. Prominent IRA figures from the past stood around outside the house and in knots in the street. I had known some of them and exchanged pleasantries. My contact took me into the house and introduced me to Bernie, Martin's wife, and his children, now fully grown. I was made to feel welcome. They said they appreciated my visit.

There was none of the alcohol in evidence normally associated with an Irish wake. Martin was teetotal. There was plenty of tea on the go. I was offered a cup, a warm welcome on a bitterly cold Irish night. I looked around the room. There was a notable absence of IRA memorabilia. No wooden Gaelic crosses fashioned by IRA prisoners in Long Kesh and the Maze. There were photographs of Martin and religious artefacts and pictures on the wall but nothing to suggest that the man lying in the open coffin had for years been the most significant IRA leader on the island of Ireland. I approached the coffin and looked at the face I had known for so long and so well. He was laid out as Martin McGuinness, peacemaker, politician and Deputy First Minister, with jacket and tie. In death he looked more recognisable than he did when a shocked world first saw the haggard face of a man who was plainly seriously ill – thought to be the result of a rare genetic disease known as amyloidosis, a terminal disease that attacks the body's vital organs but not the brain.

I said my goodbyes, chatted to a few more people, reminiscing about the time I had first met Martin in the abandoned gasworks in the Bogside shortly after 'Bloody Sunday' when he said he'd rather be mowing the lawn and cleaning the car. I then drove back to my hotel in the small hours of the morning and had a cold beer. I sat and reflected on the evening and the memories it brought back before heading to my bed.

I got to St Columba's Church, Long Tower, where the requiem mass was to be held, early the following morning, knowing that there would be standing room only. It was freezing cold and I pulled the hood of my anorak over my head to ward off the biting wind. I joined the crowd outside waiting for the previous funeral to finish. There was no orderly queue and I was told that once the heavy doors of the church were open, it was a free-for-all to get a seat in the gallery upstairs as most of the body of the church had been reserved for the serried ranks of VIPs from both sides of the border – and the White House.

I took my chances, joined the crush and ended up on the hard wooden benches at the back of the gallery upstairs. I could see the altar and various priests going backwards and forwards making sure everything was in order but could see nothing of what was happening down below in the body of the church. At one point before the requiem mass began, there was a spontaneous round of applause and then another even louder outburst. The first round was for Arlene Foster, the leader of the DUP and Northern Ireland's First Minister. The applause was a sign of appreciation for her courageous gesture in attending the funeral that must have outraged many of her DUP supporters and been difficult for her. The second round of applause was for US President Bill Clinton, who had done much to advance the peace process: from granting Gerry Adams a visa to visit America in January 1994 – seven months before the IRA ceasefire the following August – to shaking Adams's hand on the Falls Road in November 1995, fifteen months after the ceasefire had been declared.

During a lull in proceedings, I managed to change my seat so I could now look down on the congregation and the array of VIPs seated below. Gerry Adams welcoming President Clinton and shaking his hand once more; the Irish Taoiseach, Enda Kenny, with the Irish President, Michael D. Higgins; the DUP's Peter Robinson, Arlene Foster's predecessor as First Minister; Ian Paisley Jr, who before the funeral had paid a generous tribute to the man who became his father's friend and partner in government; the leaders of Sinn Féin, North and South; and the Northern Ireland Secretary, James Brokenshire. Tony Blair and the UK's then Prime Minister Theresa May were notable for their absence, but Alastair Campbell was there to pay his respects. McGuinness's coffin, simply decorated with an Irish tricolour, stood in the aisle in front of the altar.

The tributes were long and full. Most passionate was Bill Clinton, speaking largely without notes.

> He was part of the rage of his time. He hated discrimination. He decided to oppose it with every means available to the passionate young – including violence.

> He risked the wrath of his comrades and the rejection of his adversaries. He made honourable compromises and was strong enough to keep them and came to be trusted because his word was good. He persevered and he prevailed, a passionate believer in a free, secure, self-governing Ireland.[2]

He urged the congregation to honour McGuinness's legacy by completing the work that he had begun. As he returned to his seat, he touched the coffin.

Thousands followed the cortège to the republican plot in the cemetery in the Creggan estate that looks down on the Bogside. Significantly no IRA beret and black leather gloves lay on top of the coffin, as would once have been expected in recognition that it was the funeral of an IRA commander. Nor were there any shots over the grave by masked IRA men as a salute to their former comrade. Such signs would have sent out the wrong message. To Sinn Féin it was important to show the world that McGuinness, having been a man of war, had died as a man of peace. He was undoubtedly a peacemaker but, as Robert and Michael Oatley both agree, as a man of war he was a leader of an organisation responsible for the murder, torture and deaths of over 2,000 people.[*]

Two months later, on 12 May 2017, I attended Brendan Duddy's funeral, held in St Eugene's Cathedral, overlooking the Bogside. Brendan had suffered a debilitating stroke from which he never fully recovered. It left him unable to speak and unable to walk. It was desperately sad to see someone who had been so energetic and such a tireless worker for peace through four decades reduced to a shadow of his former self. The weather was grim; it was raining and the sky was heavy with dark clouds. The Cathedral was packed. Brendan's contribution was recognised in Ireland if not in England. Personal representatives of the Taoiseach and the Minister for Foreign Affairs sat in the front row of the Cathedral. The family asked me to pay tribute to Brendan. I described him as 'the secret peacemaker' who deserved the Nobel Peace Prize as much as John Hume and David Trimble, who had jointly received it. The coffin left the Cathedral to the strains of Derry's unofficial anthem, Phil Coulter's 'The Town I Loved So Well'. Outside the crowds waited in the rain to bid Brendan farewell. Among them was Michael Oatley, trying to remain anonymous and declining journalists' requests for interviews. Michael later wrote his own tribute to Brendan:

> Brendan believed passionately that peace could be achieved through dialogue and, which is truly remarkable, that it was his personal task to try to make this happen.

[*] Loyalist paramilitaries were responsible for 1,050 deaths and the security forces for 367 (McKittrick, Kelters, Feeney and Thornton, Lost Lives, p. 1,476).

We became very close, with a synchronisation of minds and complete trust under acute pressure. We were for a while closer than brothers. Brendan's sense of commitment was the more extraordinary. I was trained and paid to look for solutions while he was a private citizen who simply chose this path for himself because he believed that he could see possibilities in the situation which others ignored. His high intelligence, breadth of understanding and empathy gradually revealed themselves to me as with the peeling of an onion. He was humane, imaginative, ingenious, creative, and very brave. No one did more, and no one risked more. His contribution to peace was, literally, essential to the process. There would have been no Good Friday Agreement without the persistence over many years, and the courage, of Brendan Duddy.[3]

In my last interview with Robert on 26 July 2022, he paid his own tribute to Brendan.

None of my role could have happened, nor Michael Oatley's role either, if Brendan hadn't been there and if Brendan hadn't doggedly stuck to it, unbelievably so. Most people would have given up, but for him it was obviously a crusade that he had to bring IRA violence to a halt, to an end and then there would be peace in Ireland.[4]

There were funerals of other crucial peacemakers too. John Hume died on 3 August 2020 at the age of eighty-three. As a constitutional politician, he was likened to the nineteenth-century nationalist political giants Daniel O'Connell and Charles Stuart Parnell. The priest, Father Paul Farren, paid tribute to John, and then to his wife, Pat, for her indefatigable support in his unceasing efforts for peace.

We should never underestimate how difficult it was for John to cross the road and do what was intensely unpopular for the greater good ... even in the darkest moments, when people would have been forgiven for having no hope, John made peace visible for others.[5]

David Trimble, John Hume's fellow recipient of the Nobel Peace Prize, died as Baron Trimble of Lisnagarvey on 25 July 2022, aged seventy-seven. Delivering the eulogy at his funeral the minister, the Very Reverend Dr Charles McMullen, spoke of his enduring legacy:

> The reward for all of us has been a radically changed landscape here in Northern Ireland, which has saved many lives and allowed a generation to grow up in relative peace. History will be exceedingly kind to David.[6]

Finally there was another funeral of someone who should rightly be counted among the peacemakers: Queen Elizabeth II, who died on 8 September 2022 at the age of ninety-six, having reigned for a record seventy years, the longest of any British monarch. By shaking the hand of Martin McGuinness she set the royal seal on the peace process, giving credibility to the former IRA leader's claim that the republican movement was sincere in wishing to share the future with unionists. The part that the new Sovereign, Charles III, will play in the future of Northern Ireland and the United Kingdom, will be for future historians to record.

Those were the peacemakers who were laid to rest. What then of the 'Final Farewell' in the title of this Epilogue? The Final Farewell was Brexit, as the UK left the European Union following an advisory referendum. The danger had always been that Brexit risked destabilising the peace that was achieved in the Good Friday Agreement and all that went before it. I asked Senator George Mitchell, who so skilfully and patiently steered the Agreement to its successful conclusion, if he thought Brexit threatened its survival.

> Yes, it does. Brexit was a decision democratically taken in a democratic society and therefore it must be respected. But it's not a good result. I believe history will judge this to appear to be an unwise decision for the UK and for the Republic of Ireland. The Good Friday Agreement did not end, once and for all time, the political differences in Northern Ireland. It recognised the existence of those differences and simply said that they will be resolved by democratic and peaceful means, not through the use of violence. No one I'm aware of back in 1998 anticipated Brexit. I said on the very day the Agreement was reached that it did not guarantee by

itself political stability, peace or reconciliation. It simply made them possible.[7]

In the end Brexit was about the border between Northern Ireland and the Irish Republic, the contentious issue that since partition in 1921 has been at the root of the conflict. At the time of the Good Friday Agreement in 1998, both the United Kingdom and the Irish Republic were members of the European Union and therefore goods and citizens could move freely between both jurisdictions without checks. Effectively the border ceased to exist. At midnight (Brussels time) on 31 January 2020 all that changed when the UK officially withdrew from the European Union following the referendum. The options on the ballot were clear: 'Remain' or 'Leave'. Leave won the referendum with 51.89 per cent of the vote. Remain lost with 48.11 per cent. Significantly the result in Northern Ireland was turned on its head with 55.8 per cent voting Remain and 44.2 per cent voting Leave. Brexit meant the issue of the border, effectively dormant since Good Friday, returned to haunt Northern Ireland, Westminster and Dublin. Another way had to be found to avoid a reinstatement of the land border between Northern Ireland and the Irish Republic, a tempting target for IRA dissidents.

The compromise, presided over by the then Prime Minister, Boris Johnson, was known as the Northern Ireland Protocol accompanying the Brexit withdrawal agreement, making Northern Ireland part of the EU single market. The Protocol placed a notional watery border in the Irish Sea. This meant that goods arriving in Northern Ireland, including some goods from other parts of the UK, were subject to search and Customs approval at the port of entry in accordance with EU single market rules so goods destined for the Irish Republic could move freely across the land border. These goods included certain UK foodstuffs which were subject to examination to make sure they met EU standards. Johnson had originally declared that a border in the Irish Sea would happen 'over my dead body'.[8] The Prime Minister was forced to eat his words, as the alternative, a return to a land border, was unthinkable as it would undermine one of the cardinal principles underpinning the Good Friday Agreement. Unionists were furious, seeing the Protocol – on top of the shortages it initially caused – as a further erosion of the union and rekindling, yet again, the ever present fear of a united Ireland.

In protest, the DUP, now the second largest party in the Northern Ireland Assembly, withdrew from the Assembly and the Executive, leaving the corridors of Stormont once again echoing to the sound of silence. The party said it would only return once a satisfactory solution to the Protocol had been achieved. This was just one of the multiple challenges the new Prime Minister, Liz Truss, faced when elected as leader of the Conservative Party and therefore Prime Minister, not by the nation, but by the votes of 141,725 Conservative Party members, following the resignation of Boris Johnson on 7 July 2022 as the result of a series of scandals and statements that raised questions about his integrity. And the political upheavals were to continue when, after only forty-five days in Downing Street, Liz Truss resigned as Prime Minister because her radical mini-budget, drawn up with her short-lived Chancellor, Kwasi Kwarteng, had crashed the markets, triggering an economic crisis. Another leadership election was held, and was won by her rival in the previous one, Rishi Sunak.

How did this seismic change in the relationship between the UK and Europe and the UK and Ireland come about and where did responsibility for it lie? Initially the impetus came from the ambitious firebrand and militantly anti-EU politician Nigel Farage, who exploited anti-European feeling and prejudice through his Brexit-hungry party, the UK Independence Party (UKIP), striking fear into Prime Minister David Cameron's ruling Conservatives. Cameron was worried that Farage and his many devoted followers might drain votes from the Government and potentially deny the Conservatives victory at the next election. The Prime Minister, conscious that the issue of Europe had been poisoning British politics for years,[9] decided to settle the issue once and for all by calling a referendum, confident that Remain would win. It was a grievous miscalculation, severely damaging Cameron's legacy, just as Iraq had damaged Tony Blair's. To contextualise, all the other political parties supported a referendum of one kind or another. Cameron's was based on a simple majority with no thresholds.[10]

Brexit was cataclysmic, not least for Northern Ireland, potentially affecting the future of the hard-won Good Friday Agreement in which Robert, Michael Oatley and Brendan Duddy had all played crucial parts in their different ways and at different times. Robert was deeply depressed by the triumph of Brexit.

I was horrified. I thought we would win the referendum, just as
David Cameron did. I was stunned by the results coming in. The EU
was critical for the Good Friday Agreement. It brought both sides of
the island together. If we're not very careful Good Friday could go up
in smoke and Boris Johnson is the clown who achieved this.[11]

I finally brought Robert back to the words that were the genesis of
this book. Did he really say to Martin McGuinness at that seminal
meeting at Brendan's house in 1993, 'The final solution is union. This
island will be as one'? Does he think those words will come true? He
believes that in the fullness of time 'the border will go down' given
changing demographics and the possibility of a border poll.

The demographics among Northern Ireland's 1.9 million people
are indeed changing – and in one direction. Censuses are held every
ten years. The results of the 2021 census, announced on 22 September
2022, marked a historic moment. For the first time in the province's
101-year history, the largest proportion of its citizens came from a
Catholic background. The figures were 45.7 per cent Catholic and
43.5 per cent Protestant.[12] The comparable figures at the time of the
previous census in 2011 were 45.1 per cent Catholic and 48.4 per cent
Protestant. Significantly 9.3 per cent said they didn't belong to any
religion, potentially strengthening the centre ground, epitomised by
the growth of the non-sectarian Alliance Party. The new Catholic
preponderance was clear but not sufficient to trigger the border poll that
Sinn Féin wanted for two main reasons: not all Catholics are necessarily
nationalists; and the margin, though significant, is still relatively small.
The decision to trigger a border poll at the time of the publication of
the latest census rests in the hands of the Northern Ireland Secretary,
Chris Heaton-Harris (or his successor), a Brexiteer and former Chief
Whip appointed to the Cabinet by the new Prime Minister Liz Truss.

What followed was an almost unprecedented period of political chaos
and instability. Liz Truss resigned after only forty-four days as Prime
Minister after announcing a mini-budget of tax cuts which triggered
a financial crisis and sent the markets into a tailspin. Critics and the
Labour opposition pointed out that the tax cuts were unfunded and
relied on excessive borrowing. Another leadership ballot followed and
Rishi Sunak, Boris Johnson's former chancellor whom Liz Truss had
defeated in the previous leadership ballot, won unopposed to become

the UK's first Asian and Hindu Prime Minister. Restoring devolved government in Northern Ireland was one of the new Prime Minister's top priorities, stalled by the DUP until the contentious Northern Ireland protocol was resolved – a decision that the Government put on the back-burner until some point, to be decided, after New Year 2023. Whenever new Assembly elections are held, it is expected that Sinn Féin will be the beneficiary, as it was the last time in 2022.

Sinn Féin has dramatically changed politics in Ireland, with the party wedded to the border poll enshrined in the Good Friday Agreement. In the North, Sinn Féin is now the largest party in the devolved Assembly, having won the election on 7 May 2022 with twenty-nine seats (of ninety) with its Vice-President, Michelle O'Neill, becoming First Minister Designate. Meanwhile in the South, Sinn Féin is close to becoming a partner in government. It was expected that Sinn Féin would be the beneficiary of the new Assembly elections, as it had been at the previous elections on 7 May 2022. At the time of writing, the Northern Ireland Secretary, Chris Heaton-Harris, has postponed them until early 2023 to allow time for the negotiations to try and resolve the political impasse at Stormont to succeed. The DUP refuses to return to the Assembly until the Protocol is resolved to its members' satisfaction. Until then, the political stalemate continues with the people of Northern Ireland denied local political representation in the province's devolved administration. Who would have thought, when the hunger striker Bobby Sands was elected to Westminster in 1981, a month before he died, having gone without food for sixty-six days, that Sinn Féin would rise to become the largest political party on the island of Ireland? It is a remarkable transformation.

I remember asking Lord Prior, formerly James Prior, the Northern Ireland Secretary who finally resolved the hunger strike, if he thought the republican movement's strategy of the Armalite and the Ballot Box had worked. I posed the question in 2014, two years before he died. He thought for a while before answering.

I expect with the benefit of hindsight, one has to say, 'Yes it did.'
However unpleasant that sounds. I'm afraid it did work. I'm
afraid throughout history that's been the case: that violence, where
you feel that strongly about the government of the day, probably
does work. It may not work quickly and it may not be seen to be

working quickly, but in the long run one has to look back and say, 'Yes. It did work.'[13]

The transformation from war to peace has been remarkable thanks to the efforts of many individuals on both sides of the border and in Westminster and Downing Street. But the crucial role that has not been recognised, because by its very nature it has until now been secret, is the part played by MI6 and MI5, made possible, as Robert acknowledges, by the late Brendan Duddy.

> Brendan was absolutely crucial, right from the beginning of the Troubles. Without him, nothing would have happened. There would have been no contact with the IRA at various stages. He put his life in their hands. He possibly nearly sacrificed his own life in keeping the back channel open. He should have had recognition of some sort, but it may have meant endangering his life by pinning a medal on him. But there should be something, some mark, to say he passed this way. And there's nothing.[14]

Brendan also, for his part, hugely admired Robert.

> He was a true gentleman. I admire the guy so much. The world is full of everybody who does the right thing, and then occasionally there's people who cross the line. If he hadn't done what he did, we'd still be hearing the bombs going off today – and there would have been no Good Friday Agreement. Robert is the kind of guy who in other days you would pin medals on.[15]

Brendan was sorry to see Robert go, although he was never fully aware of the circumstances in which he went. He never saw Robert or heard from him again. Brendan treasured his parting gift: Robert Kee's *The Laurel and the Ivy*, inscribed with the quote from Virgil, 'One day it will be good to remember even these things.'

Robert still has the decanter, glasses and tray originally intended for the follow-up meeting between the IRA and the British that never happened as planned. He occasionally uses them and perhaps thinks, 'It will be good to remember these things.'

Appendix I:
Death of a Suspected Informer

The power over life and death (see p. 214) is thought to have been exercised in 1986 in the 'execution' of the IRA's Quartermaster in Derry, Frank Hegarty, who was believed to have been recruited by the British army's innocuously named Force Research Unit, the FRU. Its job was to recruit and run agents – a mirror of what MI5 and MI6 were tasked to do. McGuinness always denied any involvement in Hegarty's death. Brendan would have been fully aware of the case and the memory of it may still have been there on his journey into the Donegal hills and during his unnerving interrogation by McGuinness.

Hegarty is believed to have provided his army handlers with the location of a cache of arms imported from Libya in the mid-1980s. The cache was hidden on a beach in Donegal. Shortly before the Garda Síochána, the Irish police, uncovered the hide, Hegarty was exfiltrated by his handlers and flown to a safe house near Gatwick airport. He was desperate to return to Derry, believing he could talk his way out of trouble. Approaches were made and McGuinness is believed to have given Hegarty 'safe passage' to return. Once back home, he was interrogated, sentenced to death as a British agent and shot in the back of the head. His body was found dumped at the side of a lonely country lane.

Appendix II:
Tribute to Brendan Duddy
at His Requiem Mass

There are certain moments in my forty-five years of covering the conflict that I'll never forget. One of them is from 1998, the year of the Good Friday Agreement, when I was standing by a public telephone in the middle of the new shopping mall in the centre of Derry. I had a mountain of coins ready to feed into the slot.

I thought I had finally discovered the identity of the person who hitherto had only been referred to as 'The Link' in the secret back-channel talks between the British Government and the IRA that ran intermittently from 1973 to 1993. This was the moment when I would discover whether I was right or wrong. His name was Brendan Duddy and I was now about to ring his office. The phone rang. Someone answered. I gave my name and waited while I was put through. I fed more coins into the slot in case my time ran out. Brendan came on the line. 'I've been waiting to hear from you,' he said, to my astonishment. That was the beginning of a relationship with Brendan and his family that lasted from that day to the sad moment today when Brendan is laid to rest.

Brendan agreed to meet. We sat and talked for several hours in the tiny parlour with a smouldering peat fire in the corner where he had secretly hosted the MI6 officer, Michael Oatley, and a variety of IRA leaders on and off for twenty years. He once described the significance of that room to me.

There's a notion that big things happen in the Oval Office in Washington or the Grand Hall in the Kremlin, but it doesn't happen that way. It happens less formally and more simply. And when you get a situation where eventually someone is dying for a cup of tea and he says, 'I'll make a cup of tea' and you have to ask somebody who you are not very happy about, 'Would you like tea?', it breaks down. And then of course somebody says, 'When you're there, would you get a bucket of coal?'

That was pure Brendan.

Into the small hours of the morning, over a bottle of Irish whiskey, he told me a story that could have come straight out of the pages of an airport thriller. It was a Long Night's Journey into Day. I woke up the following morning with a dreadful headache, scarcely believing the extraordinary story Brendan had told me the night before. I thought perhaps I'd been dreaming. He only did so after I had assured him that I would never broadcast or write anything about what he said until he thought the time was right. It was to be almost another ten years before he gave me the green light. That's when I first referred to Brendan by name in my documentary *The Secret Peacemaker*.

One of Brendan's greatest regrets was that he was unable to help end the 1981 hunger strike led by Bobby Sands. He once showed me a 'com' smuggled out of the Maze from Bobby Sands just before he died after sixty-six days on hunger strike.

To you and yours, may I be permitted to say a last goodbye. If my passion is to mean anything, may it mean peace and freedom for you and all of yours. May I be permitted to say I much appreciate all the efforts you've done on our behalf.

He broke down as he read it.

During the years when his name was not known, Brendan became referred to in some sections of the media as 'The Mountain Climber'. Other sections used the same codename to describe Michael Oatley. The reality was that both deserved the sobriquet. Both were climbing the same mountain with the same aim – peace – to try and persuade the IRA to end its campaign and concentrate on an exclusively political route to achieve its long-fought-for goal of a united Ireland.

Brendan's purpose was to try and convince the IRA, via Michael Oatley, that the 'Brits' were serious in reaching a settlement, as the IRA thought it had been conned into the ceasefire of 1975.

Others on all sides climbed the mountain too – including his wife Margo, his remarkable family and close friends like Bernadette Mount, who smuggled IRA leaders across the border. All supported him through every step on Brendan's perilous ascent.

It was a dangerous journey that he undertook, from being interrogated at a posh house outside Dublin by the IRA leaders Seamus Twomey and Billy McKee at an Army Council meeting on New Year's Eve 1974 to being interrogated by four senior IRA/Sinn Féin leaders upstairs at his home in 1993. He emerged shaken. Brendan walked the tightrope and courageously lived to tell the tale.

Brendan's legacy – and the legacy of Martin McGuinness too – is the part they both played in helping bring about the peace we enjoy today. It's ironic that both passed away within weeks of each other – marking the end of an era and the eventual transition from war to peace.

Brendan's contribution is incalculable and is only just being belatedly – and rightly – recognised. John Hume and David Trimble deserved the Nobel Peace prize – but Brendan Duddy deserved it too.

Brendan. Thank you. We will all miss you.

Peter Taylor, St Eugene's Cathedral, Derry
Monday 15 May 2017

Appendix III:
A Difference of Opinion

CHARLES MOORE, *Daily Telegraph*, 1 NOVEMBER 1999

Spooked by the IRA

Did you ever wonder why the British state failed to defeat republican terrorism over the past 30 years, notwithstanding its vastly superior resources? If so, take a look at Michael Oatley's article in yesterday's Sunday Times – which affords a fabulous insight into the degenerate, post-imperial mindset of some of our secret servants. Mr Oatley was a senior figure in MI6 who 'liaised' with the Provisionals during the Troubles. He now thinks that the Unionists, the press and the 'Right wing' of the Tory party should stop insisting on the decommissioning of IRA weapons and acknowledge the sincerity of Gerry Adams and Martin McGuinness. Afford these honourable gentlemen the flexibility they need – he suggests – and they will thereby be able to show their own supporters that politics works and that the gun is redundant.

Mr Oatley is clearly suffering from a spook's variant of the 'Stockholm syndrome' – whereby captives start to view the world from the standpoint of the kidnappers. Certainly, he is hostage to just about every republican myth about the 'peace process'. Why did the first IRA ceasefire end? According to Mr Oatley, because John Major's government unfairly injected the precondition of decommissioning after the republicans had 'unilaterally' called a halt to violence in 1994. (Nothing could be further from the truth. Decommissioning was insisted on by London and Dublin at the time of the 1993 Downing Street Declaration as one of the criteria for establishing whether the ceasefire was permanent.)

These are not just points of scholarly interest: republicans take them seriously because they desperately require validation for their violent actions in the eyes of nationalist Ireland. By accepting them at their own estimation, Mr Oatley has underwritten the notion that the republicans were cheated of their just deserts by Perfidious Albion. And if they don't get what they want now, they will no doubt cite his view as yet another justification for a return to violence. At a minimum, he will have made it very much harder to persuade republicans of the idea even of token decommissioning.

In Unionist eyes, Mr Oatley's remarks will validate the idea that talks on Ulster's new political structures are mere window dressing to conceal the fact that the province's future is really being carved up in secret between unaccountable secret servants and the Provisionals. It will certainly do little to strengthen David Trimble's hand. So whose agenda is Mr Oatley serving and for whom does he speak as an ex-officer of SIS? He has, after all, recently visited the north-west of the province and has maintained his contacts there. The Conservatives should ask written questions in the Commons to ascertain whether he had any contact with a minister or an official on this subject before publication. If not, Peter Mandelson should immediately repudiate him, for giving a misleading impression of British state thinking. If the answer is yes, the implications are even more shocking – of MI6 colluding in a campaign to urge British citizens to submit to blackmail.

MICHAEL OATLEY'S REPLY TO CHARLES MOORE, *DAILY TELEGRAPH*, 3 NOVEMBER 1999

Why the IRA wants peace

Fun for the Editor, whose allegiances are no secret, to call me a post-imperialist degenerate because of views I expressed in the Sunday Times. (I began my career in colonial Africa, so why 'post'?) But the serious attention he gave them was limited.

And the last part of his note, constructing Le Carré-esque scenarios, whereby Old Spook plays a role in some extraordinary agency conspiracy, was well over the top! Old Spooks, I can tell him from the heart, are a bore and a liability to successors and, when they speak publicly, which they should of course never do, we cover our ears. I have not spoken to anyone in government about Irish matters since retiring from SIS in 1991.

I believe that decommissioning is not an issue on which the Belfast Agreement should be allowed to founder; that the majority in both communities in Ulster do not wish it to be; that mainland voters have been misled as to its significance; that pressing republicans on the matter is counter-productive; that there are understandable reasons for this; and that identification of decommissioning as a yardstick of republican sincerity damages prospects for peaceful settlement. I believe that it has done so since the republican leadership first signalled interest in pursuing a non-violent strategy in 1991.

I believe that a disservice is done to the democratic process in the United Kingdom by presenting only one side of this coin. And that this also damages Unionism: Unionists will gain no credit with the mainland electorate by getting hung up on decommissioning while claiming a right to conduct arcane ceremonies around other people's backyards.

There are more complex and interesting reasons than the mindset of such as me for the Government's inability to defeat republican terrorism. If there is only a little water, fish can swim. For two decades, military commanders and Northern Ireland secretaries of state have accepted that the activity can be contained, but not eradicated. It may wither, but people die in the meantime.

The IRA first signalled interest in adopting a political strategy in 1991. Two years later, the government included decommissioning in the Downing Street Declaration. Decommissioning was recognisably unattainable, its inclusion certain to damage political moves in the IRA. But these survived, and in October 1994 a ceasefire was announced. The government declined to accept the sincerity of the statement, demanded a reformulation, and again pressed for decommissioning.

Sir Hugh Annesley, the former RUC chief constable, later explained how unhelpful this was: 'It was clear from all intelligence assessments that the Provisionals were not going to hand in their arms. I believe that, whilst decommissioning was important politically, it was not as important operationally as some people have attempted to make out.' Albert Reynolds, a former Irish prime minister, believed he had obtained John Major's recognition that decommissioning would impede agreement.

In March 1995, Sir Patrick Mayhew produced requirements for phased decommissioning before Sinn Féin could be admitted to talks. Sinn Féin rejected them. Sir Hugh again: 'When the stalemate about decommissioning became more rigid, I think it became progressively more difficult for the leadership of Provisional IRA to hold in check those who wanted to go back to violence.' Which is my point. (Is Sir Hugh also suffering from Stockholm syndrome?)

George Mitchell produced a more realistic formula, but no sooner were peaceful negotiations once more in sight than the government announced elections for a Northern Ireland Forum. Sinn Féin was unprepared for elections. It saw a trap. The result was the Docklands bomb.

This pattern of government response to an opportunity to pursue peaceful solutions is what I call picador politics. The history of these events and the prominence in them of the issue of decommissioning is indeed 'of more than scholarly interest'. It shows how to construct a cul-de-sac. I do not think the majority on the British mainland or in Ulster wish to go down it.

Is it gullible of me to join the Prime Minister in accepting the sincerity of Gerry Adams and Martin McGuinness? I should be surprised if most participants in the Mitchell review did not accept it by now. I have had unusual opportunities over the years to observe broadening attitudes in the republican leadership, willingness to engage in dialogue with people offering fresh perspectives, re-examination of the justification and effectiveness of their campaign, leading finally to its abandonment.

Formerly a professional student of terrorist organisations, I can appreciate the difficulties of the small leadership group in keeping its supporters with it in a radically modified strategy. It must be hard, mustn't it? With a membership originally committed to violence? Compare the problems of our own party leaders in developing policy consensus and party discipline.

Republicans are determined that their movement will not be destroyed by false promises. For some, politics is on trial. This is no reason to question the sincerity of those trying to show that the course is worth pursuing. Pressure for decommissioning touches old wounds. All-out sectarian conflict is still imaginable. The IRA in its modern form emerged from such conflict. It was a response, like the introduction of British troops and the imposition of direct rule, to the apocalyptic experience of thousands of Catholics fleeing in terror as their homes burnt, our very own example of ethnic cleansing. The issue, for the paramilitaries on both sides and for the rest of us, is not whether guns are held or can be obtained. It is whether they are to be used.

MI6's Controller for Middle East and Counter Terrorism 1984–88, and Europe 1988–91

Timeline

Events specifically related to 'Operation Chiffon' are shown in italics.

1956–62	IRA border campaign.
1968–72	Civil Rights campaign.
1969	
12–14 Aug	Battle of the Bogside.
14 Aug	Deployment of British troops to Belfast and Derry.
28 Dec	Formation of Provisional IRA (PIRA).
1970	
3 Jul	Falls Road curfew. Families in three thousand homes locked in for thirty-six hours. Fierce gun battles. Four civilians killed by the army.
1971	
6 Feb	First British soldier shot dead by PIRA.
15 Apr	Billy McKee arrested and jailed. Begins hunger strike for political status.
9 Aug	Introduction of internment. Long Kesh internment camp opened to hold detainees.
9–11 Aug	Ballymurphy riots. Paratroopers shoot dead at least nine civilians.
Aug	Army's interrogation of IRA suspects, the 'Hooded Men'.
Oct	*Frank Steele (MI6) arrives in Belfast.*

1972

30 Jan	'Bloody Sunday'. Soldiers of Parachute Regiment shoot dead thirteen civil rights marchers.
4 Mar	Abercorn restaurant bombing in Belfast. Two dead. Seventy injured.
13 Mar	Harold Wilson, leader of the Opposition, secretly meets IRA in Dublin.
24 Mar	William Whitelaw becomes Northern Ireland Secretary.
30 Mar	Stormont Parliament suspended. Direct Rule from Westminster introduced.
18 Apr	Widgery Report into 'Bloody Sunday' largely exonerates the army.
13 Jun	IRA press conference in Derry invites William Whitelaw for talks.
20 Jun	*Frank Steele meets Gerry Adams and David O'Connell outside Derry.*
26 Jun	IRA ceasefire. Whitelaw grants IRA prisoners 'Special Category Status'. Billy McKee ends hunger strike.
7 Jul	*Cheyne Walk talks. Whitelaw meets leadership of PIRA.*
9 Jul	PIRA ceasefire ends in Lenadoon Avenue, West Belfast.
21 Jul	'Bloody Friday'. IRA bombs in Belfast kill eleven people.
31 Jul	Operation Motorman. Army clears 'no go' areas in Derry. *Brendan Duddy facilitates removal of IRA weapons to avoid a repetition of 'Bloody Sunday'.*
20 Dec	Diplock Report ends jury trials in conflict-related cases. Cases now heard before single judge.

1973

1 Jan	UK and Irish Republic join European Economic Community (EEC).
Mar	*Michael Oatley arrives in Northern Ireland.*
May	*Frank Steele departs Northern Ireland.*
9 Dec	Sunningdale Agreement sets up power-sharing executive at Stormont with closer links to Dublin.

1974

28 Feb	British General Election. Conservative Prime Minister, Edward Heath, replaced by Harold Wilson leading minority Labour government. Merlyn Rees becomes Northern Ireland Secretary.

15 May	Loyalist Ulster Workers' Council calls strike opposing Sunningdale Agreement. Power-sharing executive collapses.
17 May	Loyalist paramilitaries plant car bombs killing twenty-two people in Dublin and five more in Monaghan.
4 Sept	Billy McKee released from jail.
5 Oct	IRA bomb Guildford pubs, killing four soldiers and one civilian.
21 Nov	IRA bomb Birmingham pubs killing twenty-one people.
Autumn 1974	*Michael Oatley and Brendan Duddy activate back channel to PIRA.*
10 Dec	*Feakle talks between clergymen and PIRA leaders.*
20 Dec	PIRA declares temporary ceasefire.
25 Dec	*Brendan Duddy meets Ruairí Ó Brádaigh at his house in Roscommon.*
31 Dec	*Brendan Duddy meets Provisional Army Council (PAC) near Dublin.*

1975

7 Jan	*Exploratory meeting between Michael Oatley and Billy McKee at Brendan Duddy's house.*
20 Jan	*First full meeting between British representatives and republican movement. 'Structures of disengagement' discussed. Ten-point agreement finally reached.*
9 Feb	PIRA announce indefinite ceasefire.
11 Feb	Incident Centres established as part of ten-point agreement in which Sinn Féin monitors ceasefire.
Mar	*Michael Oatley departs Northern Ireland.*
31 Jul	UVF kill three members of the Miami Showband. Two attackers also killed when their bomb explodes prematurely.
1 Sept	PIRA uses cover name 'South Armagh Republican Action Force' to kill four loyalists at Tullyvallen Orange Hall, County Armagh.
2 Oct	Shankill Butchers under UVF's Lenny Murphy begin 'reign of terror', killing four Catholics working at wholesale wine warehouse.

1976

| 4 Jan | Loyalists kill three Catholic brothers at Whitecross and three members of a Catholic family in Gilford. |

5 Jan	'Republican Action Force', suspected flag of convenience for South Armagh PIRA, kill ten Protestant workers in minibus at Kingsmills, South Armagh.
7 Jan	SAS deployed to South Armagh.
23 Jan	IRA ceasefire ends.
1 Mar	Special Category Status abolished. 'Criminalisation' policy begins. Internment ends. Maze prison H Blocks now hold prisoners sentenced by the Diplock courts.
16 Mar	Harold Wilson resigns as Labour Prime Minister.
5 Apr	James Callaghan succeeds Harold Wilson as Prime Minister.
1 May	Kenneth Newman becomes Chief Constable of the Royal Ulster Constabulary (RUC).
10 Sept	Roy Mason becomes Northern Ireland Secretary.
15 Oct	Blanket protest begins after republicans refuse to wear prison uniform.
1977	RUC's Castlereagh 'holding centre' and other interrogation centres produce results. Detainees pressurised to sign statements. Widespread allegations of assault during interview (known as ADI).
7 Oct	Desmond Irvine, Secretary of Prison Officers Association (POA), shot dead in Belfast by PIRA.
11 Oct	Lenny Murphy, leader of 'Shankill Butchers', jailed for twelve years.
1978	
Mar	'Dirty'/'No wash' protest begins in the Maze H Blocks.
2 Nov	Army's secret assessment of PIRA, 'Future Terrorist Trends', leaked.
26 Nov	Albert Miles, Governor of the Maze prison, shot dead by PIRA. Continuing attacks on prison officers and governors.
1979	
16 Mar	Judicial Bennett Report on allegations of ill-treatment in police custody concludes that there were cases in which injuries sustained were not self-inflicted.

30 Mar	Conservative Northern Ireland spokesman, Airey Neave, assassinated in Westminster by Irish National Liberation Army (INLA) while driving out of House of Commons car park.
3 May	Margaret Thatcher wins General Election and becomes Conservative Prime Minister.
4 May	Humphrey Atkins becomes Northern Ireland Secretary.
6 May	John Hume becomes leader of the Social and Democratic Labour Party (SDLP).
27 Aug	IRA assassinate Lord Mountbatten in County Sligo and kill eighteen soldiers at Warrenpoint, County Down.
5 Dec	Charles Haughey becomes Taoiseach.

1980

1 Jan	John Hermon becomes RUC Chief Constable, succeeding Sir Kenneth Newman.
27 Oct	First IRA hunger strike, led by Brendan Hughes, begins with Five Demands to improve prison conditions, including the right for prisoners to wear their own clothes, effectively the restoration of special category status.
18 Dec	*Michael Oatley and Brendan Duddy, via the back channel, intervene to try to negotiate a compromise agreement to end the hunger strike. Prime Minister Thatcher signs off the compromise. Michael Oatley meets Brendan Duddy at Aldergrove airport with the document but it arrives too late. The hunger strike has already been called off with one prisoner close to death.*

1981

21 Jan	Former Stormont Speaker, Sir Norman Stronge (86), and son shot dead by PIRA at Tynan Abbey, South Armagh.
5 Feb	Prisoners demand change in prison policy. Compromise over prisoners' access to their own clothes falls apart.
1 Mar	PIRA leader in H Blocks, Bobby Sands, begins second hunger strike. Others follow.
9 Apr	Bobby Sands elected as Westminster MP in Fermanagh-South Tyrone by-election.

5 May	Sands dies after sixty-six days on hunger strike. Nine other hunger strikers follow him to their deaths. *Brendan Duddy tries to intervene to end the protest without success.* Mrs Thatcher determined not to give in to the strikers' demands.
20 Aug	Sinn Féin's Owen Carron wins Fermanagh-South Tyrone by-election caused by death of Sands. Michael Devine of Irish National Liberation Army [INLA] is the tenth and last hunger striker to die.
13 Sept	James Prior becomes Northern Ireland Secretary.
3 Oct	Hunger strike ends as families request medical intervention for their relatives. Concessions agreed including prisoners being allowed to wear their own clothes.

1982

20 Jul	PIRA bomb Green Jackets' military band in Regents Park and Blues and Royals' parade in Hyde Park, killing eleven soldiers.
20 Oct	Sinn Féin contests Assembly election for first time and wins five seats with 10 per cent of the vote.
16 Nov	Lenny Murphy, UVF leader of loyalist 'Shankill Butchers' gang, shot dead by the IRA following his release from jail.

1983

9 Jun	Gerry Adams and John Hume elected to Westminster. SDLP receives 17.9 per cent of the poll and Sinn Féin 13.4 per cent.
25 Sept	Thirty-eight PIRA prisoners escape from the Maze prison.
13 Nov	Gerry Adams elected President of Sinn Féin.
17 Dec	PIRA bomb outside Harrods department store in London kills five people.

1984

12 Oct	PIRA's Patrick Magee bombs the Grand Hotel in Brighton where the Conservative Party was holding its annual conference. Five people killed. Mrs Thatcher narrowly survives.

1985

28 Feb	IRA mortar attack on RUC station in Newry kills nine officers.

	John Hume meets members of PAC but walks out after refusing to be video-ed.
15 May	Sinn Féin wins fifty-nine council seats in Northern Ireland local government elections.
Aug/Sept	Huge shipments of arms from Libya destined for the IRA land in County Wicklow.
15 Nov	Anglo-Irish Agreement signed by Prime Minister Margaret Thatcher and Taoiseach Garret FitzGerald. Violent unionist protests.

1986

15 Oct	Sinn Féin's annual conference, Ard Fheis, permits successful candidates to take their seats in the Irish Parliament, Dáil Éireann. Ruairí Ó Brádaigh and his supporters walk out in protest.

1987

8 May	SAS kill eight members of PIRA active service unit in ambush at Loughgall RUC station.
8 Nov	IRA bomb Remembrance Day service in Enniskillen, killing eleven Protestants.

1988

11 Jan	Gerry Adams meets John Hume. Beginning of Hume–Adams dialogue.
6 Mar	SAS kill three unarmed members of IRA in Gibraltar planning to bomb British military band.
16 Mar	Loyalist Michael Stone attacks funeral in Belfast of the three IRA volunteers shot dead in Gibraltar. Stone kills three people including IRA member Kevin Brady.
19 Mar	Two corporals in civilian clothes 'executed' by IRA after accidentally running into Kevin Brady's funeral. Father Alec Reid administers the last rites.
15 Jun	PIRA bomb kills six soldiers on army 'Fun Run' in Lisburn.
1 Aug	*Robert invited to join MI5.*
20 Aug	PIRA bomb bus carrying soldiers at Ballygawley, County Tyrone. Eight killed.

| 30 Aug | SAS kill three PIRA volunteers outside Drumnakilly, County Tyrone. |
| 19 Oct | Mrs Thatcher's government introduces broadcasting restrictions. |

1989

24 Jul	Peter Brooke becomes Northern Ireland Secretary.
22 Sept	PIRA bomb Royal Marines' School of Music in Deal, killing ten bandsmen.
3 Nov	Peter Brooke admits military defeat of PIRA unlikely and reminds journalists of Cyprus's move to independence following violent campaign by EOKA 'terrorists'.

1990

30 Jul	Ian Gow MP, close ally of Mrs Thatcher, killed by IRA boobytrap bomb at his home in Sussex.
9 Nov	Peter Brooke announces Britain has no 'selfish or strategic or economic interest' in Northern Ireland.
22 Nov	Margaret Thatcher resigns in wake of Poll Tax demonstrations.
27 Nov	John Major becomes Conservative party leader and Prime Minister.

1991

Feb	*Michael Oatley holds unauthorised meeting with Martin McGuinness arranged by Brendan Duddy. Oatley reports back to Northern Ireland Office (NIO) Permanent Under Secretary (PUS), Sir John Chilcot.*
7 Feb	IRA mortars Downing Street as Cabinet discusses Iraq war.
	MI5 Operation Chiffon begins. Robert contacts Brendan to take over from Michael Oatley.
23 May	*Robert meets Brendan in Derry to take over from Michael Oatley. MI5's Operation Chiffon begins.*

1992

| 17 Jan | PIRA remote control bomb at Teebane, County Tyrone, kills eight Protestant workers returning home in a minibus after working on an army base. |
| 5 Feb | Loyalist Ulster Freedom Fighters (UFF) gun down five Catholics in Sean Graham's Belfast bookmakers in revenge for Teebane. |

6 Feb	Albert Reynolds becomes Taoiseach.
16 Feb	SAS kill four PIRA volunteers after they had opened fire on an RUC station in Coalisland, County Tyrone, with heavy calibre machine gun.
9 Apr	John Major returned as Prime Minister in British General Election. Sinn Féin vote declines from 11.4 per cent to 10 per cent. Gerry Adams loses West Belfast seat.
10 Apr	PIRA Baltic Exchange bomb in City of London kills three people and causes around £800 million damage.
11 Apr	Sir Patrick Mayhew becomes Northern Ireland Secretary.
16 Dec	Sir Patrick Mayhew, in Coleraine speech on 'Culture and Identity', says Sinn Féin could be included in talks if it ends its campaign. Does not rule out Irish unity being on the agenda.

1993

20 Feb	Sinn Féin Ard Fheis. Martin McGuinness says republican movement prepared to be 'open and flexible to serious proposals which can lead to a realistic agreement'.
21 Feb	*McGuinness tells Brendan 'the conflict is over but we need the British to tell us how to make peace'.*
22 Feb	*Brendan conveys McGuinness's message to Robert at Heathrow Hotel. Robert writes aide memoire of message.*
23 Feb	*Robert assured by Brendan and emissary from McGuinness that message is intended for British government. Message, as written by Robert in his aide memoire, then delivered to Prime Minister John Major in Downing Street.*
	Plans laid for exploratory meeting on 23 March between Martin McGuinness and Gerry Kelly and Robert and John Deverell at Brendan Duddy's house in Derry.
20 Mar	PIRA plants bombs in Warrington that kill two young boys out shopping.
	Robert and John Deverell forbidden to attend meeting with Martin McGuinness.
23 Mar	*Robert ignores the order and goes to meeting with Martin McGuinness and Gerry Kelly. Robert tells them, 'The final solution is union. This island will be as one.' As cover story Deverell and Robert give Sir John Chilcot the impression that it was Brendan Duddy who had met McGuinness and Kelly. The deception becomes a ticking timebomb.*

10 Apr	John Hume and Gerry Adams resume talks to develop their peace initiative.
24 Apr	PIRA's Bishopsgate bomb in City of London causes £500 million damage. Forty-four people injured. News photographer killed.
23 Oct	PIRA volunteers Thomas Begley and Sean Kelly bomb Frizzell's fish shop on Shankill Road believing UDA/UFF leadership meeting in room above the shop. Nine Protestant civilians and bomber Thomas Begley killed.
28 Oct	Gerry Adams carries coffin at Thomas Begley's funeral.
30 Oct	Greysteel massacre. UFF retaliatory attack for Shankill bomb. Six Catholics and two Protestants gunned down.
1 Nov	John Major says it would 'turn my stomach to talk to Gerry Adams and the Provisional IRA'.
	New intelligence reveals that a British official has talked to Martin McGuinness. It soon becomes clear that the official was Robert. Robert admits his role and tells Stephen Lander 'the sorry tale'.
28 Nov	Secret talks revealed in *Observer* scoop.
29 Nov	Sir Patrick Mayhew faces the House of Commons.
	Robert hands in his resignation and retires.
10 Dec	*Sir Patrick Mayhew writes to Robert expressing admiration for his 'great dedication and courage'.*
15 Dec	Downing Street Declaration signed in London by John Major and Albert Reynolds. Confirms the people of Northern Ireland would decide the province's future and demands PIRA permanently end its campaign.

1994

5 Jan	Sinn Féin publishes its account of the secret talks in 'Setting the Record Straight'.
29 Jan	President Bill Clinton issues Gerry Adams with limited duration visa to visit America.
March	PIRA mortar attacks on Heathrow airport. None explodes.
2 Jun	RAF Chinook helicopter crashes in atrocious weather on the Mull of Kintyre killing John Deverell and twenty-nine British intelligence officers flying to a security conference in Scotland.

18 Jun	UVF gunmen kill six Catholics in attack on pub in Loughinisland, County Down.
31 Aug	*IRA announce 'a complete cessation of military operations'. Robert receives congratulatory phone calls on ceasefire from senior MI5 colleagues.*
13 Oct	Combined Loyalist Military Command (CLMC) announces ceasefire. Its leader 'Gusty' Spence expresses 'abject and true remorse'.
9 Dec	First official meeting between British officials and Sinn Féin held at Stormont. Decommissioning of IRA weapons becomes stumbling block.

1995

8 Sept	David Trimble elected leader of Ulster Unionist Party (UUP).
30 Nov	President Clinton visits Belfast and shakes hands with Gerry Adams.

1996

9 Feb	PIRA ends its seventeen-month-old ceasefire by exploding 1,000 lb bomb at South Quay in London's Docklands. Damage amounts to estimated £150 million. Two men working in newspaper kiosk killed.
10 Jun	US Senator George Mitchell chairs all-party talks – without Sinn Féin.

1997

1 May	Labour leader Tony Blair wins landslide victory in British general election. 'Mo' Mowlem becomes Northern Ireland Secretary. Gerry Adams re-elected as Westminster MP and Martin McGuinness as MP for Mid Ulster.
27 Jul	PIRA announces new ceasefire.
26 Aug	Independent International Commission on Decommissioning (IICD) established under Canadian General John de Chastelain.
15 Sept	Sinn Féin signs up to the Mitchell Principles on non-violence and is admitted to all-party talks, along with political representatives of the loyalist paramilitaries.
11 Dec	Prime Minister Blair invites Gerry Adams and Martin McGuinness to Downing Street.

1998

10 Apr	Good Friday Agreement signed by all participating parties except Ian Paisley's DUP who refused to take part in all-party talks because of unresolved issue of decommissioning.
22 May	Good Friday Agreement ratified by referendums on both sides of border.
15 Aug	IRA dissidents of the Real IRA explode car bomb in Omagh killing twenty-nine people. The deadliest attack of the Troubles.
16 Oct	John Hume and David Trimble awarded Nobel peace prize.

1999	Impasse on decommissioning continues.
2 Dec	PIRA appoints an interlocutor to the IICD.
3 Dec	Irish Government formally amends Articles 2 and 3 to the Irish constitution.

2000

| 28 Jul | Last republican and loyalist prisoners released. |

2005

| 28 Jul | Gerry Adams publicly announces 'the war is over'. |
| 25 Sept | Last IRA weapons put 'beyond use'. Decommissioning completed. |

2007

| 8 May | Ian Paisley becomes First Minister with Martin McGuinness as Deputy. |

2008

| 4 Mar | Ian Paisley resigns as First Minister and leader of the DUP after party hostility to his sharing power with Martin McGuinness. |
| 5 Jun | Peter Robinson succeeds Ian Paisley as First Minister and DUP leader. |

2012

| 27 Jun | Martin McGuinness shakes hands with the Queen in Belfast. |

2014

| 8 Apr | Martin McGuinness joins royal toast at state banquet at Windsor Castle in honour of Irish President, Michael D. Higgins. |

12 Sept	Death of Ian Paisley.

2016

11 Jan	Arlene Foster succeeds Peter Robinson as First Minister and DUP leader.
23 Jun	EU referendum: 51.89 per cent vote Leave, 48.11 per cent vote Remain. In Northern Ireland 55.8 per cent vote Remain.

2017

9 Jan	Martin McGuinness resigns as Deputy First Minister over 'cash for ash' affair. Assembly and power-sharing executive suspended.
21 Mar	Death of Martin McGuinness.
12 May	*Death of Brendan Duddy.*

2020

31 Jan	Brexit. UK leaves European Union (EU). Northern Ireland Protocol implemented as part of withdrawal agreement covering checks on goods entering Northern Ireland from Great Britain, EU and abroad. Unionists protest the Protocol weakens the Union.
3 Aug	Death of John Hume.

2022

7 May	Sinn Féin becomes largest party in Northern Ireland Assembly elections.
25 Jul	Death of David Trimble.
6 Sept	Liz Truss elected leader of the Conservative Party by the membership and becomes Prime Minister.
8 Sept	Death of Queen Elizabeth II.
22 Sept	Results of 1921 Northern Ireland census announced: 45.7 per cent Catholic, 43.48 per cent Protestant, 9.3 per cent not belonging to any religion.
20 Oct	Liz Truss resigns after forty-five days as Prime Minister.
25 Oct	Rishi Sunak elected leader of the Conservative Party and becomes Prime Minister.
9 Nov	Northern Ireland Secretary, Chris Heaton-Harris, postpones Assembly elections until early 2023 to allow time for negotiations on the Northern Ireland Protocol.

Notes

INTRODUCTION

1 Personal letter to Robert from one of his former colleagues, undated.
2 Jonathan Powell, interview with the author, London, 2014.
3 Ibid.

1. FINDING ROBERT

1 The 'republican movement' originally meant the IRA but conveniently became the umbrella term embracing both the IRA and its political wing, Sinn Féin.
2 Virgil, *Aeneid*, Book I, line 203.

2. MEETING FRANK STEELE

1 Maurice Zinkin and Iftikhar Malik, 'Frank Steele, OBE', *Asian Affairs*, Vol. 29, Issue no. 2 (1998), p. 253, published online 18 June 2010, www.tandfonline.com/doi/abs/10.1080/714041355.
2 Ibid.
3 Brian Faulkner was the unionist Prime Minister of Northern Ireland from March 1971, four months before the introduction of internment, until his resignation in March 1972 when Direct Rule from Westminster began.
4 Two of the most glaring examples of discrimination were that workers at Belfast's biggest employer, the giant Harland & Wolff shipyard that built the *Titanic*, were almost exclusively Protestant, while in the overwhelming nationalist city of Londonderry/Derry the local

government electoral boundaries were politically gerrymandered to produce a unionist council.

5 Sydney Elliott and W. D. Flackes, *Northern Ireland: A Political Directory, 1968–1999*, Blackstaff Press, Belfast, 1999.

6 'Bloody Sunday: 50 Years On', BBC Radio 4, Archive on 4, Peter Taylor, 22 January 2022.

7 Peter Taylor, *Provos: The IRA and Sinn Féin*, Bloomsbury, London, 1997, p. 24.

3. 'BLOODY SUNDAY' AND BEYOND

1 Taylor, *Provos*, pp. 114–15.

2 Peter Taylor, 'Ulster, Five Long Years', a *This Week* Special, Thames Television, 8 August 1974.

3 Peter Taylor, *Provos*, Episode One, 'Born Again', BBC1, 23 September 1997.

4. FACE TO FACE WITH THE IRA

1 Frank Steele, interview with the author for *Provos*, Episode One, 'Born Again'.

2 Elliott and Flackes, *Northern Ireland. A Political Directory*.

3 Frank Steele, interview with the author for *Provos*, BBC1, 1997.

4 Ibid.

5 CAIN Archive (Conflict and Politics in Northern Ireland), PREM 15/1009, Top Secret Note of a Meeting with Representatives of the Provisional IRA, https://cain.ulster.ac.uk/publicrecords/1972/index.html.

6 Taylor, *Provos*, p. 138.

7 Ibid., p. 139.

8 Brendan Hughes, interview with the author for ibid., p. 137.

9 Frank Steele, interview with the author for ibid., p. 140.

10 Ed Moloney and Bob Mitchell, British Cabinet Account of 1972 Ceasefire Talks, *The Broken Elbow*, 21 January 2014, https://thebrokenelbow.com/2014/01/21/british-cabinet-account-of-1972-ira-ceasefire-talks/.

5. BACK TO THE WAR

1 *Taig*: an offensive term used by Protestants for Irish Catholics and nationalists.

2 Frank Steele, interview with the author for *Provos*, BBC1, 1997.

3 BBC Online, *On This Day*, 10 July 1972, 'Whitelaw's Secret Meeting with IRA'.

4 https://thebrokenelbow.files.wordpress.com/2015/06/tuzo-13.jpg.

5 Frank Steele, interview with the author for *Provos*, BBC1, 1997.

6 Taylor, *Provos*, p. 149.

7 Ibid., p. 150.

8 Gerry Adams, *Before the Dawn: An Autobiography*, Mandarin Paperbacks, London, 1996, p. 210.

9 'Remember Bloody Sunday', *Inside Story*, BBC1, 28 January 1992.

10 The National Archives, Cabinet Papers, 'No-Go Areas and Operation Motorman', CAIN Archive, 31 July 1972.

11 Peter Taylor, *Talking to Terrorists: A Personal Journey from the IRA to Al Qaeda*, Harper Press, London, 2011, p. 12.

12 David McKittrick, Seamus Kelters, Brian Feeney and Chris Thornton, *Lost Lives: The Stories of the Men, Women and Children Who Died as a Result of the Northern Ireland Troubles*, Mainstream Publishing, Edinburgh, 1999, p. 240.

6. MEETING BRENDAN DUDDY

1 Anthony Bevins, Eamonn Mallie and Mary Holland, 'Major's secret links with IRA leadership revealed', *Observer*, 28 November 1993.

2 This and subsequent quotations in this chapter, Brendan Duddy, interview with the author for *The Secret Peacemaker*, BBC2, 26 March 2008.

7. MEETING MARTIN MCGUINNESS

1 Taylor, *Provos*, p. 153.

2 Geoff Gilbert, 'The Irish Interpretation of the Political Offence Exception' in *International and Comparative Law Quarterly*, Part 4, October 2022, pp. 66–84; published online by Cambridge University Press, 7 January 2008: https://www.cambridge.org/core/journals/international-and-comparative-law-quarterly/article/abs/irish-interpretation-of-the-political-offence-exemption/3181BB7E2ED8F916992CD4DEE7DDB7FB.

3 Ibid., pp. 151–2.

4 Ibid., p. 153.

5 Ibid., p. 155.

6 Malcolm Sutton, *An Index of Deaths from the Conflict in Ireland, 1969–1993*, Beyond the Pale Publications, Belfast, 1994, pp. 39–54.

8. ENTER 'THE MOUNTAIN CLIMBER'

1 Michael Oatley, family archive and communication with the author.
2 Robert, interview with the author, 2021.
3 Brendan Duddy, interview with the author for *The Secret Peacemaker*, BBC2, 26 March 2008.
4 Bernie Mount, interview with the author for *The Secret Peacemaker*, BBC2, 26 March 2008.
5 This and subsequent quotations from Michael Oatley in this chapter, interview with the author, London, 1997.
6 Speech by Ian Paisley at DUP Annual Conference 1984, https://cain.uls ter.ac.uk/issues/politics/docs/dup/ip_1984.htm.
7 Peter Taylor, *Brits: The War Against the IRA*, Bloomsbury, London, 2001, p. 172.
8 McKittrick, Kelters, Feeney and Thornton, *Lost Lives*, p. 480.
9 Ibid.
10 Patrick Maume, *Dictionary of Irish Biography*, https://dib.ie/biography/rees-merlyn-a9415.
11 McKittrick, Kelters, Feeney and Thornton, *Lost Lives*, p. 497.
12 Ibid.
13 Ibid.
14 Taylor, *Brits*, p. 174.
15 Ibid.
16 Niall Ó Dochartaigh, *Deniable Contact: Back-Channel Negotiation in Northern Ireland*, Oxford University Press, 2021, p. 124.

9. SIDESHOW

1 Marie Louise McCrory, *Irish News*, 22 July 2005.
2 McKittrick, Kelters, Feeney and Thornton, *Lost Lives*, p. 161.
3 Taylor, *Brits*, p. 110.
4 Hansard, Vol. 826, Col. 1586, Northern Ireland, 25 November 1971.
5 Merlyn Rees, in Taylor, *Provos*, p. 132.
6 Brendan Anderson, *Joe Cahill: A Life in the IRA*, The O'Brien Press, Dublin, 2002, pp. 249–50.
7 *Provos*, Episode One, 'Born Again', BBC1, 23 September 1997.
8 Ibid.
9 Taylor, *Brits*, pp. 166–7.
10 Ibid., p. 176.
11 Ibid.
12 Ibid.

10. THE BAMBOO PIPE IN ACTION

1 Michael Oatley, interview with the author for *Provos*, 1997.
2 Brendan Duddy, interview with the author for *The Secret Peacemaker*, BBC2, 26 March 2008.
3 Michael Oatley, interview with the author for BBC2 documentary, *Ireland After Partition*.
4 Taylor, *Talking to Terrorists*, p. 18.
5 Billy McKee, interview with the author, in ibid., p. 19.
6 Ibid.
7 Billy McKee, interview with the author, 2014.
8 Michael Oatley, interview with the author.
9 *The Secret Peacemaker*, BBC2, 26 March 2008.
10 Ibid.
11 Bernadette Mount, interview with the author for ibid.
12 Ibid.
13 Frank Cooper, interview with the author for *Provos*, 1997.
14 Information provided by the participants: Brendan Duddy and Michael Oatley master interviews with the author; Brendan Duddy at home, Derry, 2008, with subsequent updates; Michael Oatley at the Langham Hotel, London, 2000, with recent updates from his personal family archive: 'An Irish Adventure', 'Blue Pencil' and 'Bogside Rambles'.

11. NEGOTIATING WITH THE IRA

1 Extract from republican movement minutes, shown privately to author in 1997.

12. TIT FOR TAT

1 Taylor, *Brits*, p. 182.
2 McKittrick, Kelters, Feeney and Thornton, *Lost Lives*, p. 534.
3 Ibid.
4 Ibid., pp. 555–6; Peter Taylor, *Loyalists*, Bloomsbury, London, 1999, pp. 147–8; Stephen Travers, interview with the author.
5 Taylor, *Loyalists*, p. 148. They were subsequently released under the 1998 Good Friday Agreement, *Guardian*, 14 December 2011.
6 McKittrick, Kelters, Feeney and Thornton, *Lost Lives*, p. 560.
7 Taylor, *Brits*, p. 182.
8 Taylor, *Provos*, p. 195.
9 Taylor, *Loyalists*, p. 153.

10 Martin Dillon, *The Shankill Butchers: A Case Study of Mass Murder*, Hutchinson, London, 1989, p. 255.
11 McKittrick, Kelters, Feeney and Thornton, *Lost Lives*, p. 609.
12 Ibid., p. 611.
13 Alan Black, interview with the author, in Taylor, *Brits*, p. 189.
14 Ibid.

13. THE COUP

1 The author's confidential interview with retired RUC Special Branch officer.
2 Taylor, *Brits*, p. 201.
3 Peter Taylor, *Beating the Terrorists? Interrogation in Omagh, Gough and Castlereagh*, Penguin Books, London, 1980, p. 71.
4 *Index on Censorship*, Vol. 7, Issue no. 6, 1 November 1978.
5 Taylor, *Beating the Terrorists*, p. 158.
6 Taylor, *Brits*, p. 202.
7 Ibid., pp. 202–3.
8 Ibid., p. 207.
9 Taylor, *Provos*, p. 207.
10 Taylor, *Beating the Terrorists*, p. 345.
11 Ed Moloney, *A Secret History of the IRA*, Penguin Books, London, 2nd edn, 2007, p. 170.

14. THE SECOND FRONT

1 Taylor, *Provos*, p. 204.
2 Ibid., p. 217.
3 Ibid.
4 Ibid., p. 221.
5 Memorials, Prisons Service Trust (PST), www.pst-ni.co.uk/memorials/.
6 *This Week*, Thames Television, 22 September 1977.
7 Taylor, *Provos*, p. 218.
8 Ibid., p. 219.
9 Ibid., p. 221.
10 Ibid., pp. 221–2.
11 Cathal Crumley, interview with the author.
12 Taylor, *Provos*, p. 222.
13 Roy Mason, *Paying the Price*, Robert Hale, London, 1999, p. 211.
14 Ibid., p. 210.

15 Hansard, Vol. 959, Col. 1505, Debate on NI Emergency Provisions Act, 6 December 1978.

16 https://alphahistory.com/about-alpha-history.

17 Hansard, Vol. 959, Col. 1573, Debate on NI Emergency Provisions Act, 6 December 1978.

18 Taylor, *Provos*, p. 216.

19 'The Long War', *Panorama*, BBC1, 29 February 1988.

20 Taylor, *Provos*, pp. 216–17.

21 John Courtney, *It Was Murder*, Blackwater Press, Dublin, 1996, p. 19.

22 McKittrick, Kelters, Feeney and Thornton, *Lost Lives*, p. 794.

23 Toby Harnden, *Bandit Country: The IRA and South Armagh*, Hodder & Stoughton, London, 1999, p. 149.

24 Courtney, *It Was Murder*, p. 18.

25 Taylor, *Brits*, p. 222.

26 Harnden, *Bandit Country*, p. 144.

27 Taylor, *Brits*, p. 223.

28 *Provos: The IRA and Sinn Féin*, Episode 2, 'Second Front', BBC1, 30 September 1997.

29 The INLA had the same aim as the Provisional IRA, to end British rule and reunify Ireland, but its politics were more revolutionary.

30 *Provos*, Episode 2, 'Second Front', BBC1, 30 September 1997.

31 Margaret Thatcher, *The Downing Street Years*, HarperCollins, London, 1993, p. 389.

32 *Provos*, Episode 2, 'Second Front', BBC1, 30 September 1997.

15. 'THE MOUNTAIN CLIMBER' RETURNS

1 Taylor, *Brits*, p. 233, and continuation of original interview with author.

2 *Provos*, Episode 2, 'Second Front', BBC1, 30 September 1997.

3 Brendan Duddy, interview with the author.

4 Michael Oatley, interview with the author for *Provos*, Episode Two, 'Second Front', BBC1, 30 September 1997.

5 Ó Dochartaigh, *Deniable Contact*, p. 173.

6 Taylor, *Brits*, pp. 232, 233 and 235.

7 Thomas Hennessey, *Hunger Strike: Margaret Thatcher's Battle with the IRA*, Irish Academic Press, Sallins, 2014, p. 117.

8 Ibid.

9 Michael Oatley, interview with the author for *Provos*, Episode Two, 'Second Front', BBC1, 30 September 1997.

10 Ó Dochartaigh, *Deniable Contact*, p. 176.

11 Ed Moloney, *Voices from the Grave: Two Men's War in Ireland*, Faber & Faber, London, 2010, p. 238.

12 The Republican Hunger Strikes: 27 October–19 December 1980, PRONI NI/12/196A, https://cain.ulster.ac.uk/proni/1981/proni_NIO-12-196A_1980-nd.pdf, p. 19.

13 Thatcher, *The Downing Street Years*, p. 391.

16. THE FINAL SHOWDOWN

1 Moloney, *Voices from the Grave*, p. 241.

2 Ibid., p. 240.

3 Michael Oatley, interview with the author in London, early 1997, for *Provos*, Episode 2, Second Front, BBC1, 30 September 1997.

4 Brendan Duddy, *The Secret Peacemaker*, BBC2, 26 March 2008.

5 Michael Oatley, interview with the author in London, early 1997, for *Provos*, BBC.

6 Archive on 4: 'The Hunger Strikes', BBC Radio 4, 1 May 2021.

7 McKittrick, Kelters, Feeney and Thornton, *Lost Lives*, p. 849.

8 Hennessey, *Hunger Strike*, p. 154.

9 David Beresford, *Ten Men Dead: The Story of the 1981 Hunger Strike*, Grafton Books, London, 1987, p. 83.

10 Ibid.

11 Hennessey, *Hunger Strike*, p. 156.

12 Bobby Sands, www.bobbysandstrust.com.

13 Hennessey, *Hunger Strike*, p. 161.

14 Ibid., p. 164.

15 Archive on 4: 'The Hunger Strikes', BBC Radio 4, 1 May 2021.

16 Thatcher, *The Downing Street Years*, p. 391.

17 Taylor, *Provos*, p. 240.

18 Ibid., pp. 240–1.

19 Beresford, *Ten Men Dead*, p. 113.

20 Taylor, *Provos*, p. 242.

21 Margaret Thatcher Foundation, Speeches, etc., 5 May 1981, https://www.margaretthatcher.org/document/.

22 Thatcher, *The Downing Street Years*, p. 391.

17. THE RISE OF SINN FÉIN

1 *New York Times*, 29 May 1981.

2 Taylor, *Provos*, p. 243.

3 Brendan Duddy, interview with the author for *The Secret Peacemaker*, BBC2, 26 March 2008.

4 Denis O'Hearn, *Bobby Sands: Nothing But an Unfinished Song*, Pluto Press, London, 2016, p. 114.

5 Taylor, *Provos*, p. 244.

6 Brendan Duddy Archive, University of Galway, Pol 35/166, The Red Book Manuscript, 10.50 p.m., 11 July 1981. The Red Book is the compilation of contemporaneous notes made by Brendan Duddy. See also Hennessey, *Hunger Strike*, p. 347.

7 Duddy Archive, The Red Book Manuscript, 10.50 p.m., 11 July 1981.

8 Ibid.

9 Ibid.

10 Taylor, *Provos*, p. 239.

11 Ibid., p. 248.

12 Ibid., p. 250.

13 Ibid., p. 251.

14 Hennessey, *Hunger Strike*, p. 448.

15 Ibid., p. 393.

16 Brendan Duddy, interview with the author at home in Derry in 2007.

18. THE ARMALITE AND THE BALLOT BOX

1 Taylor, *Provos*, p. 282.

2 Ibid.

3 McKittrick, Kelters, Feeney and Thornton, *Lost Lives*, p. 909.

4 Ibid., p. 908.

5 Taylor, *Provos*, p. 283.

6 Ibid., p. 284.

19. THE BRIGHTON BOMBER

1 Patrick Magee, *The Brighton Bomb*, BBC1, 14 September 2004. This and subsequent quotes from Patrick Magee, interview with the author.

2 Thatcher, *The Downing Street Years*, p. 380.

3 Ibid., p. 382.

4 'IRA Blitz Brits', *An Phoblacht*, October 1984.

5 Patrick Magee, *Gangsters or Guerrillas? Representations of Irish Republicans in 'Troubles Fiction'*, Beyond the Pale Publications, Belfast 2001.

20. STALEMATE

1 Taylor, *Provos*, p. 285.

2 'IRA–Libya weapons compensation inquiry to begin at Westminster', BBC News, 9 September 2015, https://www.bbc.co.uk/news/uk-north ern-ireland-34195268.
3 Taylor, *Provos*, pp. 290–1.
4 Ibid., p. 269.
5 McKittrick, Kelters, Feeney and Thornton, *Lost Lives*, p. 1,026.
6 Taylor, *Provos*, p. 270.
7 Ibid., pp. 274–5.
8 Taylor, *Brits*, p. 277.
9 www.irishcentral.com, 30 September 2011, https://www.irishcentral. com/news/martin-mcguinness-ashamed-of-the-ira-enniskillen-bombi ngs-video-130843268-237415101.
10 Taylor, *Provos*, p. 298.
11 Sean Hartnett, 'The Inside Story of the Brutal Killing of Wood and Howes', *Independent*, 18 September 2016.
12 Mary Holland, '"Good enough for him," youth said', *Irish Times*, 21 March 1988.
13 Taylor, *Provos*, p. 306.
14 Ibid., p. 304.
15 Ibid., p. 308.
16 Ibid., p. 309.
17 McKittrick, Kelters, Feeney and Thornton, *Lost Lives*, p. 117.

21. BIG CHANGES

1 Taylor, *Provos*, p. 316.
2 Ibid.
3 Ibid., p. 318.
4 Ibid., p. 320.
5 Michael Oatley, interview with the author for *Provos*, Episode Two, 'Second Front', BBC1, 30 September 1997.
6 Albert Reynolds, *My Autobiography: With Jill Arlon*, Transworld Ireland, Dublin, 2009, pp. 160–1, 288.
7 Michael Oatley, interview with the author for *Provos*, Episode Two, 'Second Front', BBC1, 30 September 1997.
8 Ibid.
9 Ibid.
10 Michael Oatley, interview with the author, 1997.

22. ROBERT: THE THIRD MAN

1 Quotations from Robert and the narrative that follows are taken from a number of visits and interviews: 11–12 August 2021, 6–7 September 2021, 17–18 Feb 2022, 3–4 March 2022, 25–26 July 2022 and 13–14 Oct 2022.

23. OPERATION CHIFFON

1 Christopher Andrew, *Defence of the Realm: The Authorized History of MI5*, Allen Lane, London, 2009, p. 783.
2 Ó Dochartaigh, *Deniable Contact*, p. 226.
3 https://cain.ulster.ac.uk, Employment in Northern Ireland.
4 Brendan Duddy, interview with the author for *The Secret Peacemaker*, BBC2, 26 March 2008.
5 Robert, interview with the author, 2021.
6 Ibid.
7 Ibid.

24. BRENDAN: A TERRIFYING INTERROGATION

1 See Appendix I, p. 317.
2 'IRA declares Christmas Truce', *New York Times*, 23 December 1972.

25. TREADING WATER

1 Robert, interviews with the author, 2021–22. All other quotes from Robert in this chapter are from the same interviews.
2 McKittrick, Kelters, Feeney and Thornton, *Lost Lives*, p. 1,269.
3 Ibid., p. 1,270.
4 Ibid., p. 1,278.
5 Ibid., p. 1,285.
6 Interview with Sir Patrick Mayhew, *Provos*, 'Endgame', BBC1, 14 October 1997.
7 Taylor, *Brits*, p. 322.
8 Sinn Féin, *Setting the Record Straight*, 5 January 1994, p. 16.
9 Ibid., p. 18.
10 'Conflict is over' message, in Taylor, *Brits*, p. 330.
11 Ó Dochartaigh, *Deniable Contact*, p. 237.
12 John Major, interview with the author for *Who Won the War?*, BBC1 Northern Ireland, 29 September 2014.
13 Ibid.
14 Taylor, *Brits*, p. 323.

15 Sinn Féin, *Setting the Record Straight*, Report of a meeting with British Government representative, 24 February 1993, p. 20.
16 Ibid., p. 21.
17 Ibid., pp. 18–19.

26. TALKS ABOUT TALKS

1 Sinn Féin, *Setting the Record Straight*, p. 22.
2 Ibid., p. 20.
3 McKittrick, Kelters, Feeney and Thornton, *Lost Lives*, p. 1,314.
4 Ibid.
5 Ibid., p. 1,317.
6 Robert, interview with the author, 2021.
7 Ibid.
8 Ibid.

27. OUT ON A LIMB

1 This and subsequent quotes by Robert in this chapter, interviews with the author 2021 and 2022.
2 Duddy Archive, University of Galway, Pol 35/266, p. 11.
3 Sinn Féin, *Setting the Record Straight*, p. 22.
4 Duddy Archive, University of Galway, Pol 35/266, p. 15.
5 Sinn Féin, *Setting the Record Straight*, p. 8.

28. GETTING READY

1 Robert, interview with the author 2021.
2 Harnden, *Bandit Country*, pp. 244–5.
3 Richard English, *Armed Struggle: The History of the IRA*, Macmillan, London, 2003, p. 296.
4 Taylor, *Brits*, p. 327.
5 Sinn Féin, *Setting the Record Straight*, p. 26.
6 Robert, interview with the author, 2021.
7 Ibid., pp. 30–1.

29. ROBERT COMES CLEAN

1 Robert, interview with the author.
2 Taylor, *Provos*, p. 338.
3 *Irish News*, 18 March 2022.
4 Taylor, *Loyalists*, p. 224.

5 McKittrick, Kelters, Feeney and Thornton, *Lost Lives*, p. 1,335.
6 Ibid.,
7 Taylor, *Brits*, p. 331.
8 Sinn Féin, *Setting the Record Straight*, p. 40.
9 Taylor, *Sinn Féin*, p. 40.
10 Brendan Duddy, interview with the author for *The Secret Peacemaker*, BBC2, 26 March 2008.
11 Hansard, Vol. 231, Col. 35, 1 November 1993.
12 Robert, interview with the author, 2021.
13 Robert, interview with the author, 2022.
14 Robert, interview with the author, 2021.
15 Ibid.
16 Hansard, Vol. 233, Col. 785, Northern Ireland, 29 November 1993.
17 Hansard, Vol. 233, Cols 789–90, Northern Ireland, 29 November 1993.
18 Ibid.
19 Personal letter from Sir Patrick Mayhew to Robert, 10 December 1993.
20 Personal letter to Robert from one of his former colleagues, undated.
21 Personal letter to Robert from one of his former colleagues, undated.

30. PEACE COMES DROPPING SLOW

1 Taylor, *Brits*, p. 336.
2 John Major's speech at the 1993 Lord Mayor's Banquet, 15 November 1993, https://johnmajorarchive.org.uk/1993/11/15/mr-majors-spe ech-at-the-1993-lord-mayors-banquet-15-november-1993/.
3 Paul Bew and Gordon Gillespie, *Northern Ireland: A Chronology of the Troubles, 1968–1999*, Gill & Macmillan, Dublin, 1999, p. 288.
4 Taylor, *Brits*, p. 335.
5 Michael Oatley, interview with the author, 1997.
6 Robert, interview with the author, 2021.
7 CAIN Archive (Conflict and Politics in Northern Ireland), 31 July 1972, https://cain.ulster.ac.uk/othelem/chron/ch94.htm
8 Bew and Gillespie, *Northern Ireland*, p. 288.
9 Sinn Féin, *Setting the Record Straight*, p. 32.
10 John Major, *The Autobiography*, HarperCollins, London, 1999, p. 457.
11 Taylor, *Brits*, p. 337.
12 McKittrick, Kelters, Feeney and Thornton, *Lost Lives*, pp. 1,363–9.
13 Taylor, *Brits*, p. 337.
14 Ibid., p. 338.
15 Robert, interview with the author, 2021.
16 Sir John Chilcot, conversation with the author in Oxford, late 1994.

17 Taylor, *Loyalists*, p. 233.

31. THE ROAD TO GOOD FRIDAY

1 Tim Pat Coogan, *Michael Collins*, Arrow Books, London, 1991, p. 276; Margery Forester, *Michael Collins: The Lost Leader*, Sphere Books, London, 1972, p. 256.
2 Jonathan Powell, *Great Hatred, Little Room: Making Peace in Northern Ireland*, The Bodley Head, London, 2008, p. 83.
3 Ibid., p. 84.
4 Ibid.
5 Taylor, *Brits*, p. 341.
6 McKittrick, Kelters, Feeney and Thornton, *Lost Lives*, p. 1,389.
7 Michael Oatley, interview with the author for *Provos: The IRA and Sinn Féin*, BBC1, 1997.
8 Taylor, *Brits*, p. 359.
9 Powell, *Great Hatred, Little Room*, p. 87.
10 Tony Blair, interview with the author on the twentieth anniversary of the IRA ceasefire in 2014.
11 Taylor, *Brits*, p. 361.
12 Powell, *Great Hatred, Little Room*, p. 22.
13 Ibid.
14 Taylor, *Brits*, p. 262.
15 Alastair Campbell, *The Blair Years: Extracts from the Alastair Campbell Diaries*, Hutchinson, London, 2007, p. 290.
16 Taylor, *Brits*, p. 365.
17 Northern Ireland Assembly, The Belfast Agreement/Good Friday Agreement 1998, Summary.
18 Iconic, https://www.youtube.com/watch?v=MY4U59eb_0c.
19 Campbell, *The Blair Years*, p. 288.
20 Taylor, *Brits*, p. 365.
21 *Ireland After Partition*, BBC2, 14 June 2021.
22 Tony Blair, interview with the author at Mr Blair's office 2014 for *Who Won the War?*, BBC1 Northern Ireland, 29 September 2014.
23 Andrew, *Defence of the Realm*, p. 783.

32. ENDGAME

1 *Guardian*, 12 January 2018.
2 Moloney, *A Secret History of the IRA*, p. 562.
3 Ibid.

4 Michael Oatley, 'Forget the weapons and learn to trust Sinn Féin',
   Sunday Times, 31 October 1999.
5 Charles Moore, 'Spooked by the IRA', *Daily Telegraph*, 1 November 1999.
6 Final Report of the International Commission on Decommissioning, 28
   March 2011.
7 *Who Won the War?*, first shown on BBC NI on 29 September 2014 and
   then on BBC2 on 9 October 2014.
8 Ibid.
9 Robert, interview with the author, 2021.
10 Brendan Duddy, interview with the author.
11 *Guardian*, 20 June 2014.
12 *Christian Today*, 20 January 2014.
13 BBC News, 9 February 2016, https://www.bbc.co.uk/news/uk-northern-
   ireland-35529566.
14 Ibid.
15 *Belfast Telegraph*, 9 February 2016.
16 Martin McGuinness, interview with the author for *Who Won the War?*,
   BBC1 Northern Ireland, 29 September 2014.
17 Ibid.
18 Robert, interviews with the author, 2021–2.
19 Martin McGuinness, interview with the author on the twentieth
   anniversary of the IRA ceasefire in 2014.
20 Gerry Adams, interview with the author on the twentieth anniversary of
   the IRA ceasefire in 2014.
21 *Who Won the War?*, BBC.
22 Ibid.

EPILOGUE

1 *Belfast Telegraph*, 19 October 2014.
2 *Derry Journal*, 25 March 2017.
3 Michael Oatley, family archive.
4 Robert, interview with the author, 2022.
5 *Guardian*, 5 August 2020.
6 BBC News, 1 August 2022, https://www.bbc.co.uk/news/uk-northern-
   ireland-62371935.
7 Senator George Mitchell, interview with the author on the twentieth
   anniversary of the Good Friday Agreement, 2018.
8 ITV News, 12 June 2021.
9 *Guardian*, 13 March 2017.

10 BBC News, 19 September 2019, https://www.bbc.co.uk/news/uk-polit
    ics-49753420.
11 Robert, interview with the author, 2021.
12 Northern Ireland Statistics and Research Agency (NISRA), 22 August
    2022, nisra.gov.uk. https://www.nisra.gov.uk/system/files/statistics/cen
    sus-2021-main-statistics-for-northern-ireland-phase-1-statistical-bulletin-
    religion.pdf.
13 *Who Won the War?*, BBC2, 9 October 2014.
14 Robert, interview with the author.
15 Taylor, *Talking to Terrorists*, p. 39.

Bibliography

Adams, Gerry, *Before the Dawn: An Autobiography*, Mandarin Paperbacks, London, 1996.

Anderson, Brendan, *Joe Cahill: A Life in the IRA*, The O'Brien Press, Dublin, 2002.

Andrew, Christopher, *The Defence of the Realm: The Authorized History of MI5*, Allen Lane, London, 2009.

Beresford, David, *Ten Men Dead: The Story of the 1981 Hunger Strike*, Grafton Books, London, 1987.

Bew, Paul, *Ireland: The Politics of Enmity, 1789–2006*, Oxford University Press, 2007.

Bew, Paul and Gordon Gillespie, *Northern Ireland: A Chronology of the Troubles, 1968–1999*, Gill & Macmillan, Dublin, 1999.

Bolton, Roger, *Death on the Rock and Other Stories*, W. H. Allen/Optomen, London, 1990.

Campbell, Alastair, *The Blair Years: Extracts from the Alastair Campbell Diaries*, Hutchinson, London, 2007.

Coogan, Tim Pat, *Michael Collins*, Arrow Books, London, 1991.

Courtney, John, *It Was Murder*, Blackwater Press, Dublin, 1996.

Dillon, Martin, *The Shankill Butchers: A Case Study of Mass Murder*, Hutchinson, London, 1989.

Elliott, Sydney and W. D. Flackes, *Northern Ireland: A Political Directory, 1968–1999*, Blackstaff Press, 1999.

English, Richard, *Armed Struggle: The History of the IRA*, Macmillan, London, 2003.

Fitzpatrick, Maurice, *John Hume in America: From Derry to DC*, Irish Academic Press, Newbridge, 2017.

Forester, Margery, *Michael Collins: The Lost Leader*, Sphere Books, London, 1972.

Harnden, Toby, *Bandit Country: The IRA and South Armagh*, Hodder & Stoughton, London, 1999.

Hennessey, Thomas, *Hunger Strike: Margaret Thatcher's Battle with the IRA*, Irish Academic Press, Sallins, 2014.

Hermon, Sir John, *Holding the Line: An Autobiography*, Gill & Macmillan, Dublin, 1997.

Holland, Jack and Susan Phoenix, *Phoenix: Policing the Shadows: The Secret War Against Terrorism in Northern Ireland*, Hodder & Stoughton, London, 1996.

Jeffery, Keith, *MI6: The History of the Secret Intelligence Service, 1909–1949*, Bloomsbury, London, 2010.

Kee, Robert, *The Green Flag: A History of Irish Nationalism*, Weidenfeld & Nicolson, London, 1972.

—, *The Laurel and the Ivy: The Story of Charles Stewart Parnell and Irish Nationalism*, Hamish Hamilton, London, 1993.

Leahy, Thomas, *The Intelligence War Against the IRA*, Cambridge University Press, Cambridge, 2020.

Lynch, Robert, *The Partition of Ireland, 1918–1925*, Cambridge University Press, Cambridge, 2019.

McKittrick, David, Seamus Kelters, Brian Feeney and Chris Thornton, *Lost Lives: The Stories of the Men, Women and Children Who Died as a Result of the Northern Ireland Troubles*, Mainstream Publishing, Edinburgh, 1999.

Magee, Patrick, *Gangsters or Guerrillas? Representations of Irish Republicans in 'Troubles Fiction'*, Beyond the Pale Publications, Belfast, 2001.

Major, John, *The Autobiography*, HarperCollins, London, 1999.

Mallie, Eamonn and David McKittrick, *Endgame in Ireland*, Hodder & Stoughton, London, 2001.

Mason, Roy, *Paying the Price*, Robert Hale, London, 1999.

Maume, Patrick, *Dictionary of Irish Biography*, https://dib.ie/biography/rees-merlyn-a9415?

Moloney, Ed, *A Secret History of the IRA*, Penguin Books, London, 2nd edn, 2007.

—, *Voices from the Grave: Two Men's War in Ireland*, Faber & Faber, London, 2010.

Ó Dochartaigh, Niall, *Deniable Contact: Back-Channel Negotiation in Northern Ireland*, Oxford University Press, 2021.

O'Hearn, Denis, *Bobby Sands: Nothing But an Unfinished Song*, Pluto Press, London, 2006.

O'Rawe, Richard, *Blanketmen: An Untold Story of the H-Block Hunger Strike*, New Ireland, Dublin, 2016.

Powell, Jonathan, *Great Hatred, Little Room: Making Peace in Northern Ireland*, Bodley Head, London, 2008.

—, *Talking to Terrorists: How to End Armed Conflict*, Bodley Head, London, 2014.

Reynolds, Albert, *My Autobiography: With Jill Arlon*, Transworld Ireland, Dublin, 2010.

Sharrock, David and Mark Devenport, *Man of War, Man of Peace: The Unauthorised Biography of Gerry Adams*, Pan Books, London, 1998.

Sutton, Malcolm, *An Index of Deaths from the Conflict in Ireland, 1969–1993*, Beyond the Pale Publications, Belfast, 1994.

Taylor, Peter, *Beating the Terrorists? Interrogation in Omagh, Gough and Castlereagh*, Penguin Books, London, 1980.

—, *Stalker: The Search for the Truth*, Faber & Faber, London, 1987.

—, *Families at War: Voices from the Troubles*, BBC Publications, London, 1989.

—, *States of Terror: Democracy and Political Violence*, BBC Books, London, 1993.

—, *Provos: The IRA and Sinn Féin*, Bloomsbury, London, 1997.

—, *Loyalists*, Bloomsbury, London, 1999.

—, *Brits: The War Against the IRA*, Bloomsbury, London, 2001.

—, *Talking to Terrorists: A Personal Journey from the IRA to Al Qaeda*, Harper Press, London, 2011.

Thatcher, Margaret, *The Downing Street Years*, HarperCollins, London, 1993.

Townshend, Charles, *The Partition: Ireland Divided, 1885–1925*, Allen Lane, London, 2021.

Urban, Mark, *Big Boys' Rules: The Secret Struggle Against the IRA*, Faber & Faber, London, 1992.

White, Robert W., *Ruairí Ó Brádaigh: The Life and Politics of an Irish Revolutionary*, Indiana University Press, Bloomington, 2006.

Index

A Note on the Author

PETER TAYLOR is acknowledged to be one of the BBC's most distinguished and respected journalists, best known for his coverage of the Irish conflict and political violence over the past fifty years. He has won many awards for his work, including Journalist of the Year, the James Cameron Award and Lifetime Achievement Awards from both BAFTA and the Royal Television Society. He was also presented with an Honorary Doctorate in Peace and Security Studies from Bradford University, and with an OBE. Peter has written nine books, eight of them related to Northern Ireland, terrorism and political violence. His Bloomsbury trilogy, *Provos, Loyalists* and *Brits*, is recognised to be a definitive history of the conflict. Operation Chiffon now completes the picture and makes the trilogy a unique quartet.

A Note on the Type

The text of this book is set Adobe Garamond. It is one of several versions of Garamond based on the designs of Claude Garamond. It is thought that Garamond based his font on Bembo, cut in 1495 by Francesco Griffo in collaboration with the Italian printer Aldus Manutius. Garamond types were first used in books printed in Paris around 1532. Many of the present-day versions of this type are based on the *Typi Academiae* of Jean Jannon cut in Sedan in 1615.

Claude Garamond was born in Paris in 1480. He learned how to cut type from his father and by the age of fifteen he was able to fashion steel punches the size of a pica with great precision. At the age of sixty he was commissioned by King Francis I to design a Greek alphabet, and for this he was given the honourable title of royal type founder. He died in 1561.